Cracking Up

Studies in Theatre History and Culture

HEATHER S. NATHANS, *series editor*

Cracking Up

Black Feminist Comedy in

the Twentieth and Twenty-First

Century United States

Katelyn Hale Wood

UNIVERSITY OF IOWA PRESS *Iowa City*

University of Iowa Press, Iowa City 52242
Copyright © 2021 by the University of Iowa Press
www.uipress.uiowa.edu
Printed in the United States of America

Text design by Richard Hendel
Cover design by Lindsay Starr

Printed on acid-free paper

Library of Congress Cataloging-in-Publication Data
Names: Wood, Katelyn Hale, 1985– author.
Title: Cracking Up: Black Feminist Comedy in the Twentieth and
   Twenty-First Century United States / Katelyn Hale Wood.
Description: Iowa City: University of Iowa Press, 2021. | Series: Studies
   in Theater History and Culture | Based on the author's dissertation
   (doctoral—University of Texas, 2014). | Includes bibliographical
   references and index.
Identifiers: LCCN 2020042470 (print) | LCCN 2020042471 (ebook) |
   ISBN 9781609387723 (paperback) | ISBN 9781609387730 (ebook)
Subjects: LCSH: Stand-up comedy—Social aspects—United States. | Stand-up
   Comedy—Political aspects—United States. | African American Women
   Comedians—Biography. | African American wit and humor—History and
   criticism. | Feminism—United States.
Classification: LCC PN1969.C65 W66 2021 (print) | LCC PN1969.C65 (ebook) |
   DDC 792.7/6028096073—dc23
LC record available at https://lccn.loc.gov/2020042470
LC ebook record available at https://lccn.loc.gov/2020042471

Contents

Acknowledgments *vii*

Introduction *1*

1 Laughter in the Archives
Jackie "Moms" Mabley *25*

2 I Love You Bitches Back
Spect-actors and Affective Freedom in
I Coulda Been Your Cellmate! *53*

3 The Black Queer Citizenship of Wanda Sykes *83*

4 Contemporary Truth-Tellers
A New Cohort of Black Feminist Comics *110*

Conclusion *147*

Notes *153*

Bibliography *173*

Index *185*

University of Virginia have been endless sources of inspiration and generosity. Lanice Avery, Anne Meng, and Ashon T. Crawley: I am so grateful our paths have crossed. Thank you to Kate Burke and Jim Benedict, Spencer White, Jessica B., and the sweetest of neighbors in Rose Hill. All of you have helped me feel at home.

I am blessed to have a gaggle of queers/chosen family, whose love, creativity, and laughter I've felt and channeled through each stage of this project. Ryan Henneberry, Nikiko Masumoto, Michael Graupmann, Michael Slefinger, Jesús Valles, Ralph Hardesty, Betsy McCann, Kirsten LaMantia, Michelle Hill, Shelby Autrey, Mel Messer, Amy Engleman, and Justine Fanarof are each inspirations in their own right. Thank you for the texts, calls, dinners, drinks, pep talks, care packages, postcards, and for asking about the book and also not asking about the book. I cherish y'all.

Trevor Reichman and Justin Doak gave me much-needed space to finalize this manuscript, as well as too many joy-filled meals to count. My thanks extend to the rest of the Reichmans. I am forever grateful to have found my way into their world and family.

My unending appreciation and love go to the Wood/Bova family, who encouraged me as I ventured from home to graduate school and beyond. I hold so dear the constant support of my godmother Jude Bova and the privilege of being Christina Wood's twin. Rosemary Bova-Wood watched me pull out of her driveway thirteen years ago wrapped in inherited self-determination and the knowledge that she is cheering me on no matter the distance. Thank you, Mama.

Nicole Martin: no way, no how would this book exist without you (at least the good parts). Thank you for your countless pieces of superb and heartening advice over the years as this project developed, and always for your steady, gracious, joyous friendship.

I met Lauren Reichman at the beginning of my academic career, and at the start of writing what would become this book. I didn't know (but also totally knew in my heart of hearts) that she would be beside me at its completion and beyond. My anchor, my favorite, my beloved: thank you a million times over for everything, and for all that is to come.

To note: chapters 1 and 3 draw from previous publications and have been heavily revised and added to: Wood, Katelyn Hale, "Laughter in the Archives: Jackie 'Moms' Mabley and the Haunted Diva," *QED: A Journal in GLBTQ Worldmaking* 1, no. 3 (2014): 85–108; and Wood, Katelyn Hale, "Cracking Up Time: Black Feminist Comedic Performance and Queer Temporalities in the Standup of Wanda Sykes," *Departures in Critical Qualitative Research* 5, no. 3 (2016): 10–32.

Introduction

n the culture galleries on the top floor of the National Museum of African American History and Culture in Washington, DC, a dynamic, pulsing energy circulates and envelopes patrons. An abundance of visual art, food, dance, film, performance, and music curatorially spin in architectural circles and curves, showcasing the awe-inspiring work of Black and African American creative innovators. One does not move from room to room so much as one slides from space to space, the life force of Black artistic practice spiraling in its depth and breadth.[1]

A short homage to Black comedians is tucked away among the theatre and live performance displays. Despite the expansive feeling of the rest of the floor, this is an intimate alcove. Three ten-foot panels displaying stand-up comedy greats draw and demand attention. Backlit by bright blue bricks and flanked by two equally sized photos of her male successors, Dick Gregory and Richard Pryor, Jackie "Moms" Mabley takes center "stage" in a black and white poster vignette. Mabley sits in a chair, slightly hunched over in her comedic persona's signature costume: a mismatched floral muumuu and house coat, floppy hat, argyle socks, and slippers. She holds a microphone in her right hand and a handkerchief in her left. The photo was taken toward the end of Mabley's life and career. Her age shows in the soft wrinkles on her face. But a sense of contentment is also evidenced from her wizened features: half-squinted eyes and a wide grin. Above Mabley's left shoulder, a signature quotation from her stand-up routines reads, "I just tell folks the truth. If they don't want the truth, then don't come to Moms."[2]

I just tell folks the truth. If they don't want the truth, then don't come to Moms.

JACKIE "MOMS" MABLEY

Jackie "Moms" Mabley at the National Museum of African American History and Culture, Washington DC. Photograph by Jerry de Wilde, 1972; used with permission.

Jessica Williams and Phoebe Robinson at the premiere of their 2018 HBO special 2 Dope Queens. *HBO.*

Slide forward to 2018. More than four decades after entertainment photographer Jerry de Wilde snapped this image of Mabley performing, Jessica Williams and Phoebe Robinson excitedly enter the stage at Kings Theatre in Brooklyn to kick off their filmed HBO special, a derivative of their weekly WNYC podcast, *2 Dope Queens*. Dressed fashionably and, like Mabley, in clashing florals, the duo begins riffing in a back-and-forth routine, citing the kinds of people who owe Black women apologies. Their list begins with white women who appropriate Black culture. They then roast white men who call Black women "chocolate." Their bit comes to a climax as Williams assertively adds, "You know what, this might be a little controversial, just a white guy that should apologize—" she takes a breath and firmly declares, "Thomas Jefferson." Robinson cuts in with indignity, "Of course. Not maybe. No, *definitely!*"[3] Williams, adopting the vocal tone of an ironic half-apology, sighs and shrugs, "I just think some people are really into history, so I know that's gonna rub some people the wrong way." She quickly shifts to earnest exasperation: "But also,

3

oh my fucking goodness, I can't believe that." Robinson chimes in, agreeing: "And also, people who are like, 'His love [for] Sally.' No, it's not. Sally Hemings was not a *lover*. That got real."[4] The audience, whose excitement seemed suspended as they wondered where the women were going in the opening act of their show, laugh in relief and then cheer as Williams and Robinson high-five and continue with their introduction. The comics, unwilling to yield to a hesitant audience, followed in the footsteps of fellow Black feminist comic Mabley. Tea was spilled, history was cracked up and out, truth left hanging in the air of the ornate, even gaudy, theatre. Mabley, Williams, and Robinson demonstrate the cornerstone of Black feminist stand-up comedy: joke-telling as truth-telling in the name of Black women's expression and freedom.

Black feminist comedy evokes a politic of joy while telling necessary truths about race, gender, sexuality, and citizenship from the perspectives of Black women and Black queer women in the United States. Both visceral and epistemological, Black feminist comedy and laughter hold space for the pleasures, communities, and spiritual experiences that thrive in the face of, and in spite of, legacies of racialized grief. From the early twentieth century through present-day comedy platforms, Black women comics have deployed the art of joke-telling to "stand up" against oppression and "stand up" for joyful expression. In line with traditions of Black art and performance more broadly, the stakes of Black feminist comedy have "been relevant beyond the shaping of Black subjectivities. They have developed and exposed the character of the entire nation."[5] Performance archives may characterize Black women comedians and their work as marginal, but they are integral in the trajectory of stand-up comedy and important figures of theatre and performance history in the United States.

In four case studies, *Cracking Up* archives and analyzes the performative labor Black feminist comedians do to (re)form and assert citizenship in the United States. I argue that Black feminist comedic performance and the laughter it ignites are vital components of feminist, queer, and anti-racist protest. Through archival research and performance analysis, I study Black women stand-up comedians from the United States, including: Jackie Mabley, Mo'Nique, Wanda Sykes, Sasheer Zamata, Sam Jay, Michelle Buteau, and Amanda Seales. I claim that Black feminist comedic performance "cracks up" historical legacies of racialized and gendered violence in the United States.

4

That is, as Mabley and the 2 Dope Queens showed, Black feminist comedy exposes structures of marginalization and oppression that attempt to silence Black women and Black queer people.

"Cracking up" is the foundational concept that unifies each Black feminist comic in the following four chapters. I use the term to denote a performance strategy and its after-effects. "Cracking up" is an idiom that originated in the United States. The term's varied meanings—to laugh out loud, to mentally or emotionally break down, to convulse in laughter uncontrollably—all point to roots in embodiment, lack of decorum, and displays of affect.[6] In line with Black feminist performance practices, and Black comedic performance histories, cracking up both breaks down and opens up. Laughter that is wild, seemingly verging on insanity, is also a vocal and communal response that reveals cultural recognition and release, letting loose what under more polite or respectable circumstances needs to be contained. I will also note that cracking up is a creation of a fissure, that, once released, perhaps can no longer be fully sutured. This is a method of speaking truth to power and to fellow Black women outside the purview of dominant culture. Cracking up makes space for a physical and emotional loss of control in a culture that too often restricts, commodifies, or demonizes Black joy and embodied expression.

A primary aim of *Cracking Up* is to showcase a genealogy of Black feminist comics and to connect a lineage of Black women artists. The artists I study have had an outsized presence in stand-up comedy with complex and emboldening performance styles, yet all have been chronically underrepresented in theatre and performance studies literature. Paying homage to these comics' skillful artistry as part of a larger history of excellent Black feminist performance artists attends to the labor of comedy, rather than siloing them as naturally gifted tokens in a white/male-dominated industry. Like Emily Lordi's study on Black women singers, *Cracking Up* interrogates the assignations of "natural" talent that link Black women performers to a lack of intellectual and artistic agency.[7] With an aim to build upon and subvert archival practices that marginalize Black performance, Black queer performance, and Black women, I hone in on the effects and affects of their popular entertainment, marking the inevitable "blind spots where some performers defy the expectations and desires of the audience member/recorder."[8] I argue throughout this book that Black feminist comics, highly skilled and politically charged, have played important roles in histories of resistant Black feminist and Black queer performance.

A second aim of this book is to document comedy's efficacy. I historicize and closely read Black feminist comedy as a modality of Black feminist and Black queer protest and coalition building. Stand-up comedy is not just a reaction to or a reflection of culture. It also holds the power to shape or, as in the case studies in this book, crack up white supremacist ideologies in the United States. The jokes examined in the pages that follow distill cultural truths by interrupting hegemonic fictions of Black womanhood and, as Matt Richardson explains in *The Queer Limit of Black Memory*, "threaten to unearth the amnesic defenses created through repression."[9] Joke-telling and laughter let loose that which has been silenced or repressed, and the comics I study reveal and question normalized structures that uphold white supremacy and heteropatriarchy (and their various offshoots of classism, ableism, and so on). When approached through the lens of social critique and justice, stand-up can create an experience that helps performer and audience script how they want to reshape their communities.

Black Feminist Theory and Performance in Comedy

Black feminism is the guiding theoretical frame in *Cracking Up*. When I began researching stand-up comedy more than ten years ago, Black women were, unsurprisingly, the comics who were most potently addressing intersectional feminist issues via joke-telling. As I discuss in more detail in chapter 4, stand-up has become more diverse and accessible to wide-ranging audiences in the past five years. But since its inception as a form of popular entertainment, Black women and Black queer women have been at the forefront of using stand-up comedy to further social justice issues pertinent to Black women and Black queer people. Black feminism guides the scholarly engagement in this book, not just because of the artists' racial identities, but because it frames the important cultural labor of their work and historicizes them within traditions of Black feminist thought and performance practices. I briefly define and preview how *Cracking Up* engages Black feminism, Black queer theories, and Black feminist performance aesthetics.

Feminism itself is a contested, highly dynamic term, movement, and discipline—always cracking up along the lines of race, class, sexuality, and gender. Black feminist theory, thought, and performance practices are unapologetically intersectional. When I invoke the term Black feminist, I am following the writing, speaking, and performance traditions that both articulate an already existing consciousness of Black women's citizenship and, as Collins defines Black feminism in "The Social Construction of Black Feminist Thought," gives Black women "another tool of resistance to all forms of their subordination."[10] That is, Black feminist theory both names what kinds of embodied knowledge has historically circulated among Black women and their allies, and is a vocabulary for strategic resistance.

Black feminism also has strong historical links to queer theory; queer theory has strong historical links to Black feminism. Both together and separate, Black feminism and queer theory disrupt and intercept linear time, historical narratives focusing only on those in power, and value judgments of who and what is worthy of the time and space for public discourse. Black feminists such as Audre Lorde and bell hooks have written extensively about the ways that heteropatriarchy furthers misogyny, homophobia, and white supremacy in US contexts. Kara Keeling cites Lorde's feminism as "also a queer theory" that confronts capitalism and heteropatriarchy and the ways such structures rely on harmful logics of reproduction.[11] Because feminism, Black studies, and queer theory are (at least for the artists in this study and for the theorists with whom I engage) so closely linked, I often evoke these terms simultaneously.

For example, I will write: "Black/queer women" to indicate both Black women and Black queer women. I may write "queer" to indicate an identity marker or framework that acknowledges intersecting modes of power and seeks to use the body, performance, or scholarship to maneuver around such restrictions. Not divorcing queerness from sexuality, I also use this term to describe desire and relationality that rejects heteronormativity and heteropatriarchy. At times, I state "Black feminist" or "Black feminism" without using the term queer alongside it. Nonetheless, queerness is ever-present in all of these artists' work, regardless of their sexual identity. Omi Osun Joni L. Jones insists that queerness and Blackness are linked insofar as they operate "transtemporally" and refuse crystallization, generating sites of possibility and movement.[12] I agree with Jones, and attempt to document how all of the women in this study use performance to name, critique, and dismantle white heteropatriarchy.

In addition to using the stage to evoke Black feminist thought, the women in *Cracking Up* align with the aesthetic and political movements toward freedom in traditions of Black and Black feminist performance. Black performance interrogates and animates the dynamics of "African dislocation, imperialist trade, capitalist accumulation, human violence, and black abjection."[13] Typically, these collective memories of trauma are ignored, disregarded, and/or silenced in service of dominant interests and ideologies that frame the United States as a site of freedom and justice for all. In direct contrast, and as a form of performance that simultaneously distills and complicates such nation-state mythologies, the joke in Black feminist comedy follows lineages of Black performance that sit at "the interstices of Black political life and art, providing the lynchpin that sustains and galvanizes art and acts of resistance."[14] Moreover, the feminist and queer sensibilities of the artists examined here also broaden what is possible within Black feminist performance traditions of communal expression. They use the stage as a site of "exacting roads to transformation," which Jones describes as a foundational tenet toward liberatory Black feminist and Black queer performance.[15]

Anchored by Black feminist epistemology, the comics in this book occupy the stage to convey knowledge gained via "outsider-within" positionalities and embody self-definition and self-determination.[16] The presence of Black women on center stage on their own terms provides subversive opportunities for both performer and audience. Artist Pearl Cleage designates artistic work committed to creating a conduit for Black women's voices a "hollering place."[17] Black feminist comedy generates a hollering place for Black women to bond over shared experiences and understand the complexities of their differences. bell hooks explains that it is harmful to "assume that strength in unity can only exist if difference is suppressed and shared experience is highlighted."[18] The hollering place is a space in which Black women can narrate and hear the various stories that constitute the specificities of Blackness, womanhood, and queer life in the public and private spheres.

When interpreted amidst the rich history of Black feminist theory and performance, Black feminist stand-up comedy situates Black women as radical agents within history, their subjecthood, and their communities, despite the imposition of dehumanizing hyper in/visibility at various intersections of systematic marginalization. Lorde states that Black women asserting their "sources of strength and support" and pursuing power and political interests is a "vital component in the war for Black liberation."[19] Hollering places for Black women and their allies exemplify the generative, powerful work of what M. Jacqui Alexander calls "knowing who walks with you." There is power in the commune and solidarity created through performance.[20] Black feminist comedians use the mic as a means to foster belonging and to exchange important ideas about identity/ies, history, and culture. Black feminist comedy mirrors traditions of fostering empowerment via Black feminist ideology in cultural spaces ranging from kitchens to classrooms to churches; it performatively models how intersectional identities and history need not be solely dictated by white, patriarchal, and heteronormative domination.[21]

Privileging the body as a site of knowledge, Black feminist comedic performance creates conditions to empower performers and audiences, and stage critical interventions. Like Mabley's truth-telling, and the 2 Dope Queens' reclamation of historical narratives that idolize Thomas Jefferson, I examine artists throughout the book who intervene in dominant history, summoning stories of Black women into the cultural fabric of US collective memory. Black feminist comedy employs performance as a form of social and political dissent whereby white supremacy and sexism are deconstructed, revealing and challenging the normalizing of racist histories. This practice, according to Diana Taylor, "also functions as an epistemology. [Performance as] embodied practice, along with and bound up with other cultural practices, offers a way of knowing."[22] Accordingly, the performances I examine in this book work *as* Black feminist critique of the state and for expressive freedom. In line with other Black feminist, Black queer, and avant-garde theatrical traditions, this book archives artists who understand that the stage can be a place of transformation, progression, and freedom, and that their Black feminist performance is in service of continued illumination rather than contained, ephemeral happenings.[23] These "bodies in dissent," to borrow language from Daphne Brooks, "traffic in cultural excess." Their performances are unabashed, but also exist within their "socially, politically, and culturally circumscribed bodies."[24] The artists here dissent against institutions that deem their bodies unruly and use comedy to assert Black feminist expression of truth and presence.

INTRODUCTION

9

Stand-Up Comedy Histories and
Oppositional Black Humor

From the violence of forced performances for slave owners to appropriative popular culture well into the twenty-first century has meant that Black performance often operated as both a stealthy and overt form of resistance, an "oppositional move within a matrix of disciplining powers reigning over the Black body," as Thomas DeFrantz and Anita Gonzalez theorize.[25] Stand-up comedy and Black humor in particular has reflected such covert and blatant subversion of power in performance history. Black women have played important roles in shaping stand-up comedy as a strategy of opposition within various live and mediated contexts.

Scholars of Black performance and comedy frequently link a primary origin of stand-up to the shameful practices of minstrelsy in the United States, whose central premise was to evoke pleasure from violence against the Black body. Rooted in what Eric Lott historicized as white fascination with and desire for Blackness, minstrel shows enacted fictions of Black culture as it existed in the white American imaginary.[26] One common act in a minstrel show was the "stump speech," in which a single male performer in blackface and formal wear gave an unintelligible extemporaneous address.[27] These performances profited from and exploded cultural fictions of Black inferiority, which, for white audiences, got taken up as cultural fact outside the theatrical space.[28]

Minstrelsy's haunted legacy of the stump speech influenced the structure of stand-up, but oppositional work of Black minstrels, who carried a more complex weight in their performances, helped to shape the spirit and tenor of Black comedy. Using the very stereotypes expected in the minstrel show, Black minstrels asserted their superior performance skills and thwarted racist representations of Black people. Black minstrel performers working at the turn of the twentieth century evoked the comedic strategy of parody to express resistance and confront oppression often under the gaze of white audiences. The emergence of parody at this time reflected W. E. B. Du Bois's concept of double consciousness, or the idea that Black bodies occupy a sense of "two-ness" in which they see themselves through their own eyes as well as those of their oppressors.[29] In *Resistance, Parody, and Double Consciousness in African American Theatre,*

1895–1910, David Krasner historicizes the ways that Black performers worked "amidst deteriorating race relations between two competing forces: the demands to conform to white notions of black inferiority, and the desire to resist these demands by undermining and destabilizing entrenched stereotypes of blacks on stage."[30] Black women minstrel performers, like Black women stand-up comics, have often existed in the margins of theatre histories. Yet these artists were key players in the development of Black comedy and parody as a form of social protest.

Black women's participation in minstrel performances, while less documented in theatre history, provide important examples of parody and protest performance in the United States. Using what Annemarie Bean theorizes as "double inversion," Black women performers challenged and changed the supposed fixed social order of gender and race on the minstrel stage.[31] Bean cites the work of Aida Overton Walker, Ida Forsyne, and Josephine Baker who all engaged in male impersonation to show the malleability of gender and race through their exceptional performance skills. Overton Walker, for example, parodied white superiority through dance and gesture in cakewalks. The dance itself was invented by enslaved people to ridicule white masters, mocking the "dissonance between a so-called high society and its brutality and violent exploitation of Black enslaved people."[32] Black women in minstrel performance used the realm of popular culture as a form of protest and reformed "what the audience expected of her as an African American woman on the popular stage."[33] Like their foremothers, the women in *Cracking Up* have intervened in a largely white and male-dominated sect of the entertainment industry, and have defied expectations of "proper" performances of Black womanhood.

Black humor prior to and beyond minstrelsy has deep and diverse roots in West African griot traditions, the satiric styling of slave humor, playing the dozens, pouring tea, and more. Black humor in written, oral, and performative traditions developed out of the diaspora, creating conditions for Black people to adapt and mold a new language of the "uniquely American comic form."[34] Bambi Haggins asserts that comedy has been crucial for the expression and formation of Black identities, and to cope with systemized oppressions and celebrate Black culture.[35] The minstrel roots of stand-up do not detract from the empowerment and pleasure Black performers and their audiences have derived from comedic performance. Such performances reflect the actuality of the Black diaspora rather than fulfill fictional stereotypes produced and consumed by white performers and audiences. Black comedians in the United States have been subverting white supremacy through stand-up since the birth of the form.[36] Haggins argues that performative protest has always been a feature of Black stand-up comedy: "Historically, the Black comic has retained the ability to get the audience laughing while slipping in sociocultural truths."[37]

Aligning with Haggins, Glenda Carpio writes that Black joke-telling draws upon a distinct "diasporic sensibility" to mark the body as a site of power.[38] In *Laughing Fit to Kill*, Carpio theorizes the Black comedic artist as a conjurer who symbolically redresses slavery through joke-telling, performances of the grotesque, satire, and re-formation of Black stereotypes. That is, the Black comedic artist reveals tropes of racial archetypes as constructions of white supremacist history through the "arsenal" of Black American humor: the insult, the tall tale, the trickster, and the "blues-infused" joke have created a foundation in which Black humor bonds performer and audience through a shared sense of time and legacy.[39]

On the Black vaudeville circuit, also called the Theatre Owners Booking Association (TOBA), Black comic entertainers flourished.[40] TOBA was formed in 1920 and consisted of a string of theatres across the South and Midwest that showcased Black vaudeville performers. The circuit provided steady work for those performers, who could showcase their talents to largely Black audiences. Black women comedians honed jocular aesthetics rooted in African American cultural traditions of folklore and dance, and also in queer theatrical tropes such as camp and drag on the TOBA circuit.[41] By the 1950s, in the working class, Black-owned performance venues of the Chitlin' Circuit, Black women performers used humor for backlash and bonding, performing a kind of "no holds barred" comedy.[42]

In civil rights era United States, theatres such as the Uptown in North Philadelphia, the Apollo in Harlem, and Chicago's Regal showcased Black comics who engaged in staunch anti-segregationist rhetoric. Jackie "Moms" Mabley was the first Black woman comic to perform without a male counterpart on the TOBA and Chitlin' circuits, and she performed sold-out sets across the northern United States well into the early 1970s. As I examine in chapter 1, Mabley set standards for Black women to tell jokes in "response to systematic oppression based on their racialized gendered identity and minority sexual orientation as asexual and hypersexual representational others."[43] Mabley pioneered an overtly political style of stand-up comedy that influenced her male mentees such as Richard Pryor and Dick Gregory. Her legacy fostered into the present day a lineage of Black feminist comics who cracked up historical legacies of racial violence and misogyny.

Stand-up comedy became a widespread form of mediated entertainment through the rise of comedy albums and television by the middle of the twentieth century. In the 1960s and 1970s, "party albums" became a way for Black comics to record the kind of raunchy performances not made for the rising popularity of network television's late night programs.[44] Although women comics at this time were sparse, comics like LaWanda Page and her sexually explicit stand-up represented this kind of adult entertainment. Mabley's popularity also sky-rocketed once her comedy became available on vinyl in the last decade of her life and career.[45] With television widely used in American households by the latter third of the twentieth century, stand-up comedy became an even more accessible and popular form of entertainment. The cable network *Comedy Central*, the first network devoted to comedy programming, premiered in 1990 and produced many stand-up specials. The 1990s also saw a resurgence in Black comedy with the premiere of *Def Comedy Jam* in 1992. The television series showcased comedians who refused assimilation and displayed "an unabashed disregard for the politics of respectability."[46] Black women made up a minority of the Black stand-ups on television at this time, but artists such as Adele Givens, Simply Marvelous, and Sheryl Underwood comedically engaged in raunchy humor and issues that directly addressed working-class Black women.[47] Stand-up comedy has undergone a renaissance in the digital age. As I detail in chapter 4, Black feminist comics are spearheading new ways to use comedy as protest across wide-ranging media platforms.

Throughout the book, I contextualize Black feminist comedy in line with these histories and Black women comics as important shapers of US performance history, stand-up comedy, and Black feminist performance at large. Black feminist comedic performances employ jokes and the resultant laughter to, as bell hooks would describe, "talk back" to the cultural, political, and historical narratives that caricaturize and confine Black women to the dominant imagination.[48] As resistant and generative performers, the Black women and Black queer women comics in *Cracking Up* occupy the stage not only as a place for enjoyment but also as a platform from which to speak bold truths about what it means to be "American" in their historical and political circumstances.

Comedy as Community

Comedy is an audience-dependent performance form. A joke does not become such until uttered to an audience who then responds.[49] Instead of the well-mannered, passive audience in modern white, Western theatre, audiences in comedic performance spaces are depended upon to create an experience of exchange, and hopefully, affirmation. From the Ring Shout to jazz aesthetics, improvisatory participation has been a key feature of Black performance rituals, breaking down the binary of audience and performer, and creating sacred spaces for unity, as well.[50] Operating within Black diasporic traditions of call and response, the laughter that derives from Black feminist comedy contributes to its subversive effects as well as its spiritual nature. Laughter from an audience amplifies the performer's message and also creates a new kind of commune.

Throughout *Cracking Up*, I use the term "audience" in multiple ways. First, when I reference "*the* audience," I am writing about the group of people for whom the comic performed immediately, in the live theatrical event. *The* audience, then, means the live audience who also contributes to my performance analysis: I often note their laughter, cheers, silence, etc. I do my best to describe and closely read *the* audience from archival materials available to me. However, I also acknowledge that there is no singular experience for witnesses of a performance that I could encompass here, and no monolithic identity of the audience other than the shared time and space of the performance itself. Even with my own shortcomings as a researcher, I still acknowledge *the* audience as active participants who shape a comedic performance and create important moments of both affirmation and tension within the theatrical event. I show throughout the book the dual role the audience plays in Black feminist comedic performance. The audience both bears witness to and generates meaning *in addition to* the performance, and also *within* it, and can participate in moments of performative rebellion. The audience is in constant conversation with the performer as a collective entity. I pay detailed attention to the exchange of comedic performance—the kind of call and response between joke-telling and laughter that defies restriction. As I examine more closely in chapter 2, for example, in Mo'Nique's 2007 performance at the Ohio Reformatory for Women, the audience of incarcerated women express power in their collectivity even while under state supervision, breaking the assumption that the audience is always in solidarity with Mo'Nique. They become what Augusto Boal calls "spect-actors," who claim their power to shape and change a theatrical experience.[51] As spect-actors to Black feminist comedic performance, the audience and its embodied response co-creates joyful and resistant community.

When I write "audiences," I mean to implicate those seeking out the performance outside the time/space of the initial event. Audiences can mean both potential and future consumers of the performance as well as mediated audiences who have already consumed the performance via a different medium such as television, film, audio, or social media. There are challenges to integrating both live and mediated audiences into a manuscript. But I evoke both *the* audience and *audiences* because they are critical to the outcomes of comedic performance, and crucial to recording the cultural significance of the event. Many times, the comics in *Cracking Up* direct their performance specifically toward Black women, women, and/or LGBT audiences. I do my best to note when such moments of a performance occur and theorize what that kind of comedy might mean for Black feminist and Black queer worldmaking.

Cracking Up intervenes in white masculinist canons of humor theory that characterize comedy as a battle for power between the joke-teller and audiences. Sigmund Freud's theory of the joke argues that joke-telling is a method of asserting dominance. His 1905 study *Jokes and Their Relation to the Unconscious*, set a precedent in humor theory as it solidified notions that successful comedy requires aggression against another for the pleasure of the voyeur. According to Freud's psychoanalytic approach to humor, the subject (joke-teller) expresses aggression toward an object under the guise of laughter. The "successful" joke form follows a simple formulation: the teller attacks an object for the comic and the listener's pleasure. The traditional joke form is centered on the punch line. The "set up" becomes subsidiary to the momentary release of laughter. For Freud, a comic's success is dependent upon an "economy of release." Mental pleasure of the listener (voyeur) is wrapped up in the *amount* of laughter directed *at* the marginalized other or, more colloquially, the "butt of the joke." The comic is no longer useful to the audience when the economy of release has run its course. Henri Bergson's theories on comedy situated the comic as disconnected from his/her subject matter and object of the joke. He calls the successful comedian a "disinterested spectator" who approaches narrative through intellect.[52] According to Bergson, the characteristics of a successful comic include inflexibility, mechanical movement, absentmindedness, and unsociability. These standards, upheld by many contemporary comedic performers, do not account for the communal nature of laughter. It assumes that comedy that yields positive results requires the performer to work from a position of power over the audience.

Contrary to these theories, *Cracking Up* positions the comic and her audiences as co-creators of joy and resistance. One of stand-up comedy's most valuable traits then, is the exchange between audience and performer. In *All Joking Aside*, Rebekah Krefting calls this exchange the "economy" of comedy, and argues that such interaction is what makes stand-up such a powerful performance form.[53] Joke-telling is a conversation between comic and audience, and when approached through the lens of social justice, such production (the joke) and consumption (the laugh, or sigh, or boo) can help reveal and shift the status quo. The act of laughter, in particular, is one that embodies and moves toward release, both in the moment of performance and as a reference for future movements toward freedom. For many racialized and queer minorities, systemic marginalization and its after-effects are woven into the public and private.[54] Laughter can seem to negate the seriousness of struggle. At other times, laughter serves as a response to struggle—its irony, ridiculousness, and outwardly futile nature. However, a claiming or reclamation of freedom through laughter is also an integral mode of uncovering, discovering, and recovering a feminist and anti-racist coalition. Speaking up and out, laughter operates as a "liberatory act" from one's jaw being tight—"the physical reality of teeth clenched, unable or unwilling to speak."[55] Laughter in the context of Black feminist comedy bursts through and forth structures that attempt to contain, silence, and marginalize Black/queer expression.

The resistant and coalitional politics of laughter and vocal response from audiences (live, mediated, future, and potential) are not to be ignored. Diane Davis asserts that laughter breaks up "phallocratic order" by "breaking up *at* it."[56] In other words, comedy's outloudness, brassiness, and riskiness, moves bodies from a state of nonbeing to undeniable liveness, holding power in vocality beyond language. *Cracking Up* privileges comedians' artistry and recognizes that stand-up is "uniquely audience dependent," even as those audiences may represent wide-ranging populations.[57] Audiences within the sphere of the comedic performance may not share common identity markers but do take on a group dynamic under the auspices of the performance. As Michael Warner notes, racialized and gendered bodies often challenge and reshape the public versus private split. He writes, "Public and private are bound up with the elementary relations to language as well as to the body."[58] Laughter and vocal response is an embodied act of recognition, visceral feedback that signals an understanding of the comic's worldview and her relation to the audience. Laughter brings the private, lived experience into the public sphere. The Black feminist comics in *Cracking Up* know that they hold power to both affirm fellow Black women and Black queer audience members, while also reaching out to potential allies.

The comedic performance strategy of "cracking up" both disrupts the status quo and activates being and belonging. Black feminist comedic performers and audiences that affirm these performances through laughter, rail against structures of anti-Black, heteropatriarchal exclusion. Their acts onstage (and often off) evince laughter and joy as vital "acts of transfer" between and among Black women and Black/queer audiences.[59] The jokes told are not only for laughs (a product-over-process approach in performance-making), but also used to center Black women and Black queer bodies who disrupt, affectively bursting forth and through restrictive and marginalizing forces.[60] I contend that Black feminist comedic performance aims to produce laughter that dislocates its audience toward embodied experiences of freedom. I mean "dislocates" not in the sense that laughter allows the audience to simply escape or feel carefree. Rather, the artists in this book assert that comedic performance is at its best when it cracks up, jolting an audience out of normative, oppressive, and marginalizing discourse, toward truth-telling and Black feminist/Black queer liberation.

Cracking Up Citizenship

As a form of performance created in, and in reaction to, shifting and unstable definitions of "American," Black stand-up comedy in the United States has frequently been bound to the performer's relationship to the nation-state, and the false ideologies of freedom for all. The United States is a nation that has failed to fully acknowledge colonialism and systemic racism as the foundation of the nation's formation. Moreover, white superiority has been implicit in the construction of US citizenship. Dominant histories perpetuate various colonial and patriarchal myths, constructing what Stuart Hall names as a national heritage that favors those in power, or "those who have colonized the past." [61] Hall explains, "These assumptions and co-ordinates of power are inhabited as natural—given, timeless, true and inevitable."[62] De-naturalizing structures that bind white supremacy to citizenship, the artists in the chapters that follow directly engage with the broken promises of the American Dream and also claim space for Black women and Black/queer audiences.

In other words, the comics in this book crack up citizenship. They reveal how cultural memory and heritage are tools leveraged to sustain seamless narratives that sustain white supremacy. To crack up US citizenship, for these performers, is to agitate, analyze, and reveal the irreconcilable nature of freedom as it is promised, and the actuality of freedom as fleeting for Black Americans. Collins localizes the discursive forces that bind the nation to white supremacy and heteropatriarchy in her writings about US national identity. Structures that hold in place legal and cultural notions of citizenship in the United States, are rooted in what Collins calls the paradox of the racial triangle. The fundamental, hierarchical structure of the racial triangle places white citizens at the top, Black people as second-class citizens, and Indigenous Americans as foreign others. Collins asserts, "The tenacity of this racial triangle explains in part how US society can undergo massive reorganization of its basic social institutions and ethnic populations in response to phases of capitalist development, yet somehow manage to replicate a seemingly permanent racial hierarchy."[63] This system, both cultural and legal, mandates that individual rights and freedoms remain in constant tension with the reality of cultural and institutional racism and sexism.

To crack up citizenship is to deconstruct and dismiss the invisible yet salient power systems that hold the racial triangle in place and to expose the "exclusionary field structured by citizenship's necessary anti-universality."[64] Fred Moten writes that Black performance exhaustively celebrates the incongruous yet interlocking cultural forces between Black joy and pervasive state-sponsored anti-Blackness.[65] Observing and commenting on citizenship from the white margins and Black patriarchal margins, Black feminist comics assert themselves as experts on the interlocking structures in the United States that uphold racism and sexism. They critique how white superiority and heteropatriarchy function as the defining sources of power in the United States *and* revel in Black women's joy as a form of resistance.

The constant push and pull between subjectivity and state-sponsored abjection is often present in Black performance, highlighting what Hartman calls, "history that hurts."[66] In this way, Black feminist comedy does not work in spite of abjection but rather *with* it via various performative and affective strategies. Darieck Scott's *Extravagant Abjection* (2010) examines the relations between Blackness and abjection and claims that Black abjection, particularly the of Black queer people, facilitates "pathways" toward freedom and survival. Reading Frantz Fanon's writings on Blackness and subjectivity, Scott claims that if abjection is inherent in the experiences of Black people in the United States, it has to, on some level, facilitate a counterintuitive power. Scott elaborates:

> Abjection in/of Blackness endows its inheritors with a form of counterintuitive *power*—indeed, what we can begin to think of as *Black* power. This power (that is also a way of speaking of freedom) is found at the point of the apparent erasure of ego-protections, at the point at which the constellation of tropes that we call *identity, body, race, nation* seem to reveal themselves as utterly penetrated and compromised, without defensible boundary.[67]

That is, despite or even because of abjection, Black people in the United States can evoke particular kinds of affective templates for dissent and empowerment. The laughing bodies created through the performances I write about animate each other by joyfully and radically bonding through common experience. Laughter is a "uniquely invigorating kind of epistemological response" to forced abjection because laughter requires vocality, embodiment, and community—the very factors that enliven being.[68] Limon offers an important articulation of the relationship among joke-telling, laughter, and abjection. Limon calls stand-up a "beautiful abstract geometry" in which the comedian carves out and "stands up" against abjection. Limon argues, "To 'stand up' abjection is simultaneously to erect it and miss one's date with it: comedy is a way of avowing and disavowing abjection."[69] The embodied and sonic nature of comedic performance and the act of laughter make abjection, on some levels, unsuccessful if not hindered.

The comics in *Cracking Up* evoke such power against abjection in their performances, using comedy to serve as counter-discourse to dominant narratives that link US citizenship to white heteropatriarchy. Black feminist comedy uses particular tropes of the body, race, nationality, sexuality, and identity to laugh through, in spite of, with, and at times, beyond abjection. For example, chapter 3 discusses the ways that Mo'Nique and an audience at the Ohio Reformatory for Women use comedy as such a disruption, to rally against the state even under its gaze. The "unruly"—loud or joyful—displays of affect in Black women function as repositories for white supremacist fears about aggression, sexuality, and resistance.

The relevance of pleasure and joy in twentieth and twenty-first century Black feminist comedic performance is a continuation of a legacy of quotidian expression that works to supersede both historical and contemporary violations of and domination over Black people in the United States. In this way, the Black feminist comic is invested in what Christina Sharpe calls "wake work," which thinks "through containment," rupturing the structural silences produced and facilitated by Black social and physical death.[70] I examine comics who are invested in this kind wake work, performers who meld together the cerebral and corporeal, demonstrating how a performer's body, her voice, and the audiences' laughter become vessels of discursive intervention. Their performances crack up the pervasive and seemingly stable nature of white supremacy and thereby expand who belongs in US collective memory.

Methods and Chapter Overview

Cracking Up follows a case-study format that contextualizes, archives, and analyzes important moments in Black feminist comedic performance. I place the artists in *Cracking Up* together because they represent excellent Black feminist performances that forward explicit movements toward freedom, social justice, and Black women/Black queer women's commune. I "crack up" methods of theatre and performance histories that privilege broad surveys over curated close-readings. Instead, this book asks readers to dive deeply into the repertoires of these comics, some of whom have achieved more visibility in popular culture than others. Bold and innovative, the comics in this book centralize the joke as a conduit for social critique.

I am a white, queer feminist, who is deeply invested in anti-racist scholarship, pedagogy, and politics. I am working against the "easy excuses of perfectionism, fear, [and] failure" that plague white academic discourse, and am instead acknowledging the cross-racial and intercultural exchange that exists between myself and the artists in the book.[71] When I close-read and analyze these performances, I am humbly aware that I am doing so from a limited perspective and with cultural blind spots. Given my white racial identity, some of the limits in my readings are unintentional, yet inevitable. Some of them are purposeful. For example, Sam Jay often uses the n—word in her performances. I choose to not type the word in its entirety, and I do not believe the ways Jay employs the word are for me to analyze or even quote. I am following Ta-Nehisi Coates's opinion that the n—word is "a signpost that reminds us that old crimes do not disappear," and that for white people, the word is a place "they can never go."[72] There are many old crimes of white womanhood that live within me, crimes that I carry even as I work to dismantle structures that uphold them. One of these crimes of white superiority is the notion that academic writings about racialized subjects from the perspectives of white authors are a form of rescue or exoticized curiosity.[73] The posture that I strive for as the author of *Cracking Up* is a dialogical one that rejects an anthropological approach of speaking for or over others. This text is not a rescue of Black women's performance, but one that centralizes and celebrates the work of highly skilled and diverse Black feminist comedic artists as shapers and critics of US citizenship, history, and social justice movements.

Jackie Mabley inaugurates the manuscript as the historical pinpoint and innovator of Black feminist comedy; and the twenty-first-century artists in the chapters that follow her both borrow from and build upon Mabley's comedic legacy. That is not to say that Black women did not participate in stand-up comedy and comedic performance more broadly during the later third of the twentieth century. Indeed, comics such as LaWanda Page, Whoopi Goldberg, Marsha Warfield, and Adele Givens (just to name a few) all persevered in an industry that marginalizes voices of color and voices of women and queer folks. The chronological gap in *Cracking Up* is not meant to ignore the efforts of other Black women comics. What I mean to convey in such ahistoricity is both Mabley's relevance to twenty-first-century stand-up, and the importance of examining performances in-depth, offering a "close-up" on the kinds of performances that can often be dismissed as peripheral to theatre history and performance studies. Thus, while *Cracking Up* does not conduct a linear historical survey of Black feminist comics of the past one hundred years, it archives and celebrates exemplars of the form. I do hope *Cracking Up* serves as an archive that honors the work of these women, and places them in future conversations that theorize the cultural significance of comedic performance and Black feminist performance practices at large.

The performances in *Cracking Up* took place in front of live audiences, but they were also recorded for mediated consumption. I understand these performances as archival representations of a particular time and place but also as reaching to present-day and future audiences. I close-read these recorded performances, engage with archival materials, visually interpret images of the performers, and position their work within their own cultural and historical conditions. I study the artists alongside theorists in the fields of Black feminism, performance studies, theatre studies, humor studies, and queer theory. Through an interdisciplinary approach, I attempt to also "crack up" the authority of a singular field of study, especially those disciplines that often marginalize voices of color. I also privilege the artists in *Cracking Up* as theorists in their own rights, as highly skilled in their craft and exemplary models of comedic performances and Black feminist performance. *Cracking Up* makes explicit how the skillful Black feminist comic reflects and produces their own kinds of Black feminist theoretical work and agency. I show throughout the book how comedy is the genre that weaves together, through vernacular rhetoric, the complexities of lived experience, history, and Black feminist theory.

I begin *Cracking Up* by showcasing the innovative yet often overlooked comedy of Jackie "Moms" Mabley. By queerly reading the piecemeal archive of Mabley in chapter 1, I claim that mainstream and scholarly texts misremember her groundbreaking work and contributions to Black queer theatre and performance history. Mabley's voice, though scarce in popular cultural memory, reverberates across space and time. I trace how Mabley's stand-up solidified important precedents for future Black feminist comics and generated purposefully intersectional and radical Black feminist rhetoric in civil rights era United States. In addition to this archival intervention in theatre and performance studies, this chapter also lays the groundwork for the theoretical underpinnings that both inform and are generated through Black feminist comedic performance in the twenty-first century.

The second chapter analyzes Mo'Nique's 2007 *I Coulda Been Your Cellmate!*, a filmed stand-up special by Mo'Nique for imprisoned women at the Ohio Reformatory for Women. Mo'Nique's performance articulates the multiplicities of identity and builds feminist community across difference. Mo'Nique and the women in the audience engage in laughter as a disidentificatory and intimate survival strategy under the gaze and restriction of state power. This chapter addresses the promises and the limits of Black feminist comedy as a method of community and coalition building. I show how Mo'Nique uses Black/feminist/queer methods of dissent—disidentification and erotic power—through comedic performance. Mo'Nique facilitates a time and place in which the rules of her performance (intimacy, liveness, joy, and improvisation) supersede the rules of the carceral state (invisibility, mundane routine, and violence).

Chapter 3 focuses on Black queer temporalities in the comedy of Wanda Sykes from 2008–16. A comedian whose mainstream success is often attributed to her liberal, though nonconfrontational performance style, I examine instances of subversion in Sykes's comedy that crack up linear progress myths in the age of a Barack Obama presidency and before/after the legalization of gay marriage. Analyzing her comedic repertoire during this time period, I theorize how Black feminist comedic performance cracks up white supremacist and heteronormative notions of heritage, citizenship, and historical narrative. Sykes's jokes create opportunities to laugh at white supremacist history; her comedy also opens up narratives about how queer bodies of color experience time not in a singular, progressive fashion, but in a constant tension with dominant ideas of national heritage, white nostalgia, and heteronormative conceptions of progress. Sykes makes visible and audible the unseen and unspoken dominance of time as a tool of state power, and in turn, critiques that power as laughable. The Black feminist comic, in this chapter, operates as critical historiographer against sociopolitical structures that refuse to critique, let alone confront, the realities of structural racism, white heteropatriarchy, and homoliberalism in the age of the Obama administration and fights for marriage equality.

In the final chapter of the book I ask, how do Black women/Black queer comics assert demands for social justice amidst anti-Black, homophobic, anti-trans, and misogynist violence in the twenty-first century? Taking advantage of the expansive opportunities in digital streaming platforms and the audiences that they bring, there is a new cohort of Black feminist comics who are using stand-up comedy for social commentary and explicitly seeking to shift the US culture and the terrain of stand-up comedy toward a Black feminist politic. In this chapter, I highlight and put in conversation the artistry of four comedians: Amanda Seales, Sasheer Zamata, Sam Jay, and Michelle Buteau. Their work both reflects and pushes forward Black feminist comedic agendas, whereby the joke curates Black feminist spaces that critique anti-Black violence, explore what "the new racism" looks like in the twenty-first century, reject cultural and institutional forms of heteronormativity, and document resistance strategies in the wake of #MeToo.

As artist, public intellectual, and cultural worker, the Black feminist comics in this study use the mic to talk back to and crack up dominant narratives that caricaturize Black culture and Black women, and express how systemic racism, sexism, and heterosexism are imposed on the everyday lives of Black women. I argue that these artists take up the political and cultural specificities of Blackness, gender, and sexuality, and articulate the power of these intersecting identities through live performance. Each artist in the following chapters melds Black feminist rhetoric with comedic performance in order to articulate the intertwined nature of struggle and joy. They joke-tell to insist on the vital presence of Black feminist action and community.

Laughter in the Archives
Jackie "Moms" Mabley

In Harlem, 1951, photographer Gordon Anderson captured a candid moment of comic Jackie "Moms" Mabley
outside the Apollo Theatre's back door.[1] Apollo man-
ager William Spayne stands at the top of three steps
leading into the theatre, gazing just beyond the camera. Mabley and an anonymous stagehand stand at the
bottom of the steps. The stagehand is dressed in a black
suit and stares thoughtfully at the camera. The three
figures are close together but Mabley is the focal point
of this photograph. On her stocky frame, Mabley is
dressed in monochromatic light (perhaps white) clothing and sports checkered capris slacks, a short-sleeved
button-up shirt, and a pocket square. She looks casual,
well-tailored, and handsome—striking in her stylish
mix of feminine and masculine attire. She accessorizes
with a short-brim sun hat, a thin watch, and a small
woven basket as her purse. Mabley's hands are clasped
together, wrapped around an unseen object, possibly
a pack of cigarettes. Even through her cat-eyed sunglasses, the camera catches her glare. Her eyebrows
are raised above the dark frames; her lips are slightly
parted and pursed as if speaking directly to Gordon.
This rare image of Jackie Mabley—offstage, and outside
the theatre where she performed more than any other
woman comic—depicts the artist as independent of her
performance persona, "Moms."

Over twenty years later and shortly before her death,
Mabley graced the cover of the January 3, 1974 issue of
Jet Magazine in a feature titled, "Moms Mabley Raps
About Old Women, Young Love." This archival snapshot
tells a much different story of Mabley than the Apollo

photograph, highlighting broad historiographical dilemmas about Mabley's public memory, namely, the conflation of comedic persona and artist, and the erasure of her Black queer performance aesthetics. The article and cover photo stage Mabley as sweet, feminine, and passive. Mabley as cover girl sits in a shimmering light pink silk robe. She dons a conical party hat and holds up a glass of champagne to ring in the New Year with a wide, warm smile. Behind Mabley is her "blind date" for New Year's Day, a young, handsome man named Norris Sutton. He is tall, lean, and wears a brown-checkered leisure suit. *Jet* depicts the couple on their first "date" at Mabley's house. The interviewer, M. Cordell Thompson, refers to Mabley only as Moms and explains that she "initially acted like any woman (young or old) on a blind date, coy and withdrawn, but after several hours, *Jet* had a good interview and Moms was offering the young Sutton a job as her chauffeur."[2] When Thompson asked Moms to offer relationship advice for *Jet*'s younger readers, she stated, "The best time is now when you can go out with who you want, love who you want and as many as you want."[3] The "date" ends with Mabley receiving "a hearty kiss" on the cheek from Sutton. Despite Mabley's words that advocate for nonheteronormative and/or nonmonogamous sexual and romantic expression, the *Jet* article assumes a heterosexual desire that Mabley subtly rejects throughout the interview.

The backstage photograph of Mabley and the widely circulated *Jet* cover exemplify tensions in how Mabley is historicized in public memory. Moms was a grandmother to "all her children" and gleefully flirted with younger men in her audiences. By contrast, Mabley was an out butch lesbian, presented herself as dapper, and was not at all compliant to performances of heterosexual femininity. Anderson's photograph at the Apollo — a somewhat inaccessible remnant of Mabley's archive — captures Mabley in her fierce queerness. Yet, *Jet*'s more mainstream artifact sidesteps the queer entanglement between Mabley's artistry and her performance persona. To the reader/audience not seeking queer possibility, the cognitive dissonance between Mabley's flaunting of sexual freedom through a grandmother persona might simply be humorous. To the queer critic, however, Moms was not a foil to Mabley's lesbian identity but was instead integral to her Black queer performance aesthetics.

Given the disparities between these two archival remnants of the first Black woman stand-up comic, this chapter asks the following

"Moms" Mabley on the cover the Jet, *January 3, 1974.* Jet Magazine.

JAN. 3, 1974/50¢   A JOHNSON PUBLICATION

Moms Mabley Raps About
Old Women, Young Love

MOMS MABLEY &
NORRIS SUTTON

questions: How can Mabley's performance archive reveal the complicated dance between Black feminist comedic artist and comedic
persona, particularly when the two entities are so separated in cultural memory? How does situating Mabley's dynamic civil rights
comedy within Black feminist and Black queer performance aesthetics re-contextualize histories of stand-up? I explore these questions
through two main arguments. First, Mabley's legacy solidifies important precedents for Black feminist comics in contemporary US
performance, cracking up power structures that attempt to silence
Black women and Black queer sexualities. Second, the lack of documentation of Mabley's career reflects historiographical deficiencies
that relegate Black queer and Black feminist histories to the silencing
margins of cultural past and present. Focusing on Mabley's artistry
via her recorded comedy albums of the 1960s, this chapter shows how
this trailblazing artist set standards for critical/cultural work unique

LAUGHTER IN THE ARCHIVES

to Black feminist comedic performance. Although these albums represent only a small snapshot of Mabley's long career, they are the richest source of her comedic material.[4] This lack in documentation also presents an opportunity to crack up the archive—to account for Black feminist/queer possibility beyond "official" records, to look and listen closer to Mabley's Black feminist and Black queer expression through comedic performance.

Throughout this chapter, Black feminist and Black queer performance strategies are central to the legacy of Jackie Mabley. This is not necessarily direct evidence of Mabley's sexuality, but this is not *not* evidence of it. Mabley was an out lesbian. Moms was a performance persona that defied boundaries and containment, and challenged heteropatriarchy, what I would call queer. These two facts may not be causal but are nonetheless intertwined. Queer is an ever-expansive doing. It is a continuous and paradoxical fight for autonomy and connection, a struggle for individual recognition and communal assembly outside the confines of social and legal constructs of "normal." I think of Mabley's queer performances as illuminatory offerings, or what José Esteban Muñoz might have called, "a kernel of political possibility within a stultifying heterosexual present."[5] Moms freely performed expression of sexual desire and political resistance outside of white heteronormative structures and restrictions. Mabley's highly crafted comedic persona, nuanced by and grounded in Black American identity, was also deeply imbued with Black feminist/Black queer aesthetic practices that privilege the body, history, sexuality, and vernacular articulation of racist/sexist/homophobic US culture.

Archiving Black Queer Absence

Mabley's fragmented archive reflects the pervasive erasure of Black feminist and Black queer histories. Moreover, it fails Mabley and glosses over the radical, risky, and joyful work of Black feminist and Black queer resistance over a career that spanned six decades. Rereading Mabley's archive with attention to Black feminist and Black queer agency requires deploying anthropologist Michel-Rolph Trouillot's concept of "thinkability." Trouillot writes, "If some events cannot be accepted even as they occur, how can they be assessed later? In other words, can historical narratives convey plots that are unthinkable in the world within which these narratives take place? How does one write a history of the impossible?"[6] Mabley serves as an example of our "incapacity to express the unthinkable" or archive Black queer histories.[7] The following example validates that, despite earnest attempts to fill in historical gaps, Mabley's Black queer artistry remains on the margins of historical representation and thinkability.

The 2013 HBO documentary *Whoopi Goldberg Presents: Moms Mabley*, at first, seems like a reparative and recuperative effort to celebrate the career of Mabley. Goldberg, the documentary producer and host, acts as investigator, trying to piece together and honor the work of one of her comedic heroes. Gazing straight into the camera, Goldberg states, "When you look at the history [of Mabley], it's the history of Black folks in America. Because all of the information is not there. I realized that I was not in a position to do a biography."[8] The film splices footage, sound clips, and interviews with other comics/cultural critics who admire her; it pays tribute to a sidelined figure in performance history. Yet even with rare footage and images of Mabley, the documentary fails to think beyond the constraints of the archive and heteronormative, liberal ideologies that silence Black queer lives and histories.

Whoopi Goldberg Presents: Moms Mabley addresses Mabley's sexuality with an impulse to reveal and then quickly dismiss its influence on her comedic persona and politics. Midway through the seventy-minute documentary, a slew of Mabley's former coworkers and her sister in-law talk about Mabley as "one of the guys" in the entertainment industry. Norma Miller, a Black American dancer often dubbed "The Queen of Swing," "reveals" Mabley's sexuality. With admiration, Miller describes Mabley as the "dominant force among Black female comedians." She explains that she met Mabley at the Apollo Theatre when they worked in variety shows together. "She and I shared a dressing room for two weeks," Miller explains. She then looks into the camera and pauses. A thin smirk spreads across her face: "She and I, and her girlfriend."[9] Her eyebrows raise in declarative punctuation.

The background swing music crescendos as the screen cuts to a photograph of Mabley, at some time in her middle age. She is unmistakably dapper and butch in a tailored, three-piece suit, light shirt, dark tie, and pocket square. Mabley holds a cigarette in one hand and the other is slipped into her pocket. One foot casually rests on a chair. Mabley gazes into the camera with a solemn, comfortable expression. She wears no makeup. Her hair is cut to a short crop. Miller continues describing Mabley's sexual and gender expression. She explains that her fellow performers nicknamed her, "Mr. Moms," as this suited her masculine dress and queer sexuality, but still rang true to her caring nature as a colleague. "When she walked off that stage she was 'Mr. Moms.' There was no question about it. . . . We never called her lesbian. We never called her gay. That word didn't fit her. We just called her Mr. Moms."[10]

Another shot of Mabley shows her in her Moms costume flanked by two young dancers. A third woman sits on the floor in between Mabley's legs. The women are glamorous and adoringly gaze at Mabley, who stares into the camera with her wide smile. Notably, Miller is the only person interviewed who refuses to conflate Mabley with her comedic persona, and who discusses Mabley's out sexuality. After this scene, Miller, who describes Mabley as a performer and person who refused normative gender binaries, is essentially silenced throughout the rest of the film.

When Goldberg responds to Miller's account, she stares right into the camera as if giving a lecture. But Goldberg's authority as the film's producer and host becomes problematic as she claims the last word about Mabley's sexuality. Goldberg states that Mabley's queerness was matter of fact, and she erases the risks and joys of being out: "At that time, it was nobody's business. I think that she was a woman among men who was equal to those men, and they treated her like a man. And I think that is what helped give her the longevity."[11] Goldberg also asserts herself as historical authority when she states, "I will assume that when Moms came out of her costume and put on that silk shirt with those pants and had those women on her arm, I think everyone was like, 'Okay.'"[12] Goldberg's seemingly progressive and nonchalant impulse to equate Mabley to "one of the guys" erases queer desire, pervasive homophobia, and Mabley's strategic queer performance practices. Mabley's queerness is never again fully addressed in the film. Even as the documentary attempts to disrupt traditional biographies and tell a nuanced story of Mabley, it reifies and perpetuates a heteronormative, liberal history of Jackie Mabley. Thus, while the film does not fully erase Mabley's sexuality, it does craft a history in which Mabley's queerness is coincidental, or at the very least, peripheral to her artistry.

The documentary furthers its historiographical deficiencies by also undermining the labor of Mabley's comedic performance. Comic (and former contemporary of Mabley's) Anne Meara, for example, dismisses Mabley's skillful and exacting style of comedy and once again conflates Moms the persona with Mabley the artist: "She was a trailblazer. And she wasn't trying to be a trailblazer."[13] Without pause, Meara slips into an (inaccurate) impersonation of Mabley's voice, gravely, low, and with a stereotypical Black vernacular: "She was just tryin' to say her stuff, you know?"[14] As if Mabley's artistry was accidental, and Moms's and Mabley's stories were one and the same, Meara disregards Mabley's virtuosity and exceptional performance skills. This harkens back to racist archetypes that characterize Black people as "naturally" gifted and happy to entertain with apolitical performance material and motives. By dismissing Mabley's sexuality or labeling her skills as "natural" talent, and ignoring links between Mabley's sexuality, her performance persona, and her politics, the documentary fails to encapsulate Mabley's impact on Black feminist/Black queer performance histories. This particular archive of Mabley, like the *Jet* article, concedes to the normative biases of the living, and dilutes significant stories of queer performance histories and Black feminist innovation in the United States.

To tell a more complex story of Jackie Mabley is to invest in understanding the imperative cultural labor of the Black feminist/Black queer comic and the legacies their performances and lives incur. Following Roderick A. Ferguson's call to write materialist histories, I historicize Mabley's work not "emptied of the racialized and classed particularized of gender and sexuality, but framed in terms of them."[15] This chapter thus centers Mabley's comedy as decidedly Black, feminist, and queer and reads against histories that attempt to quiet or make mutually exclusive such identity markers and performative strategies of resistance. Mabley's story is one that requires us to look at and listen more closely to the archive, showing the important, even if fragmented ways that, in the words of Matt Richardson, "Black queer culture and life exist in the interstices of various historical narratives of blackness, queerness, women, diaspora, and the nation."[16] Mabley's stand-up established the productive and transformative work of Black feminist comedic performance and its place in theatre scholarship, feminist theory, and Black/Black queer studies.

From Mabley to Moms:
Crafting a Black Feminist/Black Queer Comic Persona

I read Mabley as intentional in crafting Moms to showcase queerness in subversive ways, marketed to mass Black—and, later in her career, racially integrated—audiences. Through comedy and the persona of a grandmotherly figure, Mabley spoke truths about white supremacy, gender inequity, class dynamics, and sexuality in blunt, confrontational ways that otherwise may have been dangerous for a Black lesbian to do in the public sphere. Haggins defines the comedic persona as a construction of multiple ideologies pieced together by "acculturation, individual choice, and industrial imperatives" that can reveal "the inherent tenuousness of the black comic's place in contemporary American comedy."[17] Haggins focuses on comedic persona to analyze the artistry rather than biography of a comic; however, I argue that Mabley's persona of Moms did not detract from Mabley's Black queer aesthetic practices as an artist. Moms was the conduit through which Mabley enacted Black feminist and Black queer performance activism in civil rights era United States.

Mabley was born Loretta Mary Aiken between 1894 and 1897 in Brevard, North Carolina. This three-year gap exists because Mabley was never forthcoming about her age. Straddling the delicate balance between her stage persona and her personal life, Mabley played the part of Moms when reporters asked her how old she was, avoiding direct answers to the question. As noted in *Ebony* in 1974, "When it comes to her age, Moms is as evasive as a hostile Watergate witness."[18] Elise Williams explains in her biography *The Humor of Jackie Moms Mabley*, "though she on occasion revealed personal details during her performances, she characteristically avoided revealing specific, intimate details of her life to interviewers."[19] A year before her death in 1975, Mabley, bored by the question of her age from a curious reporter, dryly responded in a monotone voice, "I ain't that old. I'm not quite that old." She then lifted her cigarette, pinched between her thumb and forefinger, and took a long drag.[20]

Mabley began her performance career at the age of fourteen in order to help support her family. She left home and joined a minstrel troupe that performed all over the United States. A 1974 *New York Magazine* profile of Mabley claimed that "Moms was already 'letting granny grow' when Butterbeans and Suzie, the famous dance team, caught her on the TOBA one night in 1921."[21] Women comics who worked for TOBA often performed as the foil or sidekick to male performers. However, under the guidance of Butterbeans and Suzie, Mabley developed "Moms" as a solo act in her early twenties. She became the only woman on the TOBA circuit to perform comedy without a male counterpart.

Mabley stood out on the TOBA circuit as a solo performer and was certainly influenced and encouraged by the political performances popular among Black audiences at the time. Christine Acham points out that TOBA "formed the basis of political comedy" for Black Americans in the early twentieth century United States.[22] In the 1920s, communities of Black working-class performers and audiences found TOBA to be an outlet for cultural production and expression through working-class, nonassimilationist performances.[23] The performers of TOBA established an "empire of comedy and pathos ... for, by, and about Black folks," and Mabley's work is in line with this unapologetic and celebratory staging of Black experience and pride.[24]

The Moms persona allowed Mabley to perform alone, guarded, and outside the confines of sexually exploitative expectations placed upon other Black women contemporaries in the circuit. As a result, Mabley was able to craft Moms to focus on the intersections of race, class, gender, and sexuality.[25] Dressed in an oversized housecoat, floppy slippers, and a short wig and hat, Mabley "schooled" her audiences through jokes and storytelling. The 1948 film *Boarding House Blues* captured Mabley's early iteration of her "Moms" persona. The film follows a group of Black vaudeville performers trying to save their favorite boarding house (owned by Moms) from foreclosure. As a fundraiser, they put on a show, and Moms is one of the comedy acts. Mabley, who was at the time middle-aged and not quite as elderly as her character let on, comes onstage in her persona's signature costume, tap dances, and tells versions of what become some of her most famous routines. Hands on hips, feet turned out in too-big slippers, she laments about losing her job and losing her man, who would often call her a dog. "Sometimes, I wish I was a dog, and he was a tree, I'll tell you that much."[26]

Mabley wove her penchant for truth-telling and pleasure through comedy into her mythology of "Moms." Blending Mabley's actual biography with the creation of Moms, Mabley credited her sense of humor and self-determination to her grandmother on the 1964

Jackie Mabley as "Moms." Library of Congress, Prints and Photographs Division, NYWT&S Collection, [LC-USZ62-117535 (b&w film copy neg.)].

album, *The Funny Sides of Moms Mabley*. Moms tells the story of how her great-grandmother, Harriet Smith from Brevard, North Carolina, taught Moms to be "hip."[27] Moms exclaims, "This is the truth. She lived to be 118 years old. And you wonder why Moms is hip today? Granny hip me. She said, I done lied to the rest of 'em but I'm not gonna let you be dumb, I'm gonna tell you the truth."[28] As Moms, Mabley performs an homage to matriarchal lineage. In a gruff, low tone with sometimes slurred speech, Mabley's voice is as distinct as her comedic material. She continues, by recounting a conversation with Granny:

> One day she sitting out on the porch and I said, "Granny how old does a woman get before she don't want no boyfriend?" She was around 106 then. She said, "I don't know honey, you have to ask somebody older than me!" She said, "A woman is a woman as long as she lives. But at a certain place in time a man has to go to a place they call Over the Hill. And when you got to go son, go like a man.... And you don't have to be old because your head bald. You don't have to be old cause your hair is gray. But when your mind start makin' them dates that your body can't fill? Over the Hill, brother!"[29]

Blurring the lines between storytelling and one-liners, between fact and fiction, this particular bit reflects Mabley's political and personable joke-telling style. The porch becomes a site of Black Southern communal gathering and feminist empowerment. Mabley enacts what E. Patrick Johnson calls a "quare" performance style, or a vernacular performance/theory-making that "locates racialized and class knowledges" and employs non-normative sexuality via "an embodied politic of resistance."[30] As Granny explains, women have agency over their bodies and minds their entire lives, but men's power and desirability have an expiration date. This philosophy carried over into the ethos of "Moms," who found old men deplorable and flaunted her sexual prowess no matter her age. By revising misogynist traditions of making women the object of the joke, Mabley creates a world in which older Black women's sexual desire and confidence exist and are to be celebrated.

As Moms, Mabley foregrounded performances of pleasure and sexual agency and rejected the invisibility placed upon Black/queer women. Moms defied invisibility. She entered a stage with her arms stretched out widely. Her eyes would bug out comically at each of her punchlines. In her later years, when Mabley wore dentures, she would take them out for her performances, smacking her lips in an exaggerated way to show she was not wearing her false teeth. Moms flaunted sexual desire and ease onstage. Moms did not hide older age, she paraded around in it. Moms did not shrink, she took up as much space as possible, even occasionally laughing at her own jokes and loudly slapping her leg. Mabley's Black queer iteration of a grandmother character made space for a singular, mature, funny Black woman to express a brashness and bossiness not culturally "allowed" for Black women of her time. Mabley's performances as Moms mock and resist heteronormative femininity and sexuality. A grandmother or mammy caricature might be selfless and sexless, but Moms was self-possessed and insistent on physical and sexual pleasure.[31]

The Black queer sensibility of Moms is also found in her movement among various contradictions. Mabley's performances as Moms found possibility within seemingly disparate characteristics of subjecthood. She was quite mobile among aspects of the self—hypersexual and motherly, aging and hip, or nonthreatening and dissenting. Mabley did not just straddle these lines, she invalidated the boundaries that separate these often gendered and racialized traits. Moms was funny to audiences because she spoke the kinds of truths characteristic of older family and community members, and because she strayed from the many other roles that older women are expected to occupy in white, ageist, and heterosexist frameworks. Mabley's corporeal-centered performances displayed the Black woman's body as a site and source of pleasure, anger, sexual desire, and political resistance.

The Anti-Patriarchal Power of Moms

Like the physical act of Black feminist laughter, Mabley's explosive Black queer persona destabilized and disobeyed a heteronormative imperative. For example, Moms tells an audience during a performance recorded on her 1962 album, *Moms Mabley at Geneva Conference*, that she prefers to wear a muumuu-style dress for the embodied freedom it allows. She declares: "I like 'em! For the summer, you know? I think this is what a woman ought to wear in the summertime." She continues, gently building her voice to a guttural exclamation: "So the air can circulate, you know? See them great big fat women in the summertime, with all them corsets and brassieres on. And get that air all hemmed up in there. And when it does come out, it's terrible!"[32] Historically a muumuu or housedress is worn in the privacy of the home to cover up the body and deemphasize the feminine form. However, Moms declares to the public that she loves her muumuu because it lets her genitalia catch a breeze. Roberta Mock would argue, and I agree, that older women comics' act of addressing the "mature vagina" in performance is both unruly and productive.[33] The aging/aged body of Moms is in direct opposition to a desexualized older Black woman. The muumuu, a garment linked in the 1960s to leisure and working-class fashion aesthetics, created a discrete freedom championed by Moms. Moms is free from constraint, from boundaries. Setting standards for Black feminist comedy to eloquently "play between public and private spaces," Mabley showed how joke-telling "becomes one such means in which Black women's self-invention and desire can flourish."[34] Mabley's sexually ignited grandmother is "breezy" and unabashedly comfortable, performing the Black queer grandmother who refuses constraints of age, modesty, and physical decline.

Mabley's comedy resisted compliance with patriarchal systems and with heteronormative notions of female passivity. However, she did not just use simple comedic inversion, or reversing the butt of the joke onto the male body, for laughs. Her jokes go a step further by exposing and queering the systems that put the female body on display for the purposes of heterosexual male consumption and objectification. On *Moms Mabley Live at Sing Sing* (1970), Mabley inverts objectification of the female body onstage, instead objectifying the elderly male body in one of her many "Old Man" bits. Mabley performed at the Sing Sing Correctional Facility in Ossining, New York around the Christmas holiday. This album is the only recorded performance of her stand-up at the prison.

The crowd cheers loudly when the announcer introduces her as the "the funniest lady in the world." When Mabley yells, "Hello dollies!" the audience cheers more intensely, their applause booming and echoing. Mabley establishes Moms as a caring figure who not-so-slyly voices dissent against the carceral system. She brings the warden onstage, thanks him for inviting her to Sing Sing, and gifts him two of her albums. "Now you just go home and put them on your machine, and laugh yourself to *death*!"[35]

This performance took place well into Mabley's career; she had built a reputation for shunning older men by making sexual advances at young males in her audience. About halfway into the set Moms begins, "That old man like to run me crazy, children. I don't want nothin' old but some old money. And I'm gonna use it to put an ad in the paper for some young man!"[36] The crowd cheers, and even Moms/Mabley chuckles at her own joke. Moms continues the set by describing the "one old man" she'd ever been with: "Old men don't know how to do nothin'. There ain't nothing for him to do but be old. My old man was sitting under a tree this summer and a leaf fell on him and knocked him out. He got up on the scale to weigh [himself] and the scale didn't move."[37] Here, Mabley employs hyperbole to paint a comedic picture of the male body's weakness and uselessness.

Mabley affirms her own comedic prowess and her control over her audience. When she says, "a leaf fell on him and knocked him out." Mabley laughs low and slow as the rest of the audience in the recording howls. She continues:

> He looked at me and he said, "Tell me, just tell me, where you gonna find another man like me?" I said, "In the graveyard."
> He said, "What man can you find that will treat you like I do?"
> I said, "Hitler." He said, "If I should die what would you do?"
> I said, "Laugh." He said, "I ain't gonna argue with you. I'm going upstairs. I'm going to bed." I said, "You gonna have to wait a while 'cause I don't feel like carrying you up the steps."[38]

Mabley slowly builds up this story in speed and rhythm until the audience is uproarious in their laughter. She skillfully moves back and forth between her own voice and the character of the old man. Mabley's voice, still gruff and low in tone, is nonetheless strong and loud. It booms into the microphone and echoes at the end of her sentences. On the contrary, the old man's voice is whispery and shaky. Mabley adds a mocking undertone to the Old Man, a wink to the audience of his stupidity. In this quick exchange, she reverses normative gender coding through vocal affect. The Old Man is feminized through a weak vocality. He is quiet and struggling, whereas Moms is loud and assertive. Moms's stronger voice fuels her contentions that her old man does not meet any of her sexual or emotional needs.

Mabley cracks up patriarchy, strategically objectifying and emasculating a heterosexual male for an audience of all men. She mocks male heterosexual desire, physical strength, and the ability to take care of a female partner. The male spectators in this performance, even as they laugh, cannot identify with Mabley. If they fall into the category of the older male, they are forced into the role of the useless partner. If they are younger, they become the object of Moms's desire. Mabley exposes, destabilizes, and denaturalizes compulsory heterosexuality and "proper" performance of femininity, and asks that her audience question their role as the supposed power holders within a heterosexual dynamic.

Mabley continues with her disgust for older men in a musical number that parodies the song "Can't Take My Eyes Off of You." Mabley calls this her "Old Man Opera." Employing the structure and melody of a famous love song, the lyrics re-situate Moms as the singer in power over the Old Man, not hypnotized or distracted by heterosexual desire. The song begins:

> You're just too old to be true.
> There's nothing weaker than you.
> I have to grab you and shake
> Just to keep you awake!
> There's nothing more I can do.
> You're just too far gone to be true.[39]

Mabley not only changes the words to the original song, but also shifts the role of narrator from passive to active. Frankie Valli's original recording, "You're just too good to be true / Can't take my eyes off of you / You'd be like heaven to touch / I wanna hold you so much," locates the narrator as distant from the object of desire, idealizing them and wishing for them from afar.[40] Mabley, however, places Moms in the present moment with the old man, who is physically passive and mentally incapable according to her lyrics ("far gone"). In this queer iteration of a love song, Mabley strategically essentializes the male body as disposable, mute, and blind. Moms sings of her longing, not *for* the Old Man, but for his cessation: "You're just too weak to be true / I'm sorry I ever met you / Why don't you give me a break / and just go jump in the lake?"[41]

Mabley employs her infamous vocal virtuosity in this recording to render the Old Man abject and place Moms as Black feminist agent. Not smooth like Valli's recording, but biting and hoarse, Mabley's voice fuels her impeccable comedic timing and a fierce rejection of patriarchal power. Moms ends the song lamenting with a drawn out "my old man," the vowels dragging and elongating, so the listener hears "myyyyy oooooooold maaaaaaan." Her notes are guttural and low, denouncing the subject of her ballad. Long-held notes, according to Meta DuEwa Jones's analysis of Langston Hughes's public performance of poetry, "signifies a fierce, fearsome, can't-touch-me attitude that might also indicate a begrudging form of respect."[42] Moms both cannot and will not depend on the patriarchal figure. Mabley's performances queer the subject of the grandmother strategically and pointedly, and mark Moms as a creator of her own gendered, racialized, and sexual ideologies. Here Mabley enacts a key mode of cracking up for the Black feminist comic: vocalizing, exposing, and disposing of patriarchal scenarios that contain Black women and Black queer subjectivity.

Cracking Up the "Good Old Days"

Sexual freedom was central to the persona of Moms, as were pointed critiques of white nostalgia and patriarchy. Mabley revised the stereotypical nostalgic grandmother narrative, re-membering historical experience through Black feminist and Black queer standpoints. Performing the role of comic and cultural critic, Mabley complicated dominant narratives of the "good old days" and positioned herself as a self-possessed sexual agent. Like much of her other comedic material, Mabley weaved jokes in and out of familiar cultural scripts, riffing on and revising popular songs, nostalgic story structures, and fairy tales. Within the persona of mother/grandmother, her stand-up routines evoke a sense of domesticity—sitting down at the kitchen table listening to a family member talk about the past or tell a children's story.

For example, in her 1964 album *Out on a Limb*, Moms retells the Cinderella fairy tale, called "Cindyella." Cindyella is a little Black girl whose fairy godmother, Bobby Kennedy, turns her into a white girl so she can go to a dance. Through the wave of his two wands, the Civil Rights Bill and the Constitution, Kennedy transforms Cindyella:

On her pretty black hair she had a pretty blue ribbon. She looked down at her feet and her shoes had turned to pretty glass slippers. She went over to the mirror and to her surprise she had turned as white as snowy bleach. She said, "Mirror, mirror on the wall who's the fairest of them all?"

Moms describes this scene with sweet reverence as if reading to children. Her tone shifts quickly as she gets to her first punchline, she bluntly declares: "The mirror said, 'Snow White and don't you forget it!'" Her audience laughs heartily, Mabley's comedic timing bursts through her initially enchanting tone, and laments the futility of assimilation. Revising the original fairy-tale simile, "white as snow," to "white as snowy bleach," Mabley describes Cindyella as possessing a skin tone the color of a chemical. The state claims to emancipate Cindyella, but even as she turns white Bobby Kennedy reminds her bluntly that she is not and will never be the "fairest of them all." Mabley thus frames whiteness as a covert poison that purports to cleanse.

As Mabley's fairy-tale version goes, when the clock struck midnight, Cindyella's dress turned to rags and her skin no longer fair. Mabley builds to her punch line: "Everyone was gazin' on the floor at Cindyella. The little colored girl dancing with the president of the Klu Klux Klan. This story is to be continued. Her trial comes up next month!"[43] Here and throughout her repertoire, Mabley's comedic performances "defy traditional notions of temporality through simultaneously repeating and revising cultural scripts or scenarios."[44] The fairy tale, reifies normative gender roles, instills ideals of white womanhood, and romanticizes heteropatriarchy. Cindyella initially tells a new, hopeful story, centering a Black girl and the redemptive potential of the United States through the Civil Rights Bill, the Constitution, and help from a gender-flipping godmother, Bobby Kennedy. With humor that cuts deep, Mabley stops short of a nostalgic revision. Instead, the state cannot be trusted to protect Cindyella, and white supremacy constantly prevents a happily ever-after.

Mabley also refused and rebutted patriarchal nostalgia through her repertoire of Old Man jokes. For example, in *Moms Mabley Live at the Apollo*, Mabley performed a well-loved and often repeated bit titled, "The Good Old Days." In it, Mabley scrutinized and amended typical "good old days" narratives from nostalgic to complex, revealing how misogyny circulates in the everyday and imbues itself in cultural memory. Moms introduces the bit by quickly shifting from sentimental to potent commentary on patriarchal domination. She begins boisterously, even cheerfully: "Let me tell you about the good old days." She pauses before landing the punchline: "You couldn't do nothin'!" Moms continues describing the darkness of the "good old days":

And if you did, they'd [your parents] would knock your brains out. He hit my brother so much with a backhand, until his lips were out here. Looked like he put on a turtleneck sweater. Everything your parents pick for you to do. Who are you to love, who are you to go out with, who are even you to marry ... If Daddy said so that was it.[45]

Grounded in what Haggins calls socially defiant "commonsense feminism," Mabley resists simple nostalgia. She is frank about a childhood entrenched in patriarchy and violence.[46] When Moms states, "let me tell you about the good old days," she initially seems to reminisce about simpler times. However, the narrative quickly becomes a critique of the domestic sphere and gender inequality. Mabley proclaims Moms's subjectivity as both narrator and powerful subject within the story. When she states, "let *me* tell you about the good old days," the past moves from universal to specific—this will be Moms's story, rather than a romanticized version of history.

Mabley strategically switches between first and second person in this routine, shifting the story from stereotypical nostalgia to detailing the specifics of a Black feminist perspective. When Mabley changes the subject of her monologue by saying, "you couldn't do nothing" instead of "I couldn't do nothing" while explaining the controlling nature of her household, she demands her audience to put themselves in such a situation. After Mabley remarks, "if Daddy said so, that was it," she seamlessly switches back to first person when talking about her looks. While the matronly persona of Moms could potentially reify nostalgia, positioning her body as a caretaker/mammy of the audience, Mabley instead uses this persona to direct identification toward Black women's experience.

She continues the joke in an exaggerated tragic tone, elongating her words and reminiscing: "I was nothing but a child. Fourteen going on fifteen." Her manner quickly shifts to confident, quick, and sassy: "And just as cute as I want to be. Hair hanging down my back. See, I'm half Indian. And the other half, the beauty parlor takes care of that!" Moms laughs heartily and then shifts her voice low and slow, introducing another one of her Old Man bits: "And this old, dead, puny, moldy man." She picks up the pace and moves into playing the dozens, "I mean an old man. Santa Claus looked like his son. He was older than his mother. Even when his sister died, we went to her funeral. After the funeral the minister went over tapped him on the back, said, 'How old are you, Pops?' He said, '91.' He [the minister] said, 'Ain't no need in you going home!'"[47]

Mabley's bits were often fictionalized, but she was forced into marriage at age fourteen and was the victim of sexual assault by two adult men in her community.[48] In this recording, Mabley as Moms has a voice in her own archive—she re-members it, recalling and revising an archive that positions her as agential. Mabley is, as Elin Diamond suggests, "not only a solo woman performer in view, but a female body that [produces] new means of imbricating the psychic and the historical."[49] The process of remembering is, like theatrical and everyday performance, both an ever shifting and embodied practice. In other words, memory for an individual or a public is dynamic, and one cannot instigate memory without attention to the body. With detailed attention to her own physical beauty while rendering the old man's body near death/abject, Mabley creates a dialectical image— Moms is separated from the violence described in the story and is instead the subversive joke-teller/survivor. While being "nothing but a child" initially evokes images of an innocent, tragic victim, Moms sassily describes herself as "just as cute as I want to be." She turns the image of childhood trauma to one of agency. Thus, even under the control of her father, she declares self-possession through an understanding of natural beauty ("hair hanging down my back. See I'm half Indian.") and control over self-presentation ("the beauty parlor takes care of that!").

Mabley crafts a vocalized performance in which Moms possesses power (youth, beauty, self-determination) and the old man is voiceless, nameless, and weak. When she introduces him, she elongates "old," stretching the vowels to signify her contempt and exhaustion, as well as his age. By describing the old man as dead and moldy, Mabley reads him to abjection in the Black rhetorical tradition of signifyin(g).[50] Mabley also queers the hyperbolic, often misogynistic undertones of the dirty dozens. A "figurative, ritual insult" often aimed at a mother, Mabley flips the script.[51] Mabley does not use the mother figure as the outlet to roast the old man. Instead, she uses his own abject body against him. As hyperbole, being older than one's mother is comedic. Moreover, it denies the old man's birth and, thus, existence. Moms re-members an oppressive structure (marriage and also the script of nostalgia) to an agential one. Or, as Shane Vogel describes,

Moms deploys a Black feminist tactic of "phenomenological unfolding through space and time as she interfaces with a public, masculine and economic world."[52] The joke here is not only that Mabley inverts the past to expose patriarchal power structures but also that she shows how thinking fondly of the "old days" is a ridiculous act. In this bit, to tell the story with a sense of genuine nostalgia would be the joke in and of itself.

Free to Roam: Black Queer Disruption in the South

By the 1960s, Mabley was a household name. She was famous for her live performances in mostly northern US cities, widely distributed comedy albums, and appearances on prime-time television on programs such as *The Smothers Brothers' Comedy Hour* and the *Merv Griffin Show*. In the last fourteen years of her career, Mabley's comedic prowess reached larger and more racially diverse audiences. She used her comedic legend status to preach messages of civil rights and challenge structures of white supremacy in the United States. Mabley's earliest routines as Moms lamented her bad luck and dismissed old men, but in the later years of her career, Moms became more overtly political.[53] The persona of Moms was not only convenient for truth-telling about gender and sexuality but also for critiquing structures of anti-Black racism.

In her 1960s comedy albums, Moms was a spokesperson for civil rights protest, cracking up systems of inequity in the United States. Much of her material from this time addressed a specific kind of civil rights rhetoric that tackled issues of location, mobility, and safety for Black Americans in the Southern United States. Onstage, Moms preached the rhetoric of Martin Luther King, Jr. and Bobby Kennedy in hopeful tones, while also using comedy to articulate the ever-looming threat of violence for Black populations in the United States, particularly in the Jim Crow South. She utilized various joke formats—the pun, the stunt, and musical parody—to assert Black, feminist, and queer citizenship. These routines, funny, yet explicit in their telling of anti-Black violence, deconstruct racist systems that only grant security and full citizenship to white citizens.

One of Mabley's most popular comedic civil rights protest strategies was to deride the "backward" nature of the South. After Mabley began performing on the TOBA circuit, she never again lived below the Mason-Dixon Line and, as Moms, would frequently refer to the

South as "that other country" or a "foreign country." Distancing herself from Southern culture and pointing out the injustices of Jim Crow laws and anti-Black racism, Mabley ridiculed the South as a space without logic in order to highlight how white supremacy permeated the legal and colloquial processes of life. During a performance at the Playboy Club in Chicago in August 1961, Moms tells a story of driving through South Carolina on her way to Florida for a show. She begins, "I was on my way down to Miami." Quickly, she corrects herself, her tone turning toward mild disgust, "I mean, *they-ami*."[54] Her sarcasm is derisive. She employs this tenor and wordplay to both point out the obvious dangers of a Black woman's body in the South and, more importantly, to give the place over to the white people who are interested in maintaining state-sponsored segregation. In this instance, she emphasizes a desire for cultural separation from the South and also outright rejects the region as fully American. She continues to the main punchline of the bit:

> I was riding along in my Cadillac you know. Going through one of them towns in South Carolina. Passed through a red light. One of them big cops came over to me and said, "Hey woman. Don't you know you went through a red light?" I said, "Yeah, I know I went through a red light." He said, "Well what'd you do that for?"[55]

Feigning innocence, Moms fakes the role of a polite, mistaken, older woman. "I said, ''Cause I seen all you white folks going on the green light, I thought the red light was for us! I didn't know!'"

The palpable threat of anti-Black violence looms over the scene Mabley sets. Two months before this performance, the first group of Freedom Riders left Washington, DC on two busses, en route to New Orleans—beginning a tour of the Southern US to protest racial segregation in bus terminals. As the cohort of interracial activists rode deeper into the South, threats of violence became more pronounced. By the time they reached Alabama, white mobs attacked the bus depots, aided by law enforcement who promised residents no arrests would be made against white vigilantes. In Anniston, Alabama, the KKK set fire to the first bus of Freedom Riders. Next, in Birmingham, white supremacists dragged the activists off the bus, severely beating them while local police stood idle. Klansmen and other white Southerners terrorized the hundreds of activists who arrived in the Deep South the rest of that summer.[56] Given the pervasive links between anti-Black violence and law enforcement, Mabley implicates the police officer in this story as a threat to her safety and mobility. However, Moms escapes intimidation and persecution through witty manipulation (and, perhaps, class status in her expensive car). Timely and biting, Mabley references the dangers of interstate travel for Black people in the US and characterizes law enforcement as threatening, but not to be bested.

Like her "*they*ami" bit, Moms strategically toes the line between powerful resistance and playful ignorance in a performance recorded on *The Best of Moms Mabley and Pigmeat Vol. 1* (1961).[57] Moms quietly says to her audience, as if leaning in to share a secret, "I just got back from down there ... you know."[58] She clears her throat, perhaps waiting for a verbal or nonverbal response from the audience. When she says, "down there," her voice goes low and dips as she enunciates and elongates "there." "You know" implies that her audience is on her side—that they have experienced or are aware of Jim Crow and racial violence, and that they also see the South as backward. "You know" bonds the audience to Moms and places all of them in firm opposition to the haunted space below the Mason-Dixon Line. This generalization of the Southern United States and its anti-Black racism also harkens back to the ways in which white people have used indirect, coded language to speak of the "dangers" of predominantly Black neighborhoods as "bad." Moms continues the story:

I didn't want to go, but you know, my children are down there. ... And I tried to pass, you know? For anything except what I am, you know? And some of my friends from Montana, my children out there, sent me a cowgirl outfit. So, I wore that the whole time I was there. I wouldn't wear nothing but this cowgirl outfit. They were nice to me! I was surprised. They didn't treat me bad at all. In fact, they called me after Roy Rogers's horse: Trigger! Everywhere I go, they say "Hi Trigger!" At least I think that's what they said![59]

To a sympathetic audience, she can easily express why the South is a hostile place without much explanation, and how Black mobility requires a constant monitoring to gauge the safety of one's surroundings, or what Koritha Mitchell describes as the simultaneous mundaneness and pervasiveness of anti-Black racism.[60] Jim Crow laws and the specters of lynching, alive and well "down there," meant that despite Mabley's/Moms's success and class status, she would have to defer to state-sponsored segregation and the ever-present threat of violence and harassment.

In an effort to pass for "anything except what I am," Moms's cowgirl drag carries with it historical and cultural codes incongruous with Blackness and femininity, as the rancher operates as a symbol for white masculinity and power.[61] The joke also highlights the comedic stunt as a strategy of opposition. Mary Russo's *The Female Grotesque* defines the "stunt" as something that may be more helpful to marginalized groups within risky and unsafe places "where strategy is not possible."[62] The stunt is a performative tactic in which the forceful display of the self involves "a reshaping of the entire woman/space configuration away from the inner/outer dichotomies of bodily and spatial representation."[63] Moms makes herself hyper-visible—faking obliviousness to her outrageous outfit and an inability to hear the violent word of the presumably white residents, while affirming the real threat of anti-Black violence in the Jim Crow South. Moms was never meant to pass, but she performs resistance through the costume of a flamboyant cowgirl.[64] Mabley creates the act of the comedic stunt to ironically play up the stereotype of a happy, ignorant Black/Black queer body to invade white/heteronormative spaces. The disruption of Black respectability and propriety is a mode of asserting Black feminist/Black queer presence in an unwelcoming space. This public performance, fictional or not, fractures the image of the rural South as bucolic and serene. Mabley once again loosens the knot of nostalgia that holds tight to a happy, tranquil South.

When stating, "Hi Trigger," Mabley manipulates the usual gravely low tone of Moms and replaces it with a higher, crisper stereotype of a Southern male. "Hi, Trigger" comes out of Mabley's mouth in a slow drawl. The words themselves, while seemingly friendly, are haunted by the word Moms did not (or would not) hear. Additionally, Mabley's vocality, or what Faedra Carpenter calls "linguistic whiteface," instigates affective, mocking confrontation.[65] Linguistic white face has long been a Black comedic tactic of foiling white superiority. Carpio's study on Richard Pryor's imitation of white vocality asserts that vocal performance and Black resistance can work in tandem. She argues, "Black Americans have not only created their own stereotypes of white Americans—of 'peckerwoods' and 'honkies'—but have also directed their laughter at the stereotypes with which they have been represented, appropriating those images in order to diffuse the power of humiliation."[66] This type of performance reveals "the nature of the stereotype itself, showing what it masks and suggests, and what people, across gender and race, have invested in it."[67] "Hi, Trigger," then, is an important moment in this bit insofar as it not only exposes the threatening menace of anti-Black violence but also reveals Mabley's virtuosity, employing vocality as a strategic tool of resistance. In the telling of this fictional joke, Mabley renders white men stupid while foiling stereotypes of Black cheerfulness and willingness to accommodate, thereby inverting each group's supposedly customary power dynamics.

Mabley used song parodies to perform a desire for freedom from state-sanctioned violence. In one rhyming bit on her *Moms Mabley at the Playboy Club* (1961), Moms revises Lead Belly's "I'm Alabama Bound," rapping:

> To tell you the truth I'm scared as a son of a gun
> And baby I'm too old to run.
> So I ain't Alabamee bound
> Not this evening.
> 'Cause I'm not gonna let the Greyhound take me
>   down there and the bloodhound take me back
> You know Moms is too hip for that![68]

Recorded during a performance at the Uptown Theatre in Philadelphia five years after the murder of Emmett Till and four years before the passage of the Civil Rights Bill, Moms expresses the anguish of past state-sanctioned violence and trauma inflicted on Black bodies in the South, and also predicts the future to be grim. Again, referencing the Freedom Riders' dissenting trips to Alabama (Greyhound) and the violence those activist encountered (bloodhound), Moms gives over such corporeal risks to a younger generation. She is both "too old to run," but also, "too hip" to place herself in danger.

Another small but powerful bit from a performance at the Uptown Theatre in 1961 on *Moms Mabley Live at the U.N.* expresses the constant tension of imagining and striving for a more racially egalitarian United States, while also confronting the looming danger in fights for Black citizenship. Moms sings:

I had a dream last night.
I asked for my equal rights.
Somebody said, "Moms, you're next."
And there I stood with a rope around my neck.[69]

Without pause, a piano cuts in and Moms begins to sing to the tune of Ray Charles's "Georgia." With piano accompaniment, she belts:

In Georgia, Georgia,
No peace will I find
'Til I catch a plane up North
And put Georgia outta my mind.[70]

The piano continues, and she shouts into the microphone, "Ray Charles can have it! You hear me?"[71]

Mabley's comedic performance shifts to an angry confrontation. She gives over Georgia (and arguably the entire South) to Ray Charles not out of fear but exasperation. She refuses to identify with the original song as it romanticizes a woman who possesses the name of a state that upholds and perpetuates anti-Black laws and cultural practices. Moms, dreaming of her equal rights, implies that they are imaginable and within reach. In the meantime, Moms also asserts herself as a mobile woman who will not concede to segregation and racism. She does not, however, paint the North as a place of respite. After all, in her dream, Moms already has a rope around her neck. Her performance is a stand-in for freedom that the state will not provide. Laughter, elusive and subjective, nonetheless restores a frustrated and weary Mabley and the live audience to powerful people unwilling to be in an unsafe and unwelcoming space. Her performance allows for Mabley (as both Moms and herself) and the audience to assert that they are agents of change and will refuse to endure mythologies of freedom for all in the United States.

In another song parody, or opera as Moms called them, on the album *Moms Mabley Breaks it Up* (1968), Mabley performs the role of comic opera diva. In riffing on the operatic diva, Mabley becomes the diva. She demands her piano accompanist, Luther, play to her whim, joking that the right lighting can transform her into Lena Horne (another important Civil Rights diva). Elongating her words, and turning the word opera into three distinct syllables, she plays with (or gives the finger to) high-class vocality when she directs,

"Luther! The Opera!" This opera (unlike the Old Man routine that riffs on love songs), is really a genre mashup, a revision of Americana folk re-formed for the purpose of Black feminist civil rights proclamations. In the opera's opening melody, Moms begins slow and low: "When I was living down in New Orleans a many day ago, it wasn't yesterday. / The white folks said, 'To the North Pole woman, I'll gladly pay your way.'" After she holds a long and low note on "way," Mabley pauses and then speeds up:

So I took their money
And I took their advice
And I'm very glad to say—

She pauses and then declares, "I'm a freedom rider from the South!" The audience cheers as she finishes the punchline, "Yippee eye-o, yippie eye ay / Damn glad I got away!"[72]

Moms explains how she took the money of Southern whites to move to the North Pole, passing states above the Mason-Dixon Line like Illinois and Ohio. The Black feminist comic demands more. Nothing short of pure freedom will do. Even in her comedic turn away from the operatic diva, Mabley still takes on the empowering presence of the commanding, demanding, virtuosic solo performer. She is, as Deborah Paredez explains in her description of the performance diva, "In time with the now while insisting that it's time for what's next. Not simply in time with what is, but with what ought to be. In time with justice."[73] One of the labors of the Black feminist comic is to facilitate communal resistance, across time and space. The interplay between Black feminist comic—whose voice moves through the microphone and then speakers—and her audiences—that shout back with vocal response during the live performance or a playback of the recording—creates sonic and affective modes of community building. Mabley demands her audiences, both live and recorded, get in time with racial justice.

Luther changes the piano tune to the western folk song "Home on the Range." Moms begins sweetly: "Oh give me a home, where I'm free to roam / Where the dark and the white folks all play." However, in the line "where seldom is heard," Mabley's voice goes deep and angry: "Tote that bale / or we'll put you in jail!" The music shifts to a big-band style as Mabley finishes, "That Dixie melody is not for me!"[74] Mabley's revision of "Home on the Range," refuses a colonialist/cowboy persona that desires freedom and westward expansion with no regard to native people. Rather, being "free to roam" is about freedom from the specificity of racial violence and trauma. Not "seldom is heard a discouraging word" (that I read as a passive aggressive avoidance of conflict), but seldom is heard threats of forced labor and incarceration ("tote that bail or we'll put you in jail"). The opera parody desires and illustrates freedom without detracting from the realities of racialized violence. This "racial truth-telling," when "angled through humor[,] has the potential to defy dominant practices and ideologies that promote the erasure of material realities of rac[ism]."[75]

Mabley ends the opera with a riff on the Christian hymn, "The End of the Road." Mabley crafts a song in which time is not finite but stretches and guides her toward spiritual bliss and meeting God. "Children I can't go wrong. Moms's got to go right. I'll find my way because a guiding light will be shining / at the end of the road."[76] Like Jason King's assertion that Black music is *paraperformative, or a 'feeling beyond' that emerges as the way to higher knowledge*"[77] or Daphne Brooks's writing on Nina Simone that calls her work a re-centering, re-sounding of the Black woman's voice buried at the bottom of the archive, Mabley's operas powerfully resonate and reverberate.[78] Laughter, like music, is an organic vocal/aural experience that binds audiences and makes connections between the past and the present. This is an affective mode of queering time and space in which the Black feminist comic cracks up the constraints of positivist history as well as the split between artist and audience.

Toward a Black Feminist Comedic Lineage

Mabley's unapologetic expressions of Black feminist interventions tell more complete stories of sexuality, history, citizenship, and Black communities in the United States. Cracking up her archive reveals Mabley's skilled creation and execution of Moms. Her Black feminist and Black queer performance strategies model subversive and disruptive modes of dissent alongside unparalleled comedic artistry. Mabley set forth a road for future Black feminist comics to use the stage as a site of simultaneous joy and resistance. Her Black feminist comedy cracks up the distances between past and present, and, as the following chapters explore, the myriad ways Mabley's comedic strategies for anti-racist and feminist/queer protest ring true today.

Over the course of sixty years, Mabley paved the way for future generations of Black feminist comics. Despite the lack of archival materials about Mabley's life, her Black feminist and Black queer artistry reverberates through time and space. Taking up the specificities of their time and place, yet also harkening back to the kinds of strategies employed by Mabley, the Black feminist comics I examine in the rest of this book situate themselves within Black feminist and Black queer aesthetic practices of collapsing material and spiritual time and privileging the body as a site of knowledge production, wherein "art is an act of creation and a vehicle for resurrecting memory, future potentialities, refuse, and the human self."[79] The following chapters jump forward to the twenty-first century, when opportunities for richer archives and broader audiences become more possible with the mediation of stand-up comedy in television and the internet age. Each of the comics carves out her own space for pointed and skilled performances, following in Mabley's footsteps. Her pioneering comedic performances continue to remain relevant to understanding so much of US culture and history. Mabley's work, resonating into the present, demonstrates how Black feminist comedy takes seriously its significance in popular culture, and also joyfully rehearses strategies for social justice.

I Love You Bitches Back
Spect-actors and Affective Freedom in *I Coulda Been Your Cellmate!*

Comic and actress Mo'Nique steps out of a white stretch limo in a barren parking lot with a grey sky looming overhead. Atypically unadorned in casual blue jeans, a white T-shirt, and black leather jacket with her hair pulled back in a bun, she looks into the camera with a solemn expression and declares, "Today is the day. And to be honest, I'm not quite sure how I'm feeling. 'Cause it's not *Showtime at the Apollo*, it's not *The Queens of Comedy*. It is the Ohio Reformatory for Women, baby."[1] In these opening moments of the 2007 comedy special, *I Coulda Been Your Cellmate!*, Mo'Nique walks into the prison and is patted down by one guard and then interviews several incarcerated women. In this montage, Mo'Nique empathetically nods while speaking to the women, gives out hugs, and takes pictures. Spliced in between these shots are text of statistics about the Ohio Reformatory for Women (ORW) that note, for example, "80% of the inmates have a history of severe psychological, physical and sexual abuse."[2] As the opening scene comes to close, viewers watch a group of incarcerated women surround Mo'Nique, and in a voiceover, she says: "Some people have said to me 'Why would you pick a prison? They've done such horrible things.' But they still deserve a little bit of laughter, a little bit of joy and a little bit of feel good. And I'm hopin' we can bring them some of that today." The screen turns black, then words appear: "Sometimes laughter is the only freedom someone needs."[3]

This chapter examines how Mo'Nique's Black feminist comedic performance ignites affective and embodied pathways toward freedom for the audience at ORW, both within and against state authority. Thirty-six years after Jackie Mabley recorded her *Live at Sing Sing Prison* album, Mo'Nique takes on and expands Mabley's strategies to comedically crack up a hyper-surveilled space with Black feminist politics and aesthetic practices in *I Coulda Been Your Cellmate!* Mo'Nique's comedy and engagement with her audience instigate a Black feminist elsewhere, at once imagined and material. Freedom, or as Jonathan Chambers-Letson describes the space between the "imaginary and the corporeal," is a feeling that "glimmers as both concrete reality (as experienced in the body) *and* anticipatory dawning."[4] Laughter as freedom melds together the corporeal and the affective, a lived reality and that which is beyond the real. Oscillating between imaginary release from imprisonment and surveillance, and the physical release of laughter, Mo'Nique's performance cracks up the confines of a prison for her audience to experience affective moments of freedom.

Both the carceral state and space are cracked up in this chapter. Highly policed spaces, namely US prisons, structure the lives of the imprisoned to rigidity. Angela Davis argues that confinement, even with the goal of rehabilitation, has historically been a means of state control. "Correction" is directly linked to regimented schedules, labor, and scrutiny by prison systems.[5] The women at ORW adhere to strict protocols of routine that rely on and reward uniformity and isolation, and as I explore later in the chapter, are subject to the panopticon (unseen, yet ever present surveillance). Mo'Nique's performance allows the incarcerated audience to come together in a new mode of being, counter to the prison panopticon and its routine confinement of bodies and spirits. The prison never fully transforms in *I Coulda Been Your Cellmate!* Yet, Black feminist comedy transcends the space's norms of detention. Placing a stage, one designated for ephemeral, live experiences that disrupt the mundaneness of reality, in the center of the prison grounds, intervenes in dehumanizing protocols of the prison. The stage not only distances the incarcerated women from daily routine, but also, more importantly, facilitates different kinds of intimacies among the women and within their environment, intimacies defined by laughter and connectedness rather than confinement and control.

The audience of incarcerated women in *I Coulda Been Your Cell-*

mate! plays a key role in Black/feminist dissent within the time and space of this performance and within the pages of this chapter. Laughter from the audience is a movement toward freedom, but so are the many ways they vocalize and assert their power. Between the stage and the audience, the performance space dissolves the isolating culture of a prison. *I Coulda Been Your Cellmate!* exemplifies the affective and political ramifications of Black feminist comedy and its ability to disrupt restrictive state power, not just from the comic but also from beyond the boundaries of the stage into the audience. This chapter analyzes how Mo'Nique and the audience utilize queer minoritarian performance strategies and Black feminist sexual politics to facilitate a time and place in which the ethics of Black feminist comedy supersede the protocols of incarceration.

A Queen of Comedy at the ORW

In addition to Mabley's performance at Sing Sing, *I Coulda Been Your Cellmate!* aligns with other important genealogies of prison performances that use the stage to work within and against state power. Perhaps most notably in the lexicon of popular music is Johnny Cash's recorded album at Folsom Prison. Blues singer B.B. King also performed in more than forty-seven prisons across the United States during his career. Both musicians used their privileged position outside of the prison to critique regimes of power from within the place and time of their performances.[6] Theatre artists like Anna Deavere Smith, Jessica Blank, and Erik Jensen created documentary-style performances to tell the diverse stories of those exonerated within the US criminal justice system.[7] Rhodessa Jones directs the *Medea Project: Theatre for Incarcerated Women*, which uses theatre as an arts-based approach to rehabilitation.[8] Stand-up comedy, less serious in tone but just as serious in effect, also uses performance to reach out to incarcerated populations. Mo'Nique follows in the footsteps of all of these artistic forms, creating movements toward freedom for those currently experiencing the inhumane structures of the US prison system.

The ORW imprisons more than two thousand women. Some of the women under maximum security face the death penalty, while others have been imprisoned under minimum security for crimes such as robbery. The ORW opened in 1916 and is located on 260 acres just outside the small town of Marysville, Ohio. The Reformatory describes itself as rehabilitative. For example, the prison is one of the first in the nation to develop an in-house nursery program called Achieving Baby Care Success (ABCs), so that "mothers and infants leave the institution together."[9] ORW also offers residential alcohol and drug treatment programs, family day camps during the summer months, and short-term offender life skills courses. *I Coulda Been Your Cellmate!* however, reminds viewers of the film that the prison system is still a dehumanizing one, narrating that the women's lives "are devoid of nurturing and caring."

When Mo'Nique announces then at the start of the documentary that, "This is not the *Queens of Comedy*. This is not *Showtime at the Apollo*," she articulates a meaning deeper than a reference to the make-up of her audience of incarcerated women, most of whom are women of color.[10] Jonathon Shailor, a prison scholar and artist, notes that the precariousness and importance of performance (both doing and witnessing) within a prison space is linked to the freedom that creativity spawns. He argues in the introduction to *Performing New Lives: Prison Theatre* that, "Theatre, in contrast to just about anyone's idea of social reform is notoriously noisy, playful and subversive, and therefore likely to be suspect in most prison settings ... the needs that theatre addressees are those of self-expression and identity, freedom (of the imagination), creativity, and community."[11] Because the prison space is not designed for experiences of joy and laughter, Mo'Nique conveys the inherent riskiness and excitement of making possible the very real effects of theatrical experience within a space never intended for such community and improvisational pleasure.

While Mo'Nique is now most widely recognized for her Oscar-winning performance in the 2009 film *Precious: Based on the Novel Push by Sapphire*, her career has spanned three decades, and she has donned many different roles in the entertainment industry—such as comic, actress, author, and talk show host. Mo'Nique began performing at open mic nights at the Comedy Factory Outlet in her hometown of Baltimore in the late 1980s. Her stand-up career soon took off, and she became the first woman host of *Showtime at the Apollo* in 1989. Following suit of many Black women comics in the 1990s era of cable television comedy, the early and mid-career stand-up of Mo'Nique was raunchy and joyful, engaging in sexually explicit material and as an affirmation of Black women's power.[12] From the late 1990s and through the early 2000s, Mo'Nique's comedy preached the importance of physical pleasure and solidarity among Black women.[13] She was known to enter a stage on a throne carried by fit, attractive Black men, and she affirmed fat acceptance long before body-positive movements took off among academics and white feminists.[14] Mo'Nique launched into celebrity status beyond live comedy venues, when she began her starring role in the television series, *The Parkers*, which ran from 1999 to 2004.[15] In 2001 Mo'Nique co-starred in the comedy tour and film special *The Queens of Comedy*, a Black woman clap-back to *The Original Kings of Comedy*.

Mo'Nique began to blend her comedic persona with that of self-help expert when she became host and executive producer of the reality show *Mo'Nique's Fat Chance*. The miniseries aired on the Oxygen Network from 2005–7 and was a beauty pageant for "fabulous and thick" women. She also hosted a VH1 series, *Charm School* in which Mo'Nique "schooled" previous contestants of the show *Flavor of Love*.[16] *Ebony* described the program as a space where women were required to "hang up their hoochie dresses and don pleated skirts and crested blazers."[17] Mo'Nique told *Ebony* in 2007 that her reason for doing the show was not to judge, but rather to be a role model for the women. "I know their stories . . . . And I'm no better than those women. My path is just different."[18] This period in her career is marked by a tension between her empowering and affirming presence and her taking up of respectability politics and bootstrap rhetoric aimed at Black women. This tension is carried over into prison performances at large. Michael Baulfor argues in *Theatre in Prison* that any time artists come to make performance into a prison space, there is "a tightrope between incorporation into and resistance to the criminal justice system it seeks to exist in."[19] Mo'Nique walks such a tightrope in *I Coulda Been Your Cellmate!*, attempting to mold her performance persona as both inspirational and instructional.

I Coulda Been Your Cellmate! came at an interesting juncture in Mo'Nique's career and stand-up comedy at large. In 2007 she was established as a queen of Black comedy, but she had not reached the crossover celebrity status that came from her performance in *Precious*. Additionally, streaming services like *Netflix* had not yet developed production wings dedicated to comedy specials, YouTube was in its infancy, and access to cable television required packaged subscriptions. All of these factors made it more difficult to consume mediated comedic performance in the early 2000s. Mo'Nique self-produced this film and released it on DVD. It garnered marginal success and served as a precursor to Mo'Nique's future career as a lifestyle expert. Mo'Nique's tone throughout the film oscillates among the roles of motivational speaker, Black feminist ally, and a self-help personality who encourages individual responsibility. As explored later in the chapter, Mo'Nique's insufficient critiques of systemic oppression detract sometimes from the altruistic tone of the film. Overwhelmingly, however, Mo'Nique and the audience co-create an experience in which freedom seems both palpable and is emotionally moving.

Costume and Stage as Disidentification

After the film's introduction, a camera, at Mo'Nique's back, captures her walking down a long, white, windowed hallway. In slow motion, she strides toward a door in an orange prison jumpsuit. A deep-voiced announcer yells in a voiceover, "Put your hands together for the one, the only, *Mo'Nique!*"[20] A crowd screams in the distance as the camera stays on Mo'Nique in the corridor, walking toward what the mediated audience can assume is the prison yard. The large windows on one side of the hall make the institutional space sunny and bright. As the announcer's voice fades and the crowd's cheering continues, the camera cuts to the cold and gray prison yard. The energy of the crowd grows and the camera pans to an outdoor proscenium stage, showing the large audience of women who rise to their feet to welcome Mo'Nique.

Mo'Nique struts onto the stage. I mean, *struts*. One high-heeled sandaled foot in front of the other, she stretches her arms out wide—even shimmying a bit. She snaps her fingers to the song "Bow Down (It's A Big Girl World)" by Blondie Cant U C ("It's a big girl world, bitch, bow down").[21] Her mouth is in a wide-open smile. She reaches her arms overhead and claps to the rhythm of the song. The women in the audience cheer and clap as well. Some of them wave their hands back and forth in the air. Mo'Nique steps up to the microphone, grabs it, and screams an elongated "Hey!" She repeats this as the women yell back at her in a call and response. The song fades and Mo'Nique screams again, "What's happening! Yes, Baby!" She repeats and extends, "Yes!" With one arm raised in the air, she pumps her fist, shouting a drawn-out "Yeeeessssssss! Yeeesss! Yes!"[22] She establishes a tone for this special as audacious and celebratory.

A closer look at the set and stage reveals that Mo'Nique has taken on the role of a fellow inmate, donning a familiarly bright orange prison uniform that has been customized with do-it-yourself diva flair. Mo'Nique's costuming enacts and exemplifies Muñoz's theory of disidentification. Muñoz described this as a performance strategy of subject formation in which marginalized subjects can point to the material effects of ideology on their bodies, cultures, and lives while also working against the everyday "protocols of subjugation" and "managing and negotiating historical trauma and systemic violence."[23] As a tactic that seeks to alter cultural logic from within, disidentification "neither posits to assimilate ... nor strictly opposes it; rather, disidentification is a strategy that works on and against dominant ideology."[24] Mo'Nique's costume transforms the logic of the carceral state by upcycling the aesthetics of prison garb, refashioning it from uniform to unique, enacting a comedic disidentification for the cultural purposes of Black/woman-centered enjoyment.

The jumpsuit's neckline has been cut to a scoop, showing off her décolletage. A gold zipper runs through the center of her now romper. Along her neckline, the uniform has been "bedazzled" with multicolored plastic rhinestones. The sleeves have been cut to be three-quarter length and hit just past her elbows. The prison number, on the left side of her torso, reads 12345. Next to it hangs her prison visitor badge. The pants have been shortened and fringed to fall just below her knees—the tassels swish as she walks. Painted on the legs of the jumper are flowers and a butterfly, also accented with rhinestones. Refashioning herself from the opening shots of the film in her casual clothing, Mo'Nique is now high-femme and fabulous onstage. She wears metallic high-heeled thong sandals, gold chandelier earrings, and a chunky gold bracelet. Her hair is in a tight bun on top of her head and her dramatic rose-colored lipstick and eye shadow shimmer under the grey, gloomy sky.

The costume is recognizable as a prison jumpsuit, yet it rejects imprisonment, especially in its accessories and feminized fit, fringe and all. Explicit and a bit raunchy, the costume disregards decorum for the sake of creating community at the outset of her performance. Muñoz theorized how disidentificatory performance strategies build minoritarian coalitions:

Mo'Nique in I Coulda Been Your Cellmate!, *2007. Enliven Entertainment.*

> Minoritarian performance is sometimes an act of maroon
> banditry. It takes what it needs from the major and disorganizes/
> reorganizes it so that we can improvise new means without
> an end. By putting the major in concert with the minor,
> minoritarian performance disorganizes the major, rendering it
> inoperative. It emancipates the minor from the major and opens
> up new, previously impossible possibilities within it.[25]

In an act of solidarity with her audience, Mo'Nique's performance
negotiates between the gaze and power structures of the prison,
while instigating audience-centered strategies for self-determination
amidst a dehumanizing system.

As the audience quiets down, Mo'Nique immediately addresses her
ensemble: "I had my shit designed just for y'all." The women cheer and
she reminds them, "Now, don't y'all go fuckin' up your outfits tomorrow." She then points to her neckline, "I got my little rhinestones and
shit. I shredded my pants up. Drew a little flower on *this shit*. Baby, I
could be your cellmate, do you hear what I'm saying?"[26] She points at
the audience and shakes her hands to the rhythm of her own words:

"I. Could be. Your. Mother. Fuckin'. Cellmate!"[27] This is the first time that Mo'Nique utters the special's title and through line. This subjunctive tense, "I could be," signals to the audience that, although Mo'Nique cannot relate to the women's experience in the prison, she will work to identify in solidarity. "Could be," as Mo'Nique repeats throughout the performance, does not assume a shared understanding between Mo'Nique and the women, but rather opens up space to speak of common ideas around selfhood, race, and sexuality. Like the costuming of Moms Mabley in Sing Sing prison, Mo'Nique's prison uniform positions her as a nonthreatening comedic performer to the guards, and greatly appeals to her intended audience: those imprisoned at ORW. Unlike Mabley's motherly persona, highlighted with her housecoat and slippers, Mo'Nique positions herself as a sister, making the prison space less mundane through a bright, bedazzled costume. Designing her costume in reverence to her audience, she is not there to, as Moms says, school her "children," but to bring laughter to and laugh *with* the women incarcerated at ORW.

Mo'Nique's disidentifying costuming positions her as surrogate rebel for the audience. What Joseph Roach describes as cultural performance of substitution, Mo'Nique performs surrogation to stand in for and disturb the power structures that discipline the audience of imprisoned women. She, through a re-fashioning of the prison costume, becomes the disidentifying, yet untouchable, unpunishable inmate.[28] Her body in costume is an "effigy as it bears and brings forth collectively remembered, meaningful gestures, and thus surrogates for that which a community has lost."[29] Surrogating for the audience a creative freedom and personal style, Mo'Nique proudly boasts of her shredding the pants to knee-length, hot gluing plastic rhinestones, and drawing floral designs. With a newly femme, sexualized, short length, and low neckline outfit, Mo'Nique delights in her excessiveness and inventiveness. In a strategic request and showing concern for the incarcerated women who would be punished if they did so, she implores the audience not to "fuck up their outfits tomorrow."[30] Instead, she stands in as one who can, with little consequence, demonstrate to the prison at large an incensed yet outlandish rebellion.

The costume's bright orange color and bedazzled flare take on special signification alongside ORW's uniform policy. The women in the prison are required to wear certain colored polo shirts based on their security assignment, marking their identities and labeling the severity of their threats to the prison order. Mo'Nique matches her orange uniform with some of those audience members wearing orange polo shirts—those under maximum security. Mo'Nique thus marks herself as a stage presence most dangerous to the state. By bedazzling, tearing up the uniform, and referring to it as "this shit" Mo'Nique disidentifies, working within yet against the confines of the prison, to celebrate freedom and power not afforded to the women. The orange jumpsuit, up-cycled in an act of communion, also stands in for moving past "this shit." The costume's homemade gaudy decor reminds the women that joy, individuality, and beauty are subjective and accessible despite what they are forced to wear. The camped-out costume promises something more than reiteration of the mundane and essentialized, uniform identities.

Mo'Nique's costume could be seen as a simple, fun, or even an insulting play on the prison uniform, but the excessive and gaudy homemade look of the outfit fortifies the possibility of quotidian resistance. Muñoz's discussion of performance artist Carmelita Tropicana documents her over-the-top performance of Latina and lesbian identity to show how campiness, although "overwhelmingly associated with the gay male subculture," nonetheless plays an important role in queer and femme performative resistance.[31] Like Tropicana's bold and chintzy dresses with tropical flair, the artifice of the prison uniform holds potential to unlock genuine, joyful connection between performer and audience. The costume is "artificial respiration; it breathes new life into old situations." As Muñoz argued, "Camp is, then, more than a worldview; it is a strategic response to the breakdown of representation that occurs when a queer, ethnically marked, or other subject encounters his or her inability to fit within the majoritarian representational regime."[32] The DIY style reads as camp not in the white gay manner, but rather in its co-constitution of working class, Black, feminist, and queer aesthetics. The costume relies on "the bold assertion of working-class racialized female style without apology and without a distancing, appropriative wink."[33] Mutually constitutive rather than opposing forces, Black feminist and camp aesthetics center Mo'Nique's masquerade as a way to dissolve separation between herself and the audience. Moreover, the bold style allows the audience to surrogate as the performer and flip off the prison system. Mo'Nique's "uniform" creates community among the performer and audience, and positions the prison system as a common enemy. The costume is comical and more importantly, critical.

The stage in *I Coulda Been Your Cellmate!* also disidentifies through set design. Usually stand-up performances are characterized by a sparse set—a single microphone and sometimes a stool for the comedian to lean on or place her water. This stage, much like Mo'Nique's costume, juxtaposes extravagant and cheap, camping up the confines of a prison cell. After describing her costume to the women, Mo'Nique shifts to a serious tone. With a raspy and commanding voice, she tells the crowd, "When I came yesterday, I took a tour. And I came to see what y'all's cells looked like. I had to. Out of respect to see how y'all are livin'. Now if I had to come in here, I want y'all to see what my shit would look like." A wide grin spreads across Mo'Nique's face. Her smile is bright and mischievous. She sweeps her arm to stage left to call attention to the set and announces, "This is what *my* shit would look like."[34]

The proscenium stage is divided into three main stations. First, to stage left is a queen-size bed with a red and green checkered comforter, large gold throw pillows, and a bed skirt. The bedding is ornate and tacky. The gold fringes that border the throw pillows, for example, are gaudy, and the bedspread material looks like shiny polyester. To the right of the bed is a nightstand with a bright red cloth over it, a brass table lamp, a large vase with fake pink roses, and a telephone. Above the bed is a comically large poster of Mo'Nique. It is a soft-focus headshot in which she is wearing a low-cut black dress and a string of pearls. She gazes into the camera with a Mona Lisa–esque smile that is calm and mysterious. The photograph is styled to look like a 1980s "Glamour Shot." The seductive gaze emulating from Mo'Nique's portrait is hyperbolic in size and style. The image shows her sexual agency and cheeky self-awareness.

Mo'Nique describes this set as her version of a prison cell: "I would have me a motherfuckin' bed with linens I stole from Walmart."[35] Harkening back to the working-class aesthetics of her outfit, Mo'Nique repeats the simultaneous luxuriousness and cheapness of the stolen linens from Walmart. In a prison cell, however, such bedroom accessories are indulgent and worth celebrating. The brick wall juxtaposed against the large fluffy bed simultaneously highlights and dismisses the captivity of a prison cell through an exaggerated, lavish space.

To stage right, a fake brick wall cheats out toward the audience. It partially encloses the stage, making it seem cozy. This side of the stage operates as the "bathroom." Two plant holders with fake flowers sit to the right of a white "porcelain" toilet and bidet. Mo'Nique points to the wall as she continues the cell tour: "Now there are two things over there. One is a toilet. Y'all know that right? That other thing is called a bidet. A bidet … makes you feel good while it's getting clean, bitch. You'd be washing your ass every second." Mo'Nique bends her knees, sticking out her rear. She closes her eyes and tilts her head over her shoulder. The audience howls with laughter and applause. Mo'Nique quickly opens her eyes and stands upright, pretending to address a fellow woman at ORW, "Wait a second, bitch!"[36] And she reassumes the position. The supposed luxury of the bidet starkly contrasts with Mo'Nique's standing over the bidet with her tongue hanging out, eyes squinting, legs squatting. The audience roars and Mo'Nique laughs heartily into the microphone.

Mo'Nique disorganizes the contemporary comedy stage—so often a blank canvas that allows the performer to shine—to depict the imaginary freedom whereby a prison cell (a space void of personalization, or at least policed to be) becomes a uniquely intimate and comforting space. Mo'Nique stages a fictional counterpublic, inviting the audience to reimagine their own elsewhere. A counterpublic, as Nancy Fraser defines it, is a group that forms their own discourse and commune in response to and alongside systems of power, devising "oppositional interpretations" of identity and culture.[37] So much of counterpublic formation relies on a creation of a new kind of communal space. In *I Coulda Been Your Cellmate!* the prison yard, bleak and constrictive, becomes transformed through the stage and audience. Performative disidentifications allow marginalized groups to work within their own "social matrix" to resist state power and create potential for counterpublicity. While "counterpublics are not magically and automatically realized through disidentifications" this kind of performance creates spaces in which they become "suggested, rehearsed, and articulated."[38] Thus, while a literal escape from the confines of the ORW is impossible, performance acts as the medium through which the lived experiences of the incarcerated women become worthy of reimagination, reshaping, and reformation through the exchange of joke-telling and laughter.

This "process of scission and division" in the disidentificatory cos-

Mo'Nique in I Coulda Been Your Cellmate!, *2007. Enliven Entertainment.*

tume and set repeats yet revises the uniform of imprisonment.[39] Mo'Nique's prison uniform and cell, on the outdoor stage, show not mundane confinement, but pleasure-seeking and expressive individuality. In a call to disorder, Mo'Nique's camp aesthetic of her costume and set "extends past the proscenium arch" reaching her audience in solidarity and joy.[40] The stage and costume create a campy world that holds sacred the time and place of the performance as a collective creation of freedom, however fleeting it may be.

Erotic Rebellion

Mo'Nique's performance also cracks up the confines of the prison system through erotic expression. When recounting her tour of ORW, as an act of respect to "see how y'all are livin'," Mo'Nique explains she asked the guards about the kind of daily restrictions faced by those incarcerated. She tells the audience that the guards said the women get "tickets" for breaking the rules. Mo'Nique recalls, "[I asked] what kind of trouble can they get in? They said 'fighting, being disrespectful, fuckin'—" she pauses and finishes the list, "each other." Her tone shifts, from curious to indignant: "Then they said 'fucking themselves.'" Mo'Nique's eyebrows furrow. She places a hand on her hip, miming how she interrupted the guards. "I said, 'Wait a minute! You can't give a bitch a ticket for fucking herself! Is that a crime? That I done fuck myself?'" She elongates the word crime and her fingers flick at her waistband, pantomiming masturbation. The audience begins to build in response—laughter mixed with affirming cheers and claps. Mo'Nique yells into the microphone, no longer enraged, but wide-eyed and unrelenting in her insistence that the rule is ridiculous. Her gaze moves past the audience toward the edges of the stage where the guards are standing and exclaims, "What kind of shit is that?" Mo'Nique turns back to the audience: "We're women. We're sexual fuckin' beings." Mo'Nique motions her arm in a circle; the "we" includes herself and the incarcerated audience. With an air of calm authority, Mo'Nique continues, "So then I say, 'I understand, we ain't tryin' to break the rule. You can't play with your figgy.' So, you gotta find another place on your body that you won't get a ticket for." Mo'Nique raises her eyebrows and cocks her head to the right. A mischievous smile spreads across her face as she places two fingers on the side of her neck and begins to rub in circles. Her face becomes serious and she rubs faster and begins to moan, mocking an orgasm. As she climaxes, Mo'Nique throws her hands in the air and yells, "I'm good!"[41] The women cheer loudly as the camera pans toward the audience; many of them give Mo'Nique a standing ovation.

Is there a difference here between an actual orgasm and what Mo'Nique performs or how the audience responds? Physically, of course. Energetically, not so much. Sexual release and laughter here become parallel as embodied, self-defining practices that maneuver around and lift out of the carceral state and heteropatriarchal supervision. Orgasm and laughter function as erotic power—embodied practices that root women into their physical and spiritual desire for freedom and joy. They enact Lorde's uses of the erotic, the deeply feminine energy that is both sensual and spiritual, and a source of venting suppressed power. Black feminist laughter and orgasm are imbued with erotic power as energetic release as well as recognition and affirmation of feminist truth-telling. Laughter is an act that is deeply present, an in-the-moment burst of vocality that releases tension and manifests joyful, physical expression.

Lorde contends that the erotic functions as a source of power on

Mo'Nique in I Coulda Been Your Cellmate!, *2007. Enliven Entertainment.*

two main levels. First, the erotic arises from "sharing joy" that, in turn, "forms a bridge between the sharers that can be the basis for understanding much of what is not shared between them, and lessens the threat of their difference."[42] Laughter, in the context of this performance, operates in the same way. The women release pleasure collectively and therefore more powerfully. The bond across difference in the audience is rooted in a Black feminist assertion of pleasure, rather than a white heteronormative disciplining of Black women/women's sexuality. Second, the erotic connects communities and intensifies capacity for joy as an emotional, physical, or spiritual expression. To be in tune with our individual erotic power means, "we begin to demand from ourselves and our lives—pursuits that [work in tandem with] that joy that we know ourselves to be capable of."[43] Lyndon Gill elaborates on Lorde's notion of the erotic, writing, "The erotic accommodates the political and the spiritual alongside sensuality." In other words, the erotic does not merely bridge the personal and political, but acts as a "strategic wellspring," a life-giving and affirming framework "to confront cultural exclusion."[44] The embodied acts of pleasurable performance and laughter ignite erotic power and facilitate opportunities to express and experience joy while critiquing and resisting state power.

Mo'Nique can vocally and safely resist the state through this performance, and she can encourage her audience to resist within the system through their bodies, desires, and abilities to give themselves sexual satisfaction regardless of the prison rules. As a Black feminist surrogate rebel, her subject position as performer "reveal[s] the shams, hypocrisies, and incongruities of the dominant culture [and] confront[s] and subvert[s] the very power that keeps women powerless," including the mythology that sexual pleasure is a privilege granted to some, not an inherently human endeavor.[45] Mo'Nique's statement—"We're women. We're sexual fuckin' beings"—forecloses respectability politics and censorship of Black women's pleasure. She positions herself as leader of their erotic rebellion, instructing embodied, pleasurable modes of protest.

Erotic autonomy directly threatens state power and systems that insist on containing women's sexuality for the purpose of heterosexual family, heteropatriarchy, and objectification. Alexander expresses the implications of performative acts like Mo'Nique's when she explains, "Erotic autonomy signals danger to the heterosexual family and to the nation.... Erotic autonomy brings with it the potential of undoing the nation entirely, a possible charge of irresponsible citizenship or no responsibility at all."[46] In the case of the women at ORW, the very private act of masturbation becomes a direct threat to the state and reason for punishment. Rebellious orgasm and laughter harness "Black feminine eroticism to secure nominal Black freedoms, often inverting contemporaneous state-sanctioned logics of Black female sexuality as Black freedom's impediment."[47]

Mo'Nique's moans and the audience's coinciding laughter crack up individual and collective silence. Evelynn Hammonds famously historicized representation of Black women's sexuality and sexual autonomy as a speechless void, a space that is simultaneously ever-visible (exposed) and invisible where Black women's bodies are always, already colonized. Hammonds explains that historically, Black women have reacted to repressive forces that contain their sexuality with silence, secrecy, and partially self-chosen invisibility.[48] Yet, this erotic rebellion lies in out-loud vocality. The voice, in orgasm and in laughter, are modes of resistance and provide vocal outlets toward embodied freedom and release. Not strangely then, Mo'Nique's substitute clitoris is the pulse point on her neck. The neck is an exposed yet not overly sexualized body part. Nonetheless, it holds immense physical and energetic power. As a pulse point, this "other body part" signifies a lifeline as well. Sexual pleasure and erotic autonomy are, in the world of *I Coulda Been Your Cellmate!*, just as necessary and natural as pumping blood. The groans of her pleasure also signify exasperation toward requisite silence, experiencing the erotic in secrecy due to fear of punishment. Patricia Hill Collins insists that vocality is central to kindling Black feminist thought: "Breaking the silence represents less of a discovery of these unequal power relations than a breaking through into the public arena of what oppressed groups have long expressed in private."[49] In vocal rebellion, Mo'Nique performs and reforms the orgasm to facilitate and validate the power of the erotic as an individual and collective mode of dissent against the state.

In the space of a prison, where nonheteronormative desire and self-pleasure are grounds for punishment, Mo'Nique places erotic autonomy and queer sexualities as a central survival strategy. She comments on the women getting in trouble for "fucking each other" as not necessarily gay, but surviving, joking that although she identifies as heterosexual, if she were a cellmate she would "role-play." She begins, "Everyone said to me, 'Mo'Nique, don't go to jail and get gay.' What the fuck does that mean? 'Don't go to jail and get gay.' Now listen ladies, I know there's some gay ones in here. I am not gay. Never have been. I've been loving dick since adolescence. Dick is my friend, bitch. Dick is good to me." She takes a break from her monologue and improvises a song, "Dick is good to me." She side-steps and sways her hips, dropping low and sticking out her tongue with a playful smile. After her short dance break, she shifts to a serious tone: "Dick is good bitch. But if I have to come in this motherfucker, I will role play, do you hear what the fuck I'm sayin?" She tilts to the side, leans back and, in an exaggerated feminine voice, exclaims, "Heyyyyyy Professor Olgelvee!" Back to her deep, booming, declaration she states, "Fuck that. Once you cross these doors it's not called getting gay, it's called motherfuckin' survival. That's what it's called. It's called survival."[50]

Moving the erotic outside the confines of heterosexual rigidity, Mo'Nique contends that pleasure is a right. Through comedy, Mo'Nique reminds the women that intimacy is rebellious and necessary for living. In a frank declaration, Mo'Nique jokes that, more than loving dick, she loves her own experience of pleasure. Professor Olgelvee was the fictional love interest of Mo'Nique on her UPN series, *The Parkers*. A bumbling and nerdy man, Professor Olgelvee is attracted to Mo'Nique for her confidence and femme beauty. In essence, Mo'Nique expresses a desire to role play a world in which she holds sexual clout not in spite of, but because of her femme identity. To role play a butch-femme dynamic is to privilege her own erotic power over any attachment to sexuality. Keeling argues that a Black lesbian butch-femme dynamic, adhering to dominant behavioral and aesthetic codes linked to gender normativity, may be outdated for some, but "butch-femme also is a malleable and dynamic form of sociality that still functions as a vehicle for the survival of forms of 'Black lesbian' community as a source of erotic tension and fulfillment, and as a set of personal gender choices and expressions."[51] Mo'Nique's performance as femme diva seems less about a strict adherence to gender codes for the sake of replicating heteronormativity, and more about boldly asserting her own desires, encouraging the incarcerated women to do the same.

Mo'Nique interrupts her own joke to ask which audience member would be her sexual partner and could take care of her inside of prison. She implores the "baddest bitch" in the crowd to stand up. A Black butch woman rises from her seat and the audience members around her cheer. Explicit in her desire for a Black masculine-of-center woman to protect her, Mo'Nique yells, "You look like the toughest bitch. I'm yours, bitch." She points and emphasizes, "I belong to *you*!"[52] Other audience members stand, expressing their desire to be Mo'Nique's butch. Mo'Nique happily interacts with one audience member, who, with arms outstretched and a puffed-out chest, asserts a status as the baddest bitch in ORW. Mo'Nique asks, "You the baddest one? And you got on a pink shirt." She turns stage right and asks the first audience member that stood up, "What color your shirt?" They reveal a blue shirt, signaling a lower security status. Mo'Nique yells, "She got a pink shirt and a blue shirt. Bitch she got you beat!" The rivaling audience member pushes their hands forward in a gesture of exasperation, scolding Mo'Nique for choosing the wrong butch. Mo'Nique continues to play along, giving them one last test of worthiness: "But let me see your hair, bitch, let me see your hair!" The rivaling audience member shoves off their hood, revealing cornrows. Immediately, Mo'Nique fires back a rejection: "That bitch got a bush, bitch! She got you *beat!*"[53] This is playful connection, improvised and fashioned through Black queer kinship among the incarcerated audience and through Mo'Nique's marking of the butch women as desirable, uses the erotic to rebel amidst a system that heavily disciplines gender and intimacy.

This erotic performance of queer sexual desire and satisfaction, even hypothetical or in joke-form, "talks back" to the state. Mo'Nique makes visible and celebrates the ways women use intimacy as a means of creating a livable life under suppressive conditions. The comedic undertones reveal and fashion new possibilities for discourse around desire and queerness. Queer becomes, in Omise'eke Tinsley's words, a mode of disrupting the "normative order and powerfully so: connecting in ways that commodified flesh was never supposed to, loving your own kind when your kind was supposed to cease to exist."[54] Mo'Nique employs queer sexuality, Black butch-femme desire, and erotic autonomy to maneuver around regimes that restrict intimacy, sensuality, and self-determination. "Getting gay" is, to repeat Mo'Nique, a form of survival. Queer sexuality and the erotic dismiss the state's attempts to foreclose, shame, and punish women's abilities to seek out and act on their sexual desires. These rebellious counteractions become meaningful, imperative ways of self-satisfaction and fostering community.

The Power of Spect-actors

Central to Black feminist comedic performance is an acknowledgment and celebration of the audience as spect-actors who, like the comic, are also capable of resistant performances. I evoke Brazilian theatre artist Augusto Boal's term "spect-actors" as a useful way to frame the agential power of the audience at ORW. Boal approached theatre and performance as a "rehearsal for revolution," and developed the method of spect-actorship, to dissolve passivity in theatre and performance experiences. Spect-actors refuse to be agreeable witnesses and can reform the world of the performance.[55] The spect-actors in ORW actively weigh in on Mo'Nique's performance and claim their collective power. Unlike realist theatre where the audience remains relatively passive, audience members in the proscenium structure of stand-up are powerful, vocal participants who can approve or dismiss the comic's attempt to relate via comedic performance. In this way, the audience and comic are in constant negotiation of connection that can be precarious, on the brink of disintegration marked by an audience's silence or vocal disapproval. One moment in *I Coulda Been Your Cellmate!* proves that the solidarity between Mo'Nique and the incarcerated women, established at the top of her performance, is not necessarily static. The spect-actors in this performance understand that Mo'Nique's (and the guards') power is fictitious and that they can crack up the power dynamic between comic and audience.

Early in the show, Mo'Nique drops her persona and aggressively turns on the incarcerated audience limiting her role as surrogate rebel. This momentary turn both reveals Mo'Nique's unstable role as hero and illustrates the ways audiences, specifically in comedy, can destabilize power structures that assume their passivity. As Muñoz teaches, critics hold responsibilities to "call attention to some of the material and psychic forces that work against the disidentifying subject."[56] For the most part, I find Mo'Nique's tactics to be radical and uplifting in this performance. When she breaks out of her role as surrogate rebel, however, it becomes obvious that Mo'Nique cannot always escape "the atmospheric force field of ideology. Neither [can she] ... effortlessly come out on top every time. Sometimes disidentification is insufficient."[57]

At first, in an impromptu interlude, Mo'Nique earnestly and seriously articulates that she admires the ways women at ORW create community, a welcoming and warm one: "See I gotta tell y'all something. Before I came here, the only thing I knew of prison was this real mean, hard ya know depressed lookin' place. When I came here, I felt a warm. Like, shit, we in this bitch but we alright." The audience applauds in affirmation and agreement. They continue clapping and she avows again, "That's what I felt from y'all, baby. That's what I felt from y'all." Then, Mo'Nique brings up a subject that causes her audience to turn on her. She continues, "And just walking around, the guards . . . ." She pauses quickly, bringing her free hand in a fist at chest height in an attempt to emphasize her point, "who are some *cool ass people.*"[58] The energy instantly shifts, and the women begin to murmur. The camera has not panned to them yet, but Mo'Nique has obviously begun to lose their adoration. She keeps explaining, with a slight overreaching in her voice as she attempts to assuage the women, "I gotta tell y'all something." The crowd's dissatisfaction comes in a wave; they will not give her the chance to explain. Though the camera is not on them, the audio recording picks up murmurs and deep, booming "boos" emanating at Mo'Nique. Mo'Nique furrows her brow, half mocks a scolding, saying, "Hey bitches. Hey."[59] She attempts a smile. The camera person and film editor privilege Mo'Nique, still not cutting to the audience. The at-home audience views Mo'Nique only, but the auditory dissent from the audience is undeniable, their voices grow louder with each passing second.

Mo'Nique pauses and lets the audience boo for a few moments. It seems she will allow this moment to pass, but then she focuses in on a particular audience member or group of women toward the front of the stage. Have they said something to offend her? Or simply booed the loudest? Mo'Nique lashes out, snapping, "Well here's the thing: if you ain't do that shit, you wouldn't be in this motherfucker!" She shakes her head and points to the targeted audience member(s), indignant and scolding. The audience is still riled up, booing loudly. At this point, Mo'Nique has lost composure. She points her thumb down shaking it at the audience, bending at the waist and leaning forward to get closer to them and shouts, "Boooo! Booo!"[60] Her voice is childish and chastising. She regards her audience's disapproval as immature and rude, and yet Mo'Nique becomes the infantilized subject for the at-home audience. All the mediated audience sees is her rage at the women's refusal to comply, yet the audience voices overpower Mo'Nique. Her persona of sisterhood disintegrates, and it is unclear whether or not the women will let her back on their side.

As Mo'Nique simultaneously mocks and attacks her audience, shaking her thumb and booing, the camera finally cuts to the incarcerated audience members laughing, clapping, and cheering. It is a split second, barely acknowledging the tension from the perspective of the audience. Is this an edit? Do they really delight in her mocking and scolding them? No matter. The women have already established themselves as powerful agents, unwilling to concede to unity with the guards. This is a quick moment, no more than thirty seconds long, but the tension is nearly unbearable. At first, it seems to be a failure on Mo'Nique's part, but actually it is a victory for the women at ORW. Mo'Nique's loss of control flips the power dynamic. She is not the sole facilitator of their affective freedom. She must concede to their rebellion in this moment of the performance. The incarcerated audience demands their voices be heard above Mo'Nique's.

This is distinctive from the individual heckler, a dreaded presence in the stand-up comedy audience. The heckler disrupts the performance for individual attention. Instead, at this moment, the audience bands together, creating and reforming power dynamics within the performance space. Like Alice Rayner's theorizing of the comedy audience, their responses are not passive, but actively create new modes of being and relation. Rayner posits, "Suppose, that is, that the audience is not simply a body, collective or individual, waiting to be amused, but an after-effect of the new perception created by [the comedic performance]."[61] The event of *I Coulda Been Your Cellmate!*, a stand-up comedy show, may prompt the guards to assume that the audience simply wishes to be entertained. However, laughter, booing, cheering, and jeering become modes of asserting presence and power under the watch of the state. The incarcerated women assert ways to rebel with or without the help of Mo'Nique. They declare themselves to be spect-actors, showing the power of collective vocality. Mo'Nique's attempt to express solidarity with the guards propels the audience members to assert that, no matter the joy they all may be experiencing together, they refuse to concede to an attempt to unify the incarcerated and their guards.

While vocal protest from an audience was common practice in early modern theatre, it has nearly ceased to occur since the early 1930s under the disciplining auspices of white vaudeville theatres.[62] Unlike much commercial and western theatre in the twenty-first century, there is no assumed contract between audience and performer in stand-up comedy to "behave." Engaging in the politically and culturally rich practice of vocal dissent, the audience in stand-up comedy disregards rules of white decorum in favor of embodiment and bold assertion of agency. Like the more active audiences of early vaudevillian performances, those in their seats vocalizing protest reflect "the basic configuration of the theatrical event—the complex interaction between the cultural institution of theatre and its socially and historically constituted audience."[63] The audience in stand-up is heavily relied upon for approval, but it is rarely guaranteed. Neil Martin Blackadder observes of the tension between performer and dissenting audience: "Certainly, neither side stands to win anything tangible, but often there is more at stake than merely which group will dominate during the encounter."[64] Perhaps their intention is not as simple as an attempt to fully dominate or disrupt the performance, but the women at ORW remind Mo'Nique and the guards of their collective ability to have a voice in the dynamics of this event, and to refuse passivity.

Mo'Nique is forced to move on. As the expert performer she is, she does so seamlessly, neither apologizing for nor acknowledging the uncomfortable tension that just arose between her and the audience. The change, however, cannot be reversed. While Mo'Nique might be a powerful interlocutor between the incarcerated women and the guards, she cannot change the audience's refusal to respect the state. In this instance, the audience's counter-performance to Mo'Nique becomes a palpable way to voice dissent under the supposed safety of the ephemeral performance. Those imprisoned at ORW are not merely vocalizing their disapproval of Mo'Nique. They are demonstrating to the guards that one performance from an ally will not gain their approval or willingness to concede to humanizing the guards in an institution that refuses to humanize the imprisoned.

The women at ORW are not objects for rehabilitation at the hands of Mo'Nique. They assert their subjecthood from the presumed passive location of the audience. From outside and below the proscenium arch, the women at ORW rise up. As an alternative site for dissent, the audience reminds Mo'Nique and the prison guards of the power in numbers. Just like laughter, jeers can crack up systems of power that uphold the stand-up comic as authority.

Cracking Up the Panopticon

I Coulda Been Your Cellmate! demonstrates a tension between the women collectively recognizing their power and yet still sticking to the rules of "good behavior," given that they are surveilled by the state. Throughout the performance, for example, the prison guards surround the periphery of the stage and audience, and while those on the outskirts of the audience may see the guards, to those deeper in the crowd, the guards are invisible. Despite such invisibility, they regulate and control the space. This is a quintessential control mechanism of a prison that ensures stable power structures. Michel Foucault wrote extensively of this architecture and its ability to instill a sense of constant surveillance upon a population. For Foucault, this disciplinary tactic was a useful metaphor to describe the ever-present gaze of the state. The power of the panopticon is that it abolishes any sense of individual or collective agency, and that those who rebel will always be caught and subject to punishment. Foucault writes of the panopticon to theorize societal hierarchies outside actual prison spaces, but the women incarcerated at ORW experience its major and literal effects every day: "to induce in the inmate a state of conscious and permanent visibility that assures the automatic functioning of power."[65] Thus, the threat of punishment penetrates the behavior of the woman who refuses to partake in acts of resistance, both communal and singular.

A panopticon produces silenced and abject bodies. Yet, Black feminist comedic performance insists on embodied, joyful affect as essential to resistance and coalition building. To negate joy and the body from political resistance would be to ignore a host of vital and creative forces that spark sites of possibility and liberation, not to mention the imperative communal nature of a radical Black feminist work. While short moments throughout Mo'Nique's performance interrupt state power, in the final moments of *I Coulda Been Your Cellmate!*, Mo'Nique facilitates resonant acts of resistance that disrupt the panopticon, cracking up the seemingly stable nature of surveillance. Through physical and vocal connection, the women in ORW use the powerful position of audience to show the importance of community that erupts from and in this performative space.

When Mo'Nique explains why she wanted to perform at ORW, she becomes ardent and stern, towing the line between comic and motivational speaker. Her voice drops in tone but rises in volume. Her face is pursed and serious, and her lips tighten:

> You know why I'm talking to y'all individually baby? 'Cause I want America to see that y'all are real human beings. That you're real women. 'Cause often times we live in a society that will throw you the fuck away like you no longer exist, and like you're not valuable or worthy. So I'm talkin' to y'all for a fuckin' reason. So when they watch this tape they can see .... I want people to see you still exist up in this, motherfucker. You're real, baby, *You're real. You're real. You're real.*[66]

"You're real" functions as a declarative assertion, a speech act that refutes invisibility and nonbeing. Being placed outside of subjecthood, as Scott explains in *Extravagant Abjection*, is the process by which points of identity (race, gender, class, sexuality, and nation) become compromised and indefensible. He notes, that abjection prevents, "even if only transiently, the subject from making its 'normal' appearance."[67] Mo'Nique, standing tall with the microphone in one hand and a small towel used throughout the performance to wipe sweat from her face, breaks the rhythm of the performance to make the women at ORW visible and heard as they cheer in response to her affirmations. The women's response at the word "real" is immediate and booming, growing louder with each repeated utterance. "You're real" repeated over and over as the women cheer louder and louder creates a moment in which the panopticon's invisible power begins to loosen. "You're real," along with the accompanying applause, merges language and embodied response to acknowledges the women's agency. Their cheers and applause overlapping with Mo'Nique's words make the performance a co-creation. Mo'Nique is not talking at the incarcerated audience, but with them. This call and response is an affirmation of each other, and solidifies a community in which women at ORW remind themselves that they are individually real, disintegrating the panopticon gaze that renders them insignificant.

Mo'Nique also cracks up the fear of connection and collective rebellion that arises in the panopticon. During what feels like another spontaneous or unscripted moment in the show, Mo'Nique pauses then confidently declares, "Now I notice, they say you can't hug. You're not supposed to hug. This is a different kind of occasion. If you sittin' next to a bitch grab her and hug her. This is a different kind of show." Mo'Nique's declaration is an active effort to use the stage as a space to supersede the power of the guards surrounding the audience. The camera cuts to the audience at ORW. Two Black women in pink shirts grinning from ear to ear thoughtfully and joyously embrace. They release and then turn to the women sitting on either side of them and repeat the gesture. The camera pans to a larger section of the audience. There is an incredible lightness on everyone's face. A woman wraps her arms around the shoulders of two other women in front of her. Mo'Nique continues to encourage the women: "Reach out and touch a bitch.... There you go baby. Sometimes just to reach out and hug somebody will make all the difference in the world. To wrap your arms around another human being to say, 'Bitch, you're still loved.'"[68]

The earlier tension between Mo'Nique and the women at ORW has dissolved, and this moment seems to override any lingering separation between the audience and performer. Mo'Nique moves from surrogate rebel to advocate, sealing community and coalition and disregarding the presence of the guards. When the surveillance of the state makes itself known, Mo'Nique steps in. The guards, perhaps looking anxious off camera, signal something to Mo'Nique. She speaks on the women's behalf. She holds up her hand as the women continue to hug and shouts, "I know, Warden, I know. I know, sister. They ain't supposed to do it. But right now, everybody's watching them ... they ain't gonna do shit to nobody."[69] The panopticon, "everyone watching," may still be present, but even momentarily, the rebellion of the women comes through physical connection. The women continue to hug. Close-up shots feature women embracing one another, some in long, tight embraces. Others put their arms around each other quickly, laughing as if embarrassed.

The physical touch among the women is in direct opposition to prison rules that separate them, impose unrelenting surveillance, and punish intimacy. Mo'Nique uses her celebrity status and role as intermediary between the guards and those imprisoned to bend the rules of the institution. She risks the performance not running smoothly, as the guards have the power to shut it down. However, Mo'Nique institutes new rules regarding what kind of authority the guards have and in what ways the women are allowed to connect to one another. The crowd, powerless in the panopticon, becomes potent and visible in this comedic performance exchange. "Un-doing totalitarian space amounts to redistributing space on the basis of 'space belongs to its everyday users' that in turn necessitates bringing down the gaze of power."[70]

Vibrational Exchange, Movements toward Freedom

In the closing moments of the performance, Mo'Nique asks if there is "a sister who can sing" in the crowd. It is hard to tell whether this is an extemporaneous or staged question. The audience cheers and a group points toward one particular woman, shouting to Mo'Nique that she can sing. They push her out of her seat. She walks out to the aisle slowly, reluctantly, rolling her eyes. She is a Black woman with chin-length straight hair. She wears the high-security uniform of a pink shirt with an unzipped navy-blue hoodie and baggy pants. Her clothes are too big on her; the sleeves of her sweatshirt go past her hands, making her seem younger than she actually is. The woman walks on stage. She is obviously shorter than Mo'Nique.

Mo'Nique guides her to the center of the stage and jokes, "Now if she can't sing, we gonna womp womp this bitch out of here."[71] The woman seems to relax and laughs. Mo'Nique takes her hand. The woman says to Mo'Nique quietly, "I love you." Mo'Nique replies into the microphone, "I love you back." The woman takes a breath, brings the microphone close to her mouth and begins an a capella hymn:

I don't know about tomorrow
I just live from day to day.
I don't borrow from the sunshine
For His skies may turn to gray.
And I don't worry about my future
For I know what Jesus said.
And today He walks beside me
For He knows what lies ahead.[72]

Her voice echoes in the outdoor arena. The woman takes her time, elongating the ends of each line. She belts the words, "He walks beside me." She fills the stage and the audience cheers to encourage her. Mo'Nique throws up her hands, purses her lips, and shakes her head. She is moved, holding back tears and looking down at the stage floor. As the singer finishes, Mo'Nique grabs her hand (she never says her name) and with tears in her eyes, says, "Take your bow."[73] The crowd continues to cheer. Mo'Nique holds up her right hand to testify to the powerful impact of the woman's song. She shakes her head with tears in her eyes. The two women, alone center stage, embrace.

Mo'Nique tells the audience to "be cool" because she notices the guards growing nervous about the singer being on stage. It becomes unclear to whom Mo'Nique is speaking—the guards, or the incarcerated women—but she squeezes and shakes the singer's hand and states, "This right here is another woman. I don't know why the fuck she's here. That ain't my business. But right now, she's my sister. And we hand in hand." Mo'Nique turns to the woman and says, "When you opened up your mouth, beauty came out of it."[74] hooks declares in "Performance as a Site of Opposition" that: "Throughout African-American history, performance has been crucial in the struggle for liberation, precisely because it has not required the material resources demanded by other art forms. The voice as instrument could be used by everyone, in any location."[75] Singing and laughter are accessible, fundamental modes of freedom. Vocal affect from the gos-

An audience member sings in I Coulda Been Your Cellmate!, *2007.*
Enliven Entertainment.

pel hymn and response from the audience throughout the performance create a sacred space. These kinds of vibrations hold "power to produce new possibilities for social attunement and new modes of living."[76] The singer, Mo'Nique, and the other women at ORW co-create collectivity through call and response, intimate exchanges of touch, and a shared experience of the performance.

The shift from Mo'Nique as disidentificatory force to self-help chastiser, however, soon becomes apparent. While Mo'Nique openly cries, explaining how she so needed to hear the song the woman just sang, but she then shifts to a "tough love" speech: "When you walk outta these doors don't you look back. Do you hear me? With a voice like that, the only person who can fuck it up is you. That voice ain't from nobody else but God .... So with that voice, you gonna touch a whole lotta people." Mo'Nique looks her in the eye and implores her to not "fuck up again."[77] Mo'Nique's plea for the woman to "not fuck it up" after she leaves prison is unsettling in its assumptions and disregard for how prison systems make it difficult for former imprisoned women to thrive in the public sphere. Yet, the vibrations of the woman's song linger. Its palpable resonance supersedes Mo'Nique's own shortcomings in performing disidentification. What she lacks, her audience fills in. They cheer for their fellow community member, whose voice is the lasting force in the performance, not Mo'Nique's.

The anonymous singer, perhaps knowingly, perhaps not, helped to further a legacy of melding comedic performance and spiritual hymn. Jackie Mabley often ended her performances as Moms with a civil rights banner or Christian song. Like Mabley, *I Coulda Been Your Cellmate!* takes up traditions of similar Black civil rights strategies and offers freedom through sonic expression and vibrational exchange. Both singing and laughter resonate, energetically enhancing the present moment and persisting into the future. The audience and the singer spawn a performance of vocal affect—affirming, communal, and inherently resistant against the silencing oppressors.

"Sometimes, laughter is the only freedom one needs," the claim that introduced Mo'Nique's performance and *I Coulda Been Your Cellmate!* exemplifies the stakes of Black feminist comedy at large, but it takes on a particularly potent meaning given the context of the film's setting. Mo'Nique insists that joy is a human right and that laughter is a powerful testament to the political importance of comedy and Black feminist performance as a mode of dissent, of cracking up panoptical power structures and spaces. While the circumstances of the performance were different than that of an open mic, a show at the Apollo, or *The Queens of Comedy*, it did not stray from the essence of Black feminist comedic performance. Rather, it epitomized it by generating unity and subverting (even momentarily) state control. The prison grounds transformed and transcended into a celebratory, sacred arena. The time and place of the performance allowed women to come together, even if just temporarily, to privilege their own experiences, differences, and joys.

Cracking up the space of the prison is a movement toward freedom, even if that freedom is "flicking in and out of being."[78] Mo'Nique's ORW performance transforms space and time, establishing a connection between performer and audience member that renders the prison space less surveilling and confining. Mo'Nique and the audience push against the systems that police women's bodies and spirits. The performance and the audience as spect-actors use laughter to revalorize embodied, expressive activities that encourage dynamic knowledge production among women. Theorizing freedom as a practice, rooted in performance and repetition, is to approach and "understand freedom not as something to be had or used but instead as *something to be collectively improvised, produced and made.*"[79] *I Coulda Been Your Cellmate!* disorders both the separation between audience/performer and more importantly, disorders the prison space. The panopticon gets cracks up. Its effects disintegrate as the woman's voice echoes, emanating from her new position of power: the stage. The singer has her own space to be out loud, individuated, humanized, and celebrated.

Mo'Nique's Black feminist comedy built an intimate coalition with and among the audience members. *I Coulda Been Your Cellmate!* illustrates strategies to find freedom in the present and create futures imbued with collective and individual agency outside state restriction. In the case study in chapter 3, I continue to consider Black feminist comedic performance as a method to imagine other, more just, spaces and times. Wanda Sykes, the next exemplar of Black feminist comedy, cracks up time and space as well. Taking a turn backward, however, Sykes's work cracks up the past and dominant narratives of US history, narrating more complex and intricate stories of Black and queer US citizenship during the Obama presidency.

The Black Queer Citizenship of Wanda Sykes

My interest in the work of Wanda Sykes did not begin with a stand-up comedy special on a cable network, witnessing her perform live, or even coming across a happenstance clip from a late-night interview. While I had not been a fan, I was of course familiar with her work. For the past twenty years she has been one of the most recognizable stand-up comics in the United States, with a wide-ranging and diverse fan base. But in 2008, when a cell phone video of Sykes went viral, I began to pay attention. In front of an audience of Proposition 8 protesters, Sykes declared herself a "proud woman. A proud Black woman. And a proud gay Black woman."[1] Despite my own ambivalence about marriage equality, I remember being deeply moved by Sykes's speech. I was in the midst of navigating my own coming out narrative, and was weary of the stifling scripts that make such processes, as Eve Sedgwick describes, simultaneously "compulsory and forbidden."[2] I was in search of intersectional, joyful queer stories that were also suspicious of linear progress and static freedom granted from simply declaring, "I was born this way."[3] In 2008, the excitement of Barack Obama's presidency was muffled by the passage of anti-gay legislation in four states. Proposition 8 reversed the legalization of same-sex marriages in California.[4] In her speech, Sykes describes the complexity of this political and cultural moment in US history. The video captures the following.

It is a blindingly sunny afternoon on November 15, 2008. Hundreds of people are gathered at The Center, the Southern Nevada LGBT Community Center.

These protesters are assembled in the Center's small parking lot, performing the scripts that often bolster queer community and US social movements: waving rainbow flags, chanting, and holding signs and banners. On grainy, shaky cell phone cameras, participants of the rally record what became another public and communal performance: coming out. Sykes was in the audience that day and, without planning to, jogged onto the makeshift stage with confidence and enthusiasm.[5] The crowd cheered wildly. Sykes was a popular comedian with Black and LGBT audiences even though she had never publicly discussed her romantic relationships with women. Dressed in jeans, a t-shirt, sunglasses, and sneakers, Sykes hugged the Center's staff. At the lectern, draped in rainbow flags and flanked by large speakers in front of the Center's entrance, Sykes puffed out her chest in pride. She took a deep breath and said, "Thank you. This is beautiful. To see this many people out here." As Sykes continued her speech, she cited affective whiplash around US citizenship as the impetus that propelled her to speak up and come out:

> On Tuesday on November 4th, 8:15 [p.m.] was the happiest moment of my life. I was so proud of the country. We elected Barack Obama. And I was like, "Man we are moving in the right direction." And then at about eleven o'clock, I was crushed. We took a huge leap forward, and then got dragged twelve steps back. When California passed Prop 8, Arkansas, you know, gay couples, same sex couples can't adopt, and Florida banning gay marriage, you know, I was just, that was just heartbreaking. I felt like I was being attacked, like I was being personally attacked. Our community was attacked. I got married October 25th. My wife is here. And you know, I don't really talk about my sexual orientation .... I was just living my life. But I got pissed off.[6]

Sykes articulated how this particular cultural moment was, as Jack Halberstam would describe, a "queer time and place," meaning both relevant to LGBT lives, and also requiring queer populations to exist outside of the logics of white-American, forward-moving "progress."[7] Gay marriages across California were suddenly void, while President Obama's victory marked unprecedented evolvement in this nation's racial history, exemplifying the ways that LGBT populations so often have to manage expectations of "hopeful" progress and reorient themselves to a "life un-scripted" by the security of protection under the law.[8] For many LGBT folks, the days following the election were exhilarating and victorious, yet also enraging and saddening, sparking both bonding and division. Sykes's insistence that she came out because of the nation's seemingly simultaneous progression and retraction of citizenship illustrates the consistent negotiation and reformation Black/queer people in the United States must make in regards to time, space, and national belonging. The supposed promise of progressive, forward-moving time with the election of President Obama coupled with the reality of discriminatory laws against LGBT marriage affectively, as she described, propelled Sykes to come out of the closet. As she narrated in her speech, Sykes felt simultaneous elation about the presidential election and rage at unequal citizenship under the law. This whiplash compelled Sykes to move her sexuality from private to public sphere. The speech soon went viral and was a launching point from which Sykes began to narrate her identity and construct new comedic material that included personal intersections among her race, sexuality, and gender. After this apparently impromptu public declaration of her sexuality and marriage, Sykes began to discuss her sexuality more freely in her stand-up, and subsequently shifted her performance persona from casual observer of social justice issues to a more personal and overtly political style.[9]

This chapter examines Sykes's comedic take on Black queer citizenship during the Obama presidency. Particularly, it looks closely at the ways a mainstream, Black lesbian comic wrestles with the supposed promise of the American Dream—assured and inevitable forward progression—coupled with an intersectional knowledge that freedom and justice for all has not been and may never be fully granted. Sykes's comedy debunks myths of the US as "post-racial" or "post-gay," on a path where "it gets better" in an Obama era presidency, and challenges linear constructions of time that favor neoliberal, capitalist relationships to power and white heteronormativity.[10] Sykes expands Jackie Mabley's civil rights rhetoric, one that combines hopes for a more just United States and expresses skepticism of linear progress narratives that erase racialized/gendered violence of the past or seek to obtain a colorblind, hetero- and homonormative future. Charging audiences to think more critically about the ways queer and Black people in America experience history and progress, Sykes's performances from 2009–16, crack up time. Her performances at the White House Correspondents' Dinner, and her two comedy specials, *I'ma*

Be Me and *What Happened, Ms. Sykes?* deconstruct linear temporalities that silence the multiplicities of Black queer womanhood and mythologize US citizenship as reachable to all.[11]

Sykes began her comedy career in the late 1980s as a stand-up in Washington, DC, and in the 1990s she moved to television writing, winning an Emmy for her work on *The Chris Rock Show* in 1999. In her steady and successful acting career, Sykes kept her personal life out of the spotlight. *Wanda at Large*, her sitcom that ran for two seasons in 2003 and 2004, was highly fictionalized (Sykes played a straight woman, for one).[12] Historicizing Sykes as part of the Black comedy elite and a crossover success with white audiences, Haggins situates Sykes within Black comedy as someone who has "crafted a distinct comic persona that, onstage, has the potential to reach and appeal to multiple audiences without contorting her voice or diluting the content of the comedy."[13] According to Haggins, Sykes is in a direct lineage to Mabley, the "storyteller as truth-teller."[14] While Sykes's comedy told many cultural truths, through a politically boisterous persona, she kept her sexuality from the public eye prior to 2008.

Sykes's comedic persona prior to coming out was shaped by being a passive observer, the commentator who critiqued racial and sexual oppression and rarely made herself a main character in narratives about queer sexuality. Sykes's stand-up was politically savvy, attuned to progressive politics, and critical of right-wing conservative ideologies, but before 2008 it mostly consisted of hypothetical, third-person narratives. Her HBO comedy special, *Sick and Tired* (2006), for example, is a scathing critique of the Bush administration, but Sykes rarely places herself inside the world of her material. She proclaims in a joke about racial profiling and racist fears of Black masculinity, "When we see a white man running down the street, we think, 'He must be late!'"[15] Sykes pointedly shows how structural racism weaves itself into the everyday. Yet, as this example highlights, Sykes built a persona as a pundit. While political and vocal about racism, sexism, and gay rights, Sykes's stand-up prior to coming out was, in a way, closeted.

Grappling with a seemingly progressive moment in US racial politics and a discriminatory time for LGBT people in 2008, Sykes found a new comedic voice that intricately wove together her identities as a lesbian, Black, wealthy woman. But it is important to note that by no means did Sykes's work overtly shift from a liberal to radical political stance. Sykes's fight for marriage equality was not a critique of the institution itself, but rather a homonormative movement toward assimilation. Defined by Lisa Duggan as "politics that does not contest dominant heteronormative assumptions and institutions, but upholds and sustains them, while promising the possibility of a demobilized gay constituency and a privatized, depoliticized gay culture anchored in domesticity and consumption," homonormativity assumes that the path toward equality necessitates assimilation.[16] Under such a framework, assimilation is presumed not only as obligatory, but enjoyable. The fight for marriage equality took up a "love is love" rhetoric, erasing queer politics that, for example, critiqued capitalism, celebrated gender fluidity, or prioritized healthcare.[17] Sykes's comedy and public persona often espouse a homonormative perspective in which progress is directly linked to assimilation and achievement of the "American Dream." Coming out did not usher in a radical Black feminist and Black queer politic for Sykes's persona at large. Yet, as I argue throughout the chapter, when looking more closely at Sykes's comedic performances from 2009–16, intersectionality, skepticism of linear progress, and the repeated failure of homonormative assimilation drove the content and the tone of her stand-up, particularly attending to citizenship, US history, and what it means to be a Black lesbian during the Obama presidency.

The Pendulum of Black Queer Time

Following a lineage of Black feminist skepticism of systemic progress, Sykes's comedy in the Obama era cracked up myths of US citizenship as equal under the law, and history as a stable, fixed narrative. The Obama presidency ushered in a myriad of white congratulatory notions of the achieved American Dream and a fervor for the progressive possibilities within the realm of US democracy. Many liberals found the election of Obama indicative of post-racial achievement, but Sykes's Black feminist/queer performances found the future both bright and daunting. Like Mabley, Sykes shaped her performances through the lens of Black queer time, in which history's hands are not clean and the future is not fully imbued with hope but contains a necessary suspicion.

Black queer theorizations of time reject time as linear and inherently progressive. Black diaspora scholar Michelle M. Wright argues in *Physics of Blackness: Beyond the Middle Passage Epistemology* that cultural and political narratives rooted in linear progress assume a straight line toward a more advanced world and give credence to systems of capitalism and white heteropatriarchy. Linear progress erases the myriad ways Black people have found moments of resistance within systems of oppression, and only root Blackness in the United States in an origin of slavery. Logical paradoxes "that result from understanding time as linear and progressive" create illusions that either "we are more 'advanced'" than previous generations, or that political, social, and/or artistic work not steeped in white supremacy is inherently reactionary.[18] Wright's physics of Blackness conceptualizes time as what many others might call queer temporality, pointing to more complex histories that theorize time as dynamic and ever-shifting, a pendulum moving forward and backward within social relations. Similarly, Ferguson notes that western epistemology and rationality is based on the idea that time is linear and progressive. This premise is foundational to how dominant paradigms disavow "figures outside the rational time of capital, nation, and family."[19] Black queer time, then, helps to reframe the ways state power is always suspect, even during celebratory movements toward freedom such as the election of the nation's first Black president.

Black/queer time rejects progressive linearity in terms of the future, and also requires a cracking up of the past. For example, Siobhan Somerville calls on Black/queer populations to be weary of an "optimistic reading of the history of civil rights in the twentieth-century United States, a reading that moves gradually from discrimination against minority groups toward the fulfillment of an idealized democracy, in which all individuals have equal opportunities to inhabit the roles, rights, and responsibilities of citizens."[20] By attending to critical frameworks of Black and queer theory, as well as the lived experience of minority subjects, time transforms from static and progressive to dynamic, asymmetrical, polyrhythmic, and circular. Black queer temporalities crack up positivist histories, and open space for more critical and complex narratives about the past.

Like the Black and decolonial scholars cited, queer literary theorist Elizabeth Freeman understands queer time to be resistant of hegemonic structures and their tempos of capitalist consumption and reproductive norms. Queer time, as she explains in *Time Binds*, "overtakes both secular and millennial time. And within the lost moments of official history, queer time generates a discontinuous history of its own."[21] Blending chronology and homo/normativity, Freeman theorizes a concept she calls chrononormativity, or temporalities that resist "the institutional rhythms of capitalism, white supremacy, heteropatriarchy, and cisgender normativity."[22] I place these theorists together and quote from them at length in order to situate Sykes as a performer who, during a particularly queer time and place in the US sociopolitical landscape, grappled with how to be Black and queer, and what kinds of temporal and historiographical dilemmas such time invoked. Sykes's performances examined in this chapter cut loose chrononormativity's impact on US identity and the bootstrap American dream narrative. To crack up US citizenship and chrononormativity is to interrogate the validity of fixed history and narratives that ignore racialized/gendered standpoints of Black queer subjectivity. Sykes's comedic performances are generative survival strategies imbued with Black feminist and queer tools of resistance: self-definition, communal empowerment, and transtemporalities. Through joke-telling and subsequent laughter, Sykes's work during the Obama presidency grappled with myths of progress and time seeming constantly out of joint.

Nailing Down the Truth

After ten years of legislation, on April 28, 2009, congressional leaders, dignitaries, and First Lady Michelle Obama gathered in Emancipation Hall at the US Capitol to reveal the bust of Sojourner Truth. Truth became the first African American woman to be memorialized and honored in the Hall, which was built to "recognize the contributions of the enslaved laborers who helped build the US Capitol."[23] The bronze statue, crafted by Los Angeles sculptor Artis Lane, stands 37 inches tall and depicts Truth staring forward with a soft smile and bonnet on her head. Michelle Obama was the final speaker before the Truth sculpture was revealed. Standing proudly at a podium in front of the audience, she spoke warmly:

I hope Sojourner Truth would be proud to see me, a descendent of slaves, serving as the First Lady of the United States of America. So, I am proud to be here. I am proud to be able to stand here on this day for this dedication.... All the visitors in the US Capitol will hear the story of the brave woman who endured the greatest of humanity's indignities. They'll hear the story of

Sojourner Truth, who didn't allow those indignities to destroy her spirit, who fought for her own freedom, and then used her powers to help others.[24]

This speech framed Mrs. Obama as an emblem of the American Dream, progress personified. She painted a clear temporal line from her enslaved ancestors to her position as First Lady of the United States.

Standing in a Hall dedicated to honoring those who have been absent from the nation's collective historical conscious, Mrs. Obama alluded to the "indignities" suffered, which most certainly included racism, sexism, poverty, sexual and physical abuse, and myriad violations and violence done to Black women's bodies before and after Truth's time. But what does it mean that they remained merely implied during the ceremony? What would it require to, as Alexander proposes, "destabilize existing practices of knowing" and dissolve "the fictive boundaries of exclusion and marginalization" that keep Black women in the United States on the margins of cultural memory, particularly those boundaries that adhere to a white, heteropatriarchal view of US history and progress?[25] How can history be cracked up to tell more complex truths about the nation and its false bootstrap mythos?

Just three months after the 2008 inauguration and two weeks after Mrs. Obama unveiled of the bust of Sojourner Truth, Sykes became the first out Black lesbian and Black woman to be the keynote comedic performer for the White House Correspondents' Dinner.[26] Showcasing her newfound comedic persona, one that moved more explicitly into Black feminist and queer historiography, Sykes's said what had been implied yet tacit in Mrs. Obama's speech at Emancipation Hall, cracking up US history and cultural memory in service of truth-telling. The yearly White House Correspondents' Association (WHCA) Dinner began in 1920 to honor and celebrate efforts of the press who cover the White House beat. Attendees include White House reporters, celebrities, and politicians. From the Nixon administration through Obama's, the WHCA Dinner customarily invited a comedian to perform for the president and the guests at the Dinner.[27]

The Obama presidency ushered in a new era of comedic performance at the Dinner. Race, history, and white supremacy were welcome topics of performance, rather than invisible, ignored, or taboo.[28] Sykes became the catalyst for many other comedic moments at the WHCA Dinner that cracked up white nostalgia and narrow conceptions of US citizenship.[29] As the keynote begins, Sykes confidently walks from the end of the head table onstage to the lectern that faces the ballroom. She is dressed in a tailored, navy pantsuit, chandelier earrings, and high heels. Sykes thanks the audience and begins by making light-hearted jokes about President Obama and Joe Biden. When she moves on to speak about the First Lady, Sykes points out how beautiful Michelle Obama looks in a sleeveless bright pink dress and ornate necklace. Mrs. Obama does not break eye contact with Sykes, laughing and nodding. Sykes directs her attention back and forth between the First Lady and the larger audience, but in a moment of seriousness, Sykes lowers her tone and gestures palms-up toward the First Lady: "I have to say, to the First Lady, kudos to you for unveiling the bust of Sojourner Truth in the White House." Mrs. Obama closes her eyes and nods. The audience applauds and Sykes does as well with an affirming, "yes." Then, suggesting the following request is just between her and the First Lady, Sykes looks directly at Mrs. Obama and asks, "But, can you do me a favor and please make sure it's nailed down real well?" She drops her tone again, as if this is a secret, pursing her lips, "'Cause, uh, 'cause you know when the next white guy comes in they gonna move it to the kitchen."[30]

In C-SPAN's broadcast of the Dinner, the camera stays on Mrs. Obama for a lingering moment. When Sykes asks her to "nail down" the bust "real well," the audience lightly, if not awkwardly, laughs. Mrs. Obama looks down, her shoulders rhythmically shaking and mouths, "Oh my god." She gazes up with her head still low, one eye toward Sykes, smiling widely. Sykes responds with a chuckle as well. The aftershock of the joke becomes an intimate moment between Sykes and Mrs. Obama, two Black women in a space not designed for their presence or bonding. The rest of the audience is relatively quiet. Many attendees, on the outside of the women's understanding of Black women's marginalization in the US, are pushed to the sidelines as Mrs. Obama and Sykes engage in knowing and resistant laughter. The joke overtly cracks up the politeness to which Mrs. Obama was required to adhere to at the bust's unveiling. The First Lady's positive, physical, and vocal response of laughter is an engagement with Sykes but also an awakening that shows a knowing, communal agreement.

First Lady Michelle Obama and Wanda Sykes at the 2009 White
House Correspondents' Dinner, Washington DC. C-SPAN.

Sykes fearlessly deploys the image of "nailing down" the bust of
Truth "real well" to crack up the absence of Black feminist histories
within US history and the assumed progress of a Black presidency.
The unveiling of the bust was supposed to signify a liberatory act in
Emancipation Hall, but Sykes's embodiment of the comic as truth-
telling Black lesbian woman articulates the physical reality of past
and present domination over Black bodies. Sykes uses her keynote
address to roast those in power, and to signal that white supremacy
is still alive and present in Washington, DC, and something to be expected to return in the future. From the WHCA Dinner stage and
Washington, DC at large, Sykes reminds the audience that these
spaces are rife with histories of racist practices within US public
policy (the White House) and domesticity (the kitchen).

Sykes cracks up history by recasting Black women not as passive
subjects in the nation's past but as active (re)creators of national heritage. Hall describes national heritage as a rhetorical and discursive
practice that is bound by notions of power. National heritage is collective memory that perpetuates colonial myths deeply steeped in oppressive rationales. Hall writes, "The Heritage inevitably reflects the
governing assumptions of its time and context. It is always inflected
by the power and authority of those who have colonized the past,
and whose versions of history matter. These assumptions and co-
ordinates of power are inhabited as natural—given, timeless, true and
inevitable."[31] Implicit in the construction of US heritage—or what it

means to be a US citizen—is the cultural scenario of the systemically privileged control, commodification, and exclusion of cultural Others. "It follows that those who cannot see themselves reflected in its mirror, cannot properly 'belong,'" Hall writes.[32] Sykes critiques and deconstructs how whiteness, maleness, and heterosexuality have become synonymous with proper citizenship and narrators of US history. She asks that Mrs. Obama nail down Truth to solidify representation of American heroism beyond its colonialist "founders."

In other words, Sykes's comedy attempts the difficult feat of dismantling national heritage that sustains a seamless historical narrative of white superiority and accomplishment. Such narratives are designed to seem natural and given when, in reality, as Freeman describes, it is "actively constructed." Time itself, "is a tool for the naturalization of power relations."[33] Dominant historical narratives and time are created by and serve hegemonic systems. James E. Young articulates how cultural memory upholds the state's interest. He explains, "If part of the state's aim, therefore is to create the sense of shared values and ideals, then it will also be the state's aim to create the sense of common memory, as foundation for a unified polis."[34] In this sense, collective memory operates "to create common loci around which national identity is forged."[35] Sykes de-naturalizes the inherent whiteness of the US history in this joke, both in her delivery and content. Her body first disrupts the overwhelmingly white presence of the WHCA Dinner. Second, and more importantly, she reminds the audience that Black presence and power has always been a part of US national identity despite silencing forces.

The joke emerges as a performative device that not only places Black women center-stage in US cultural imaginary, but it also predicts a future in which racial hierarchies are inevitably repeated in the White House. For much of US history, the idea of Black liberation, let alone a Black president, has been linked with impossibility. Tavia Nyong'o elaborates, "As national surrogate and leader of the free world, the US president traditionally stood for everything that Blackness was not: commanding, legitimate, virtuous, and white."[36] Thus, the systemic operations of national heritage that seek to erase Black bodies as part of the US past and present, would, as some hoped, be dismantled with the election of a Black president. Yet, Sykes pointedly states to Mrs. Obama, "you know *when* the next white guy comes in, they gonna move it to the kitchen."[37] "You know" to Mrs. Obama is an address of understanding between two Black women who grasp that "the next white guy," is not a matter of if, but as Sykes states, "when." The pendulum of Black queer time assumes that progress will be met with racist backlash. Sykes indicts the White House as a space rife with historicized and institutionalized hegemonic practices. She also uses comedy as prophecy. Sykes names how racism and sexism are endemic to the White House, and they will not cease to exist because of a Black presidency.

In this performance, the first WHCA Dinner of the Obama administration, Sykes poignantly de-naturalizes linear progress and silenced histories of anti-Black racism. Among and directed at an audience that has upheld settler colonialist narratives of "America," Sykes's performance demands a transformational historiography. Her position as a Black lesbian accesses Black/queer suspicion of progress and employs Black queer critical historiography to "unearth the amnesic defenses created through repression."[38] Using her comedy to crack up time and history, Sykes illustrates how amnesia seeps its way into dominant narratives around racialized violence and white supremacy in the United States. Moreover, her punchline about "the next white guy" uncannily reminds audiences that, in an unjust society, history is often doomed to repeat itself.

Coming Out as Black

Sykes returned to Washington, DC in 2009 for her first comedy special after the election and White House Correspondents' performance, *I'ma Be Me*. In the opening moments of the recording, Sykes tells her audience at the Warner Theatre that she had been "holding back" at the WHCA Dinner, despite the dinner guests' scandalized reactions. Sykes exclaims to a different, much more supportive and elated audience, "Not tonight, baby! Not tonight!"[39] Sykes opens the performance with a bit about how she delights in being able express her Blackness in public after President Obama's election. Without so much pressure to follow rules of Black respectability, she jokes, she "don't have to be so dignified," can tap dance on camera, and buy watermelon without the perpetual fear that "white people are lookin' at you!"[40]

I'ma Be Me was also Sykes's first comedy special after she came out publicly, marking an important turn in her comedy as a mode of Black feminist and queer self-expression. Her audience, seemingly in the know based on their applause and vocal excitement, cheers loudly when she states, "Had a lot of changes in my personal life." She continues to elaborate, "I got married. Happily married, got married in California. Then I had to publicly come out. Had to do that. I had to do it. After Prop 8, after that, you know that Prop 8 fiasco in California, I had to come out. I had to say something. 'Cause I was so hurt and so fucking pissed."[41] Sykes explains she had not planned to come out publicly, but was emotionally compelled to do so. "I *had* to come out," she repeats, and uses "had" to communicate the high stakes of self-definition.[42] The camera closes in on Sykes as she says this line with a furrowed brow.

Just like her speech at the Las Vegas Center, Sykes cites the election of President Obama and the passing of Proposition 8 as simultaneous victories and regressions, or, the pendulum of Black queer time. The camera pans out as Sykes continues in a conversational, yet frank and serious tone. "I was up here," she says raising her hand high above her head. "Now I'm back down here," she says while gesturing toward the floor.[43] The swiftness with which Sykes and so many other LGBT people felt degraded on election night reflects the constant (re)orientation of time and space at the intersections of race and sexuality in the United States. This "objective vertigo" is described by Frank Wilderson as a "life *constituted* by disorientation rather than a life *interrupted* by disorientation."[44] This state is inherent to Blackness and, I would add, queer subjectivities. Because, as Wilderson explains, "one's environment is perpetually unhinged."[45] At the intersection between structural disorientation (that is, imposed by the state and social institutions) and personal disorientation (that is, a feeling of uneasiness or being unsafe), is the juncture where marginalized bodies experience daily and unavoidable dis-ease. Sykes's feeling of simultaneous elation, joy, anger, and disappointment shows how Black queer bodies operate under continuous temporal discontinuity or vertigo. That is, time is experienced as a forward/backward, multiplicative, and confusing entity rather than linear—and thus, heteronormative—progression for Black queer women. Sykes expressed paradoxical feelings of being "up here" (linked to her race) and "back down here" (linked to her sexuality). Her elation for Obama's election followed by her disappointment at the passage of Proposition 8 created temporal whiplash, revealing the commonplace impossibility of linear progress in the United States.

While Sykes's initial seriousness in *I'ma Be Me* illustrates the high personal stakes of the subject matter, she does not linger in this tone. Sykes comically explores the pendulum of Black queer time and belonging by revising the cultural script of coming out of the closet. In a famous bit where she essentializes queerness and Blackness, Sykes declares with conviction, "It's harder being gay than it is Black." The set up for this joke, purposefully anti-intersectional, reveals the confusing, conflicting feelings of racial progression paired with homophobic regression. Without pause, she continues:

> It is harder. It's harder being gay than it is being Black. 'Cause there's some things I had to do as gay that I didn't have to do as Black. I didn't have to come out Black. I didn't have to sit my parents down and tell them about my Blackness. I didn't have to sit them down [and say], "Mom, Dad I gotta tell y'all something. Hope y'all still love me. I'm just gonna say it. Mom, Dad: I'm Black."[46]

Stating that her gay identity is more difficult than her Black identity could potentially alienate her audiences, but Sykes's pacing is quick, ensuring she explains herself before she potentially loses her audience to hostility. They applaud and laugh when they realize she has replaced the word "gay" with "Black." She does not deny the oppressive experiences of anti-Black racism, but rather satirizes the often anti-intersectional language of "coming out" to express how both her Black and queer identities are bound by chrononormativity and subject to a racialized and queer vertigo that impact her life as a Black queer woman.

Sykes continues this bit in a hypothetical conversation where she "comes out as Black" to her parents, using the structure of "coming out" narratives to critique normative assumptions of coming out as inherently progressive. In a miniature one-woman show, Sykes quickly switches between her voice and her mother's voice. She sets the scene, sitting her parents down and gently, slowly looking out toward the audience (who stand in for her parents). Sykes says, "Mom, Dad—." She pauses for dramatic effect and says, "I'm Black."[47] Sykes immediately pops to her mother who is clearly upset. Her imagined "Mom" holds her hand out as if she cannot/will not hear what her daughter Wanda has disclosed. Playing her mother, Sykes exclaims, "OH NO LORD JESUS NOT BLACK!" while gutturally wailing melodramati-

Wanda Sykes in I'ma Be Me, *2009. Sykes Entertainment.*

cally. Sykes turns her back to the audience and outstretches her arms yelling to God, "Anything but Black, Jesus! Give her cancer, Lord, give her cancer! Anything but Black, Lord!"[48]

As Sykes turns her back to the audience, they become the people "Mom" is rejecting. Playing multiple characters in this narrative, Sykes replaces herself with the audience as she switches to the persona of her mother. The audience subsequently has the opportunity to embody empathetic simultaneity: watching the experience of Wanda "coming out," while also becoming the character of Wanda being rejected by her mother. "Mom's" response, wishing cancer on her daughter is comedic, yet searing. Coming out facilitates a death of a normative life path and/or reproductive futurism. Mom's response to Wanda coming out "as Black" is to stop the clock and pray for her daughter's physical demise rather than accept her daughter's wanting to live outside a heteronormative social order. In substituting the word "Black" for "gay," such a response sounds ludicrous, if it were not so terribly common for LGBT people.

Underscoring a Black feminist sensibility to advocate for herself as a Black lesbian woman, Sykes also purposefully uses exaggerated gestures and vocal affect to satirize her mother's reactions. Sykes, as Wanda, is quiet and calm—the rational one. She plainly explains, "No, Mom. I'm Black that's just what it is."[49] Her "Mom's" voice snaps to serious and suspicious. Sykes hunches over and points her finger out at the audience in an accusatory manner. Then her "Mom's" voice lowers, coupled with narrowed eyes and says, "No. No. You know what it is? You been hanging around Black people ... they twisted your mind!" Borrowing from the antiquated, yet still resonating trope of homosexuality as inherently predatory and cultish, Wanda's mom regresses to denial seeped in paranoia. The pace then quickens as Wanda switches between herself and mother, heightening the emotional tension between the two women. Wanda's mom quickly switches her blame to her own parenting before finally rejecting Wanda's Blackness with religious citation:

Wanda: No, Mom. I'm Black. That's just how it is.
Mom: What did I do? I know I shouldn't have let you watch
  Soul Train!
Wanda: No, Mom. It wasn't *Soul Train*. I was born Black.
Mom: You weren't born Black, I don't want to hear that. The
  Bible says, "Adam and Eve," not "Adam and Mary J. Blige!"[50]

Through this performative exchange, Sykes satirizes coming out of closet to reveal its social and political constructedness. The processual script of coming out, when substituted with Blackness, is revealed to be ridiculous. Coming out is not inherently liberatory, nor might it offer the Black lesbian body freedom.

While the closet paradigm asserts time as progressive (coming out is seen as liberating), its narrow temporal path leaves little room for the varied histories of diverse queer bodies and desires in existence beyond the parameters of the more commonly heard and understood coming out narratives of white and middle or upper class gay cisgender men. Marlon Ross declares in his critique of Sedgwick's *Epistemology of the Closet*, "this narrative of progress carries the residue, and occasionally the outright intention, born within evolutionary notions of the uneven development of the races from primitive darkness to civilized enlightenment."[51] The closet paradigm, a script racialized to the benefit of white queer people, preserves white supremacy and forecloses queer modes of self-naming for queer people of color. This is not to imply that coming out is not often met with painful impositions of heteronormativity and homophobia for white gays.[52] Rather, Sykes uses stand-up as a vehicle to convey that she (a Black lesbian) is excluded when the parameters and expectations of coming out are naturalized in accordance with raced, classed, and gendered privilege. Sykes substitutes the language of race with sexuality not to separate her Black and queer selves, but to ridicule the raceless closet paradigm and critique the false liberation of coming out.

The role-play structure of the joke between mother and daughter reanimates and reconfigures raceless cultural scripts of coming out. Sykes highlights the ridiculousness of sexuality having to be declared through the closet paradigm and the racial vertigo of white supremacy. When her mother accuses her of "catching" Blackness by telling her she has been "hanging around with Black people," and exclaiming, "they twisted your mind," Sykes especially emphasizes the disorienting, warping nature of not just coming out, but of attempts to split and separate Sykes's intersectional identity as a Black/lesbian/woman. Karma Chávez and Cindy Griffin explain that when an anti-intersectional politic reigns "within oppressed communities, it tries to purify the oppressed group and erase or negate those who would pollute the purity."[53] However, because time moves quickly in the structure of the joke, traveling between antiquated and unfair prejudice from her mother and Sykes's present-day acceptance of herself and identity, the "twisted" mind in Sykes's exaggerated performance is not her own, but rather her mother's. Sykes's Black feminist comedy demands recognition of both her Blackness and lesbian identity beyond the narrow structures of the closet that presume shame alongside queerness. By replacing the word "gay" with "Black," Sykes creates a world where the languages of sexuality and race collide and transform narratives of coming out from progressive and necessary to laughable and exclusionary.

In *I'ma Be Me*, Sykes also temporally cracks up the parent–child dichotomy by reversing the affective roles of mother and daughter. Her mother reacts harshly while she, as daughter, remains calm. Sykes performs the stoic role that lesbian, gay, bisexual, transgender, and queer children who come out to their parents often have to play, even as they put themselves at risk for rejection, abandonment, and violence. Commonly, they also become the receptacle for familial anxieties about sexuality and compliance with political, religious, and social authorities. However, even without using Black as a stand-in for gay, Sykes could easily fall into the historical trope of the tragic queer, which would render Sykes as infantile, mad, deviant, or disturbed.[54] Instead, Sykes's time-traveling comedy retells the story to reimagine (that is, create) a different coming out script. Sykes is a representative stand-in for all Black queer women, empowered to defend herself and talk back to her mother's dehumanizing reaction and control her own narrative. The stakes of such strong declarations of Black and queer existence emanating from a Black queer woman are high. Because, as Richardson writes about Black lesbian archives, to purposefully disremember Black queer people from historical narrative means that "Black queers become unrecognizable as part of Blackness and disqualified from collective grieving. To be unrecognizable as Black opens up a process of disrecognition, the transformation of Black queers into not being Black after all."[55]

I'ma Be Me demands Black feminist recognition through self-expression. At the conclusion of several of her jokes, Sykes mimics her mother and *sotto voce* scolds: "White people are lookin' at you!"[56] This repeated punch line reveals the complexities of racial visibility and the white gaze. The implication of the comment for audience members is to stop doing whatever you are doing. The first time Sykes tells this joke she recalls a time that she was dancing in the car as a child and her mother yelled at her. Sykes's mother sought to protect Wanda from an objectifying white audience and reprimands her daughter to "act dignified" as her unruly behavior was "too Black" and "improperly" feminine. Within the construction of this through line, Sykes explores the quotidian and political ways in which white heteropatriarchy functions and how her child-self located modes of Black feminist resistance through movement (dance) and enjoyment (of music).

Sykes reclaims her time as a Black queer woman in the United States. *I'ma Be Me* explains the inadequacy of chrononormativity for Black and queer communities *as well as* for heterosexual people. Regardless of economic status, gender performativity, or race, "straight" (i.e., heteronormative) time is a constricting entity that produces and reproduces fear of change beyond white, heteropatriarchal capitalist notions of productivity. In essence, Sykes asks audiences to imagine beyond the "matrix of domination" that keeps the nation in a temporal deadlock, unwilling and/or unable to articulate the intersectional complexities and consequences of power dynamics against the backdrop of public policy, historical narrative, and daily life.[57] Moreover, Sykes's comedy articulates the affective vertigo experienced by queer people of color, yet also uses the form to revise and rescript the structures that repress Black feminist and Black queer joy.

What Happened, Ms. Sykes?

In the final year of Obama's presidency, time once again seemed out of joint. On June 26, 2015, the US Supreme Court ruled same-sex marriage legal in all fifty states. For some, this was an indication of progress; for others, the decision denoted a capitalist mode of narrowing queer love. While the battle for same-sex marriage was won, white terrorism reigned throughout the nation. In one week that summer, six predominantly Black churches were set on fire, mere days after congregants at Emanuel AME Church in South Carolina were murdered by a white supremacist during an evening Bible study.[58] In 2015 and 2016, forty-eight trans women were murdered, nearly all of them women of color.[59] The relatively swift legislative support over the right of same-sex couples to marry exhibits how time can speed up with the power of collective organizing (as well as mass marketing appeal). But what of the often ignored, yet continually endemic, brutal murders of trans people in the United States? What of the haunting replication of Black churches burning in 2015 as they did in the Jim Crow South? The Obama presidency seemed to prove, if anything, that progress the American way is at best unsteady, at worst, impossible.

Sykes released a comedy special (the only one since *I'ma Be Me*) that coincided with the end of the Obama presidency and a year heavy with Black/queer vertigo. Apropos for the time, the special's title is *What Happened, Ms. Sykes?* In it, Sykes explores pertinent issues regarding career success, family life, the pain of anti-Black racism and police brutality, and the seemingly inevitable pendulum swing toward a right-wing presidency (the special was released just two weeks before the 2016 US Presidential election). Sykes's thesis asks, how did she get to where she is, and how did the US get to this queer time and place? Sykes examines these questions via her place in her home and her white family, where her Blackness renders her a stranger in the most intimate spaces as a spouse and parent. *What*

Happened, Ms. Sykes? wrestles with a reverse question asked in her work at the onset of the Obama presidency in *I'ma Be Me*. She does not ask, how is it harder to be gay than it is to be Black, but rather, how is it harder to be Black than it is to be gay? Moreover, how does the promise of neoliberal progress bring with it disappointment and dis-ease? And how might the future point toward a time in which US citizenship and belonging become even more fraught in private and public spheres for Black/queer people?

What Happened was filmed in Los Angeles's Ace Theatre and produced by Sykes's company Push It Productions. The special was marketed as a "straight forward no nonsense comedy special," for which Sykes is famous. Similar to *I'ma Be Me*, the set utilizes deep purples and blacks. The circular stage extends out to the audience and draped curtains in the background are lit with a dark violet. Sykes enters confidently in dark slacks, a plum shirt, and a slightly sequined jacket. Referencing the special's title, Sykes begins her set by looking around at the audience and asking, "Like how the fuck did I get *here*? You know, sometimes you just sit back and think about your life and think, what the fuck *happened*?"[60] "How did I get here?" and "What happened?" are questions Sykes asks to both revel in her success and explore the ways that racism and homonormativity still bring personal and political dis-ease.

Similar to "feeling up here" and "down here" after Proposition 8's passage and Obama's election, Sykes expresses a repetitive affective vertigo: "And don't get me wrong, I'm the happiest I've ever been, but never in a million years would I imagine myself in this situation." She backtracks to her personal biography: "I mean, look, here's the thing. I'm a Black woman from Virginia. And I'm not talkin' about the nice Virginia, I'm talkin' about *Virginia*." Sykes gestures her palm toward the ground, a slight scowl on her face with a graveling texture to her voice as she says, "*Virginia*."[61] Sykes was born in Portsmouth in Norfolk County. She continues, "I went to an HBCU, a historically Black college. I went to Hampton University, yes. I pledged the first Black sorority. Alpha Kappa Alpha incorporated. So, I gotta lotta *Black* goin' on."[62] Solidifying her set up, Sykes emphasizes her Black pride and familial legacy. She explains, "And I also did the show *Finding Your Roots* with Dr. Gates."[63] Here, Sykes is referring to the PBS show in which historian Henry Louis Gates helps celebrities find out their family genealogies. "Yeah. And he found that I actually come from a line of free negros. Yeah. We weren't even *one* year a slave."[64] Sykes's next punchline encapsulates her entire special, an exploration of feeling like a stranger amidst family, and the ways "progress" is more complex than it seems. Sykes takes a breath and proclaims: "And now, I'm married to a white French woman, and I have two white kids. Fucked up my legacy!"[65] With a chuckle and an obvious sense of humor about her situation, Sykes nonetheless expresses a particular kind of racialized sacrifice that she experienced after LGBT marriage equality. Sykes's vertigo may be one in which homonormativity breeds more anxiety than realized US citizenship. Amidst homonormative progress, how does Sykes's Blackness make her a stranger in her own home? In 2016, Sykes seemingly finds it harder to be Black than to be gay.

Sykes's comedic coping strategies in her home are to seek solace, an inward biting of the tongue to manage with a loving family that cannot access her cultural and racial standpoints. Sykes's performances harken back to a long, complicated script of interracial love. Stefanie K. Dunning's explores in *Queer in Black and White* how "interraciality invokes a historical narrative about the constant renegotiation of blackness throughout the history of the United States."[66] Sykes's homonormative progression requires her to negotiate her Blackness in relationship to her non-Black spouse, specifically determining from day to day if she is willing to do the emotional and political labor of reaching across racial and national lines. For Sykes, her answer in *What Happened* is to stay quiet: "I can't explain this stuff to my wife. I can't explain racial shit to her. I can't have this conversation with her. She's *French*. She doesn't know American history.... She might say something stupid. And I love her. I don't want to have to *leave* this woman."[67] Demarcating and testing the boundaries of race within interracial, queer relationships, Sykes refuses to bring her white, European wife into the folds of racialized affect but must then test her own tolerance for being an outsider among her family.[68]

Sykes gives an example of this constant tension between her split self, a resistant and politically astute Black woman, and the uncomplicated, unbothered wife and mother. She explains to her audience, "Like when the whole Ferguson thing was going on. You know I was watchin' it and everything, but what could I do, because I can't watch shit like that with her ...." Sykes, in her typical comedic style, places herself within a scene, acting out the story as she tells it. Explaining that she must watch the television standing up in case her wife comes home, Sykes stands with a pantomimed remote control in her hand, pacing. She looks out to the audience as if they are the television to which she is glued. She explains, "you know so I had the TV on and she's out and so I'm watching the television. I'm like, 'Cracker ass, crackers.'" She points toward the "television," rooting for protesters in Ferguson, Missouri who gathered after the murder of Michael Brown, the young Black man shot by a white police officer. Sykes continues with increased fervor, the audience cheering as she does: "That's right! Burn that shit down! Fuck these mother fuckers." Sykes looks behind her, "noticing" that her wife has come home and stage whispers, "Oh shit, here she comes here she comes." She runs to the customary single stool on the stand-up stage and sits down, as if it is her couch. Sykes's tone changes from outraged and frustrated to casual and delighted to see her wife. With raised eyebrows, she turns her head to the right, mimicking a conversation with her wife: "Hey baby, hey. Just watchin' some *Shark Tank*."[69]

Just like managing the homophobia of her mother in the "coming out as Black" bit, Sykes must make the switch from outraged Black US citizen to that of non-racialized spouse, consuming mindless popular entertainment, blissfully unaware of the protests happening in Ferguson, and the catalytic traction being gained in the Black Lives Matter movement. Her change in vocality, skillful and seamless, reflects how, under a rubric of homonormativity, LGBT subjects can enter into the folds of apolitical citizenship, de-racialized and de-sexualized to prove loyalty to the State and family. Sykes's casual "Hey baby, hey" mimics the ways white citizens get to choose when they participate in political outrage. Sykes represses Black and queer rage, opting for respectability and an apolitical demeanor. Becoming what Hammonds calls the "doubly invisible" Black lesbian subject, Sykes must fake ignorance to maintain interracial harmony in her household.[70]

Sykes's Black subjectivity is rendered invisible by her children as well. Key characters in her comedic performances, Sykes laments the cultural differences between her and her children, and the ways her twins assert white superiority at their very young age. Sykes's children, as she describes, are "White, white. Like *Frozen!*"[71] Twins, Olivia and Lucas, each find different ways to test Sykes's patience and her ability to address the weight of racial tensions between them.

Sykes tells the audience the most recent way these tensions played out were in the names her children began to call her. When speaking of her daughter Olivia, Sykes tells the audience: "You know what she call me?" A pause and she emphatically declares: *"Mammy."* Sykes grips her chest just as she finishes the word, wincing and sucking in air through gritted teeth she stage-whispers, "Ahhh," as if in physical pain. She rocks back and forth saying "Ooooo. Oh, that stings."[72] The children unknowingly engage with tropes of the Black mammy, a dehumanized figure whose willingness to take care of white children overshadows her own identity and whose "close association with whites enabled the rapid, more enduring assimilation of black people to white norms."[73] Albeit comedically, Sykes performs the pain of history, how repeated cultural scripts and scenarios between white children and Black women can sting even in the familial relationship of mother–child.

Placing herself within the scene, Sykes gathers herself, puts on a sweet voice and says calmly to her "daughter" in the direction of the audience, "Olivia, sweetheart, it's *Mommy. Mommy.*"[74] Sykes emphasizes the "o" sound in "Mommy," and then switches back to a harsh, higher pitched impersonation of her daughter. She repeats Olivia's response with resentment: "Mammy. Mammy!" Sykes balls up her fists and looks away, stating, "I just had to hum a negro spiritual, you know, I was like—" she puts her head down, tightly pursing her lips and hums "Wade in the Water" as she shakes her head in both resignation and frustration. The audience laughs and she looks at them to follow up: "That's what you gotta do. You gotta hum a negro spiritual to keep from killing somebody."[75]

Taking up what Ianna Hawkins Owen calls, "declarative silence," Sykes resists engaging with her daughter for the sake of self-preservation and to maintain her dignity.[76] The mammy as "misrecognized" Black woman, argues Owen, found agential power through saying nothing, holding, through "conditions of unfreedom," how "defeat and resistance can exist in the same gesture."[77] The tight pursing of her lips performs, not forced silence, but a chosen stoicism. Then, Sykes hums a spiritual that can affectively transport her elsewhere and, even in the ridiculousness of her familial situation, connect her to sonic histories of Black resistance and movements toward Black kinship.[78] Sykes thus finds ways to affectively escape what she (and other LGBT marriage equality activists) sought to attain. The promise of normativity stifles attention to interracial complexity, so Sykes moves backward in time to find resistance.

Sykes's son also makes her uncomfortable with his new nickname for her, although at first it seems to have less explicit historical weight. She tells the audience in exasperation, "[Lucas calls me] 'Mommy-boo.' Yeah. That's my nickname now. I hate it." She rhetorically asks the audience to affirm her: "It sounds racist. Don't it sound racist?" Sykes then makes the connection for the audience: "It's too close to spook! I'm like, What the fuck is this? You racist ass babies. What the fuck?"[79] The audience applauds and laughs, and Sykes chuckles as well. Yet, the resonating sting remains. The joke rests on the notions that despite the luxuries of homonormativity (capital clout and state-sanctioned legal marriage), Sykes is still a queer stranger, distanced from her family and constantly negotiating her place in their system. Sara Ahmed reminds that affective (re)orientation is a fundamental tenant of queer/queer of color experience, that "orientations toward others" shape "affecting relations of proximity and distance between bodies."[80] "What happened?" therefore, is a particularly apt question for this special, as Sykes grapples with the Black queerness of a seemingly progressed life.

"How Did I Get Here?"
Progress and Regress at the End of an Era

Throughout the rest of the hour-long performance, Sykes engages in her famous political commentary, particularly her suspicion of the soon-to-be Republican-run White House (although, like many liberals, she did not explicitly express a belief that Donald Trump was an electable candidate for president). Bookending the comedy special with reflections on her family life, Sykes repeats and then answers the performance's thesis question:

Man, how did I get here? You know what happened? I know what happened. I know exactly what happened to me. You know what? *Progress.* That's what happened. I am now legally married to the woman I love [audience applauds] in all 50 states. I have two healthy, gorgeous, smart kids. And my name is on their birth certificate. Yeah. So, you know what's happened. Progress. That's what happened. And I'm so happy, and I'm so grateful.[81]

This moment in the performance is sweet and genuine. Sykes drops her voice low and slows down, uninterested in a punchline. At first, Sykes's optimism is almost disappointing to watch. How could she end on progress, when she expressed feeling like a stranger in her own home and, as the rest of the special negotiates, the United States on the brink of a Trump presidency?

However, Sykes's homonormative comfort fails her, even as she relishes in it. Her description of gratitude continues, then takes a turn. She summarizes earnestly, "And there's nothing more rewarding than the kids. And my favorite time is the end of the day, when they go to bed. I love that. That's my favorite moment." She tells a story of how, one night, after doing the dishes, she goes upstairs to kiss her already sleeping children good night. "I go over to Lucas's room and I give him a kiss and he goes, 'Mommy-boo?'" Sykes bends over the imaginary bed and sweetly whispers, "Yeah baby?" Her voice shifts to an eerie child impersonation, one in which the voice blends youth and menacing intent: *"I can't see you."*[82] Sykes purses her lips tight and again brings her hand to her chest in pain. The audience howls, and she continues her performance of holding back rage. She places her hands on her knees, and bends over, trying to catch her breath. She then brings a clenched fist to her still pursed mouth, eyes squinting. She turns back to the imaginary bed and begins to lean in, her hands outstretched as if to wring her son's neck. The audience continues in laughter and Sykes takes a breath, drops her hands back to her knees and shakes her head. There is nothing for Sykes to say in this moment. The audience is silent for a beat as well. Sykes stands up, straightens her back. For an instant, she lifts her head slightly, and a thin smile forms on her face, hinting at the joke to come. Then again, her lips tense and her head hangs. She turns from the imaginary bed and begins to walk away, shaking her head. Into the microphone she hums deeply, "Wade in the Water" once more.

Sykes's inability to rest easy in a homonormative space exemplifies the inadequacy of assimilative progress: its myths as well as its disappointments. In *What Happened*, Sykes's homonormative home becomes metaphor for her own Black queer citizenship, and the pendulum of Black queer time in the Obama-era United States. Sykes's ending to her performance relies on the call-back to the beginning of her special. Not just, "How the fuck did I get here," but also, "How did

Wanda Sykes in What Happened, Ms. Sykes? *2016. Push It Productions.*

this happen again?" Even with the "victory" of marriage equality and the comforts of a wealthy life, her racialized body butts up against myths of progress in the most intimate time and place. Drawing once again from the convergence of the personal and political, Sykes expresses a queer/racialized vertigo in which individual and cultural progress is always already imbued with historical legacies of anti-Black racism. Tucking her child into bed at night, her body and standpoint is still illegible to her children. Sykes's confrontation with her white child "cannily engage[s] with the uncanny, with both the alterity and the familiarity of prior times, and tap[s] into a mode of longing that is as fundamental to queer performance as laughter."[83] Sykes comedically performs both her longing for a "normal" home and the impossibility of reveling in such progress.

Time moves forward, but not in a straight line. What becomes explicitly evident in Sykes's performances at the 2009 WHCA Dinner, *I'ma Be Me*, and *What Happened, Ms. Sykes?* is the foreboding sense of conservative backlash that inevitably ushered in the election of Donald Trump and the impending waves of blatant and state-sponsored white supremacy. Yet, even as Sykes celebrated the election of Barak Obama, her comedy from 2008–16 remained tied to the violence of the past and suspicious of an all-encompassing better future. From her plea to Michelle Obama to "nail down the bust of Sojourner Truth," to her frustration with anti-Black violence and police brutality, Sykes communicates to her audiences the weariness Black/queer citizens faced both during and by the end of 2016. Sykes's comedy cracks up any notion that, for Black queer subjects in the United States, time was ever straight anyhow.

Contemporary Truth-Tellers
A New Cohort of Black Feminist Comics

As it turns out, Wanda Sykes's prophetic comedy at the White House Correspondents' Dinner in 2009 aptly summarized the pendulum of US politics and culture. The election of the "next white guy" in the White House, President Donald Trump, seemed to, nearly hyperbolically, represent the ways white supremacy, xenophobia, and capitalist paranoia can rear its figurative head in the aftermath of a Black presidency. What Sykes may not have anticipated, however, was a new wave of stand-up comedy in the United States. This wave, along with a plethora of mediated platforms from which to consume such entertainment, has fostered more diverse artists and audiences that combine comedy and a desire for social justice.[1] Alongside the 2016 presidential election of Donald Trump, the ensuing rise of white supremacy and nationalism, the #MeToo movement, and Black Lives Matter, contemporary Black feminist comics are using the intensifying popularity of stand-up to directly address Black audiences and their allies, and employ comedy as a form of Black feminist/Black queer protest. Their work does not seek to find common ground with audiences who may have historically participated in the degradation of Black, queer, and trans people and women of color. Instead, taking advantage of the expansive opportunities in digital platforms and the audiences that they bring, a new cohort of Black feminist comics use stand-up to shift US culture and stand-up comedy toward a Black feminist politic.

Over four decades after Jackie Mabley's death and her trailblazing comedy, the comics in the final chapter of *Cracking Up* follow and expand important lineages of Black feminist comedic performance. They create space to examine and critique US power systems and employ laughter as a release mechanism and embodied protest. Respectability politics and liberalism have no place in the performance practices of the women in this chapter, which interweaves the artistry of four comedians: Amanda Seales, Sam Jay, Michelle Buteau, and Sasheer Zamata. Their work reflects and advances Black feminist comedic agendas, whereby jokes curate Black feminist spaces that critique anti-Black violence, explore what "the new racism" looks like in the twenty-first century, reject cultural institutional forms of heteronormativity, detail strategies for resistance in the wake of the #MeToo movement, and celebrate Black feminism and Black queer culture.

Ever-expanding mediums and platforms for audiences to consume stand-up comedy has empowered artists to be explicit in what kinds of audiences they would like to reach, and to use their comedy to commune with audiences during precarious and hostile times under the Trump administration. The opening to Amanda Seales's 2019 HBO comedy special *I Be Knowin'* especially exemplifies the power of stand-up comedy to reach a wide variety of audiences on media platforms. Even on a mass-marketed platform, Seales still aims her performance specifically at Black women and their allies who desire to connect through laughter. Seales explains her target audiences at the start of the film.

From the bottom of a staircase in a dim hallway, a camera pans to Seales as she turns a corner and begins walking down steps, speaking directly into her cellphone. The perspective for the at-home viewer quickly shifts. The camera's point of view changes to that of a social media follower, mimicking the mediated yet intimate feel of Seales speaking directly to someone watching this scene from their own cellphone. Seales's gaze is straight into the "cellphone" camera, an extreme closeup of her face. "Now y'all keep asking me, 'Amanda who is this special for?' And I keep tellin' y'all, 'It's for my sisters!'" The film camera returns to Seales as she walks through a backstage area and concedes, "But it's comedy, so it's really for everybody."[2] Quickly, she changes her mind, "Ok, maybe not for everybody."[3] She continues:

Everybody except for racists, rapists, sexists, misogynists, narcissists, ya know, folks that are just callin' the cops on Black folks who are just livin' our lives? Yeah, it ain't for you. It ain't for fuck boys or trif gals, or that one ex who still ain't paid you that money back he owed you? Uh uh. No laughs for them. It ain't for Trump voters, or coons, or people who believe that white men can't be terrorists. It ain't for homophobes, or transphobes, or xenophobes. You know that wall is some bullshit. Hmmm. It ain't for bullies. It ain't for poachers. It ain't for abusers. And even people who keep asking me, "Amanda, can I pick your brain?" No! It ain't for dudes who want head, but don't wanna eat no pussy! It ain't for you. [sigh] It also is not for people who don't take care of their kids, and it ain't for people who take their shoes and socks off on planes! Who raised you?[4]

By now, it is apparent that Seales is backstage in a theatre. She confidently walks past staff and members of her entourage who flank the sides of the hallway. She wraps up the list of people she desires to exclude from her audience: "It ain't for fronters. It ain't for fakers. It ain't for the phonies." Seales glances at the camera and says to the at-home audience, "It ain't for the haters." She looks back at her phone and chuckles, "Nah! I'm frontin'. It is for the haters, cause ya know y'all be tryin' to stop me from getting my shine." She walks into the small corridor leading to a stage. An unseen audience cheers. An assistant in the wings lightly lint rolls Seales's blazer as she finishes her own introduction, the diva readying herself for performance: "But I can't stop. I won't stop. Ya know why? Because ...." The audience continues to clap as an announcer with a deep and booming voice proclaims, "Give it up for my girl and your girl, Amanda Seales!" Seales bows her head and nods, and then jogs onto the Edison Ballroom stage with a wide smile. In this opening shot, the audience—visible to the at-home viewer and seeming to consist mostly of Black women— gives Seales a standing ovation and cheers loudly. As a cue to her fans, Seales says into the microphone, "I be ..." and they all join in a chorus, "knowin'!"[5] Seales takes the microphone off the stand and shouts, "New York!" The audience responds in cheers, and they continue in a call and response: "We did it [claps and cheers]. We here [claps]." Seales squats slightly and points to her audience, "My people!" Affirming what she means when she states that her comedy is especially

CHAPTER FOUR

Amanda Seales opening
I Be Knowin', 2019. HBO.

for Black women, Seales punctuates her opening, "The real ones! The truth-tellers. The responsible hos! I see you boos!"[6]

In a 2019 interview Seales described herself and other Black feminist comics as those at the forefront of ushering in new types of performances and who are uninterested in crossover success. Seales described her Black feminist comedy as a mode of cracking up systems of power and understanding their wide-ranging effects. Comedy, as Seales sees it, is an entry point to understanding "why the hell it is what it is, and then creating an assemblage of laughing to keep from crying and then to get to the bottom of it."[7] The "it" Seales referred to are myriad historical and contemporary modes of power that circulate in US culture. But in addition to explicit responses to racism and sexism in the United States, Seales is also unapologetic in her own Blackness, and she seeks to create Black feminist spaces that celebrate and honor Black culture without catering to the desires of "mainstream" or white audiences. Playing with the intersection of a traditional hour-long cable comedy special, social media content, and the connecting processes of live performance, Seales exemplifies how a new cohort of Black feminist comics meld the mediated and the live, and, as Seales puts it, speak to other "truth-tellers." I briefly summarize the new terrain of contemporary stand-up comedy and analyze performances from Sasheer Zamata, Amanda Seales, Sam Jay, and Michelle Buteau. Individually, these comics are skilled and innovative in crafting their comedic personas and reaching the kinds of audiences they want to uplift. Collectively, they both borrow from past Black feminist comics and forge new possibilities for the future of stand-up comedy as protest in the United States.

Black Feminist Comics at the Forefront of the Stand-Up Renaissance

Stand-up is having, what some may call, a "moment." YouTube, Instagram, Facebook, Twitter, Snapchat, and TikTok make stand-up comics and their fans more accessible to each other than ever before. Because jokes are often told in shorter bits and monologues, comics can ensure that content sharing on social media platforms happens quickly and frequently. Unlike the 1970s–90s, it is an antiquated rarity for folks to gather for vinyl parties or a rented DVD.[8] Exchange happens in an instant, and more comedians are benefiting from the kind of exposure that comes from consumers downloading and sharing content on mobile devices. Evolving mediated platforms have also made stand-up comedy widely accessible beyond cable television, local comedy clubs, and large national tours. Digital distribution companies such as Spotify, Netflix, and iTunes, as explained by Cameron Tung in the *New Yorker* article "How Podcasts Conquered Comedy," have "flattened the old order, circumventing the traditional gatekeepers of the entertainment industry. Comics are no longer quite as vulnerable to the whims of fickle bookers, the politics of clubs and theatres, or the snap judgments of [*Saturday Night Live* producer] Lorne Michaels and his army of scouts."[9] In other words, the culture and economics of stand-up have moved beyond the exclusivity of comedy clubs and hour-long specials on cable television reserved explicitly for celebrity comics. Netflix, a platform that has invested heavily in new stand-up, now has hundreds of comedy specials, which often help propel lesser known comedians into relative stardom. Comic and actress Tiffany Haddish, for example, turned down a starring role in a Netflix special and instead helped to create a six-part comedy series with the network that showcases diverse comics called *Tiffany Haddish Presents: They Ready*.[10] These platforms have redistributed and broadened who can succeed in the comedy industry and the possibilities of the medium.

Yet, racism and sexism are still at play in both production and pay for comedians. In 2018, for example, Mo'Nique implored fans to boycott Netflix after the company offered her $500,000 for a stand-up special and paid $13 million and $20 million dollars to Amy Schumer and Chris Rock, respectively.[11] Within the shifting terrain of comedy, Black women are still woefully underrepresented and undercompensated. Despite underrepresentation, however, the Black feminist comics, whose biographies I briefly narrate, are using innovative methods to push beyond the margins of stand-up, in both the production and creation of Black feminist comedy.

Sasheer Zamata gained national attention in 2014 when she joined the cast of *Saturday Night Live* (*SNL*). Zamata was hired after a very public controversy in 2013, centering on *SNL*'s lack of Black women cast members. That September, Black male cast member Jay Pharaoh declared in an MSNBC interview that *SNL*'s producers needed to "pay attention" to the program's lack of racial diversity, which set off a host of media attention.[12] Soon after, the show conducted auditions, rumored to be for Black women only. Zamata was brought on as the first Black woman cast member since Maya Rudolph left the program in 2007; at the time of her hiring, she was the fifth Black woman cast member in *SNL*'s history. During her tenure on the show, Zamata's talents were often overlooked. This pattern did not break with her last year there. With little fanfare, she left *SNL* in 2017.[13]

Before she joined *SNL*, Zamata's work as a stand-up comic, writer, and improviser with Upright Citizens Brigade (UCB), was decidedly political and often engaged in unpacking white supremacy in entertainment and in detailing how casting agents often tried to exploit her Blackness and sexuality. For example, in an April 2013 performance in New York City, Zamata lamented her experiences of going to auditions and being asked to play Black racial stereotypes under the not-so-subtle code word, "urban."[14] That year, Zamata directed a short video for UCB with a similar storyline. Before her *SNL* audition, Zamata's work was frequently featured in feminist media outlets such as *BUST* and *Jezebel*.[15] In short, Zamata's skills and interests as an artist were overlooked on *SNL* as the program played to the desires and tastes of predominantly white writers and audiences. Since departing the show, Zamata has performed politically charged stand-up, hosting live performances in Los Angeles and co-hosting a podcast called *Best Friends* with fellow comic Nicole Byer.[16] She is also a volunteer spokesperson and artistic ambassador for the American Civil Liberties Union's Women's Rights Project.[17] As Zamata's career continues to grow, and as I explore in this chapter, she uses comedy to direct pointed critiques at racism and sexism in the entertainment industry.

Sam Jay's comedy is often characterized as "observational," but unlike the stylings of humorists like Jerry Seinfeld, Jay's stand-up is hardly about the mundane. Jay, a butch lesbian, engages the intersections of gender, sexuality, class, and power as she encounters them in urban settings in the United States. In her 2018 appearance on Netflix's *The Comedy Lineup*, Jay joked that in her hometown of Boston, both her Blackness and masculine-of-center style make her a target of white anxiety and microaggressions. She enjoys making Bostonians uncomfortable with her presence as a gender nonconforming Black person. "Like it's obvious my underwear has dick holes and they shouldn't, ya know what I mean? They look at me funny. I'm a Black dyke and old ladies cross the street when walkin' down, but I like that. I like that power. I like to feel that shit."[18] In 2018, Jay became the first Black lesbian to be hired as a writer on *SNL*, and in 2020, Jay signed a deal with HBO to host a weekly late-night political talk show set to air in 2021, propelling her into a more mainstream spotlight. Yet, Jay has refused to compromise her comedic style and persona for wider audiences. As I reveal in this chapter, her stand-up intimately examines Black queer acts of resistance and critiques of neoliberal modes of assimilation.

On the comedy podcast *So Many White Guys*, Michelle Buteau explained that she began performing stand-up comedy three days after September 11, 2001, as a form of emotional release.[19] Buteau's work joyfully explores her fat-femme heterosexual identity and desires, as well as the ways structural racism weaves its way into her life as an actress. In her signature New York accent, Buteau tells a 2018 audience: "I go out for a lot of big Hollywood auditions. Most of the characters I go in for are described as 'Tired. Mom. Real-looking body. Just lost a buncha weight.' That's my look. [And] my most favorite thing I go in for is, oh my god this is so juicy, 'open ethnicity.'" She furrows her brow and asks, "The fuck is that? ... Isn't open ethnicity just, *human*?"[20] After nearly twenty years in stand-up, Buteau began her own comedy podcast that mimics the format of a late-night television show, *Late Night Whenever*. She also co-hosts another podcast with Black male comic Jordan Carlos called *#Adulting*. Buteau's comedy analyzed in this chapter empowers Black women in the wake of Donald Trump's presidency and the #MeToo movement.

Amanda Seales has been a recording artist, actress, and cultural commentator since the 1990s. She has a master's degree in African American Studies with a concentration in Hip Hop from Columbia University. After writing/producing works such as the scripted series *Get Your Life* and the HBCU-inspired game show *Smart, Funny and Black*, and appearing as a regular cast member on the HBO series *Insecure*, Seales began performing stand-up comedy. In a 2019 interview, she stated, "Comedians are the last bastion of truth and reality."[21] Seales's stand-up is explicitly political, biting, intersectional, and steeped in Black feminist aesthetics (for example, she parodies a dance from *For Colored Girls Who Have Considered Suicide When the Rainbow is Enuf* in her comedy special *I Be Knowin'*). In her 2019 special *I Be Knowin'*, Seales creates comedy that honors and celebrates Black women and Black culture in the United States, and is unapologetic in critiques of power systems.

That Shit Ain't Built for Us

As explored in chapter 3, Wanda Sykes articulated the queer and racial vertigo that comes from the "progress" of legal gay marriage. Many LGBT folks reject marriage equality as a path toward freedom, and instead seek radical structures that expand both romantic and familial relationships. In an age of post–marriage equality, Sam Jay's comedy affirms Black queerness, rejects the state as granter of Black queer humanity, and disavows homonormative pressures to assimilate. Jay diverges from Sykes's celebration of LGBT progress through state-sanctioned approval of marriage and a logic of queer liberalism on her debut album, *Donna's Daughter*. First, *Donna's Daughter* queers the format and style of the contemporary comedy album. Not at all slick in its production value, the recording sounds older than it is. Jay's voice is a bit grainy, and the echoes of the performance venue make the album sound cozy and more dated than its 2018 digital release.[22] Tracks do not flow one right into the other, but are instead interrupted by hip hop musical interludes or are spliced in between excerpts of serious voicemails or conversations between Jay and anonymous confidants. The music and conversations create a sense of intimacy, particularly in the recordings when Jay drops her comedic persona; her voice is quiet and thoughtful, and sometimes difficult to understand due to the audio's DIY quality.

Donna's Daughter also aligns with and further articulates contemporary theorizations of Black queer temporalities post–marriage equality. The set Jay performed for this album coincided with her divorce from her wife. Jay's candid account of their relationship and its complexities does not fit into heteronormative or homonormative romance narratives. Jay refuses to rest easy in static identity, explaining that, despite her masculine gender presentation and sexual desire for women, she was never as "gay" as her ex-wife. Jay laments, "I wasn't gay like her. Like, I'm gay, but she *gay* as fuck."[23] Jay resented her ex-wife who participated in performances of pride: "like, rainbows! Parades! I'm like, ugh, you a gay bitch.... What's all this gay shit you be doin'?"[24] Not feeling homophobic shame, but rather deeply suspicious of neoliberal and capitalist uptake of queerness via consumerism, Jay rejects gay pride and the notion that state-sanctioned approval yields progress for queer and Black queer people. Her rebuff of progress is not one of pessimism, but a disallowance of the structures that create, what Judith Butler calls, a "grieveable life."[25] Jay uses her comedy less to work through the internal pain of a breakup, and more to dissect how "this shit ain't built for us."

As discussed at length in chapter 3, in the age of marriage equality heteronormative assimilation has become situated within the temporal rhythms of LGBT life more than ever before. In *Queer Times, Black Futures*, Kara Keeling situates this very point:

> That a particular historical trajectory of "queer" has been domesticated in the United States—contained through the affirmation of "gay marriage" and the increased visibility and recognition through which it was achieved—is simultaneously a sign of victory for a vivacious, bold, and heterogenous movement for "LGBT rights" and evidence of a recent modulation of control vis-a-vis sexuality and the organization of social life.[26]

Jay makes similar conclusions on the track "Gays Shouldn't Marry," particularly, that gay marriage squanders queer and Black modes of communion under a guise of inclusivity. And that "progressive"

Sam Jay in The Comedy Lineup, *2018. Netflix.*

spaces carved out for Black queer people become even more sparse. Despite its seeming victory in LGBT liberation, what gets lost in gay marriage according to both Keeling and Jay, are queers and Black communes.

"Well yeah, I'm in it. I'm in the shit man. It's divorce and it's stupid," Jay laments. The incongruity in the joke becomes immediately apparent. Jay is not deploring her personal struggles with the event, but her frustration with the institutions of marriage and divorce. The stupidity of the divorce is not because of her individual pain or loss. Instead, as Jay reveals, the absurdity is structural: "This is why gay people shouldn't be gettin' fuckin' married," she declares. The audience laughs and she continues over them, "Ah no. It's, it's heteronormative shit and it ain't built for us, ya feel me?"[27] Jay elaborates:

> Like marriage is for straight people.... We shoulda fought
> for a tax break. That was the better fight. It was just a better
> conversation. It was really gonna give us what we wanted, but we
> got caught up in, "We need to get married too." But we don't. We

don't even function the same. And we knew how to be married before all these laws and shit. We were still getting married. That's the funny thing about any oppressive group. They think they can stop the group from doin' shit but they don't. Like when n— was slaves ..., you know, they were like n— can't get married but then n— would, like, jump the broom.[28] You know you can't stop that shit.[29]

Jay notes the benefits of marriage within capitalism (tax breaks) and the drawbacks of attempting to assimilate into heteropatriarchal family structures. She reminds her audience through the example of "jumping the broom" that love exists without the legitimization of the state, and it can thrive outside said structure. Critiquing the contemporary fight for marriage equality alongside historicizing Black communal ritual, Jay emphasizes that Black and queer love may open up more freedom than so-called equality under the law. Black/queer kinship, not the state, binds Black queers to each other.

Jay refuses linear progress narratives in which assimilation is cause for celebration, and instead opts for turning toward the past, reminding audiences how, historically, Black/queer kinship circumvented white heteropatriarchal suppression of intimacy and family. "We knew how to be married before" shows that Black/queer subjects have engaged in performative rites of passage that do not reproduce or attempt absorption into the majority culture. Jay embraces a Black queer historiography that narrates the ways Black/queers can turn to the past for examples of subversive intimacies prior to the reign of homoliberalism and all of its consumerist, colorblind politic. Such structures and rituals expand intimacy and family, rather than contract to fit narrow frameworks of the "family" as deemed official under law. In Savannah Shange's words, "it is a missive from the Black queer space that *demands to be thought, but refuses to be known.*"[30] To be Black is to be queer, and to be queer is to cull dominant structures that disassociate LGBT populations from intersectional and coalitional politics.

Jay brings the past and the present together in her continued rejection of gay marriage. From jumping the broom, she moves forward in time in the bit, setting a scene during the age of internet dating but just prior to marriage equality. Jay argues that these rituals were framed outside of legal marriages and the wedding industrial complex. Harkening to practices of celebration prior to the legalization of gay marriage, Jay reminds her audiences that queer communities maneuvered joyfully around laws, consumerism, and heteronormative pressures of longevity in romantic relationships:

> We were still getting married as gay people, but it just made more sense to us. You just met a chick on an app, or you met her at a bar and you were like, "Hey bitch, I love you!" And then you just … threw a barbeque. A solid ass barbeque. Like one of those barbeques that never run out of ribs like, n— we barbequein' till the night's done, ya know? And you were like, "I'm gonna die with this bitch." And then when you were done, you just threw another barbeque! That's [marriage] all heteronormative shit. That shit make sense for y'all [straight people] cause y'all make babies and shit.[31]

Both the barbeque and jumping the broom, as Jay describes them, exist as quotidian practices of refusal. Refusal is not a direct action; as Tina Campt theorizes, it is a set of "nimble and strategic practices that undermine the categories of the dominant."[32] Refusal practices are creative answers to marginalizing power structures. They are honed in response to "sustained, everyday encounters with exigency and duress."[33] These quieter strategies operate outside of the logic of white supremacy and heteropatriarchy, which Jay describes as "shit" made for child rearing. Jay cracks up logics of reproductive futurity, and the notion that heteronormative wedding rituals are joyful, or even desirable.

Jay also cracks up mythologies of queers as monolithic in their class status, existing only in densely populated cities. The barbeque, the backyard, and home-space gatherings, decenter consumerist wedding rituals and what Halberstam refers to as "metronormativity," or how the city is most conducive to queer flourishing.[34] Halberstam discusses metronormativity as a narrative trope in which queer subjects migrate from rural to urban areas in order to fully express their gender/sexual identity, and that queer community formation can thrive only in a cityscape. A barbeque wedding, however, harkens less to urban spaces whereby queer and Black cultural formations happen in the intimacy of a neighborhood. At a barbeque, formality is traded for intimate community. In the barbeque Jay describes, marriage and wedding rituals do not isolate subjects into nuclear family structures—formal invitations sent out by parents, for example, do. Instead, the casual, welcoming backyard party trades narrow rituals for extended celebration and community.

Jay also cracks up the temporal rhythms of heteronormative courtship. While under the rubric of heteronormativity, an accelerated commitment (from dating app or bar to cohabitation within a few weeks or months) is deemed juvenile and unserious, it is actually a mode of kinship queers have taken up to survive in a classed system built to ensure the success of dual income households. Jay asks that her audiences understand the ways Black queer love expands modes of kinship outside the confines of white heteropatriarchy and metronormativity. Additionally, as Jay describes, a break-up is not a shame-inducing and isolating event that dissolves and traumatizes the family structure. Instead, it is another reason to gather and be in communion ("when you were done, you just threw another barbeque!"). Turning to queer temporal relations, Jay harkens to a "backward glance that enacts a future vision."[35] Jay refuses a linear progress narrative and a futurity that depends on state-sanctioned acknowledgement and assimilation into dominant modes of family and kinship. The cyclical return to the barbeque defies norms of marriage dissolution under the state in which property is divided and families are fractured. In Jay's scenario, Black queer love is a constant, and romantic separation simply marks a change in community rather than a dissolution of family.

Jay's argument that gays should not marry is a resourceful, hopeful statement that aligns queer people and people of color. Black and queer modes of kinship and romantic/erotic love have historically and joyfully existed outside of dominant culture. Jafari S. Allen explains that central to the Black queer diaspora are communal practices of being outside structures of power. He states, "For black queers, survival has always been about finding ways to connect some of what is disconnected, to embody and re-member. This is the social erotics of love at work."[36] The social erotics of Black queer love prove that progress is both nonlinear, and a myth perpetuated in the name of neoliberal assimilation. Jay offers her audience a way of thinking about queer love beyond institutional structures, and how queerness "remains an active and energetic reservoir for connection, affiliation, and experimentation."[37] Gays not marrying is thus a protest against normativity, and also a way to connect back to the resourcefulness that arises from minoritarian practices of colloquial resistance and refusal.

Rape Jokes:
Black Women's Freedom in the #MeToo Era

During the civil rights movement in the United States, Black women led important activist efforts against sexual violence alongside demands for racial equality. Black women's protest methods were often localized and fought for justice in criminal justice systems that sustained and perpetuated brutality against Black women in the mid-twentieth century. Rosa Parks and the Women's Political Council of Montgomery, Alabama for example, spearheaded anti-rape campaigns on behalf of women such as Recy Taylor and Gertrude Perkins, whose perpetrators went unpunished at the hands of city police.[38] These campaigns implemented boycotts of local businesses, a model that inspired the Montgomery Bus Boycotts. Countless other women in the ensuing decades, such as Fanny Lou Hamer, Joan Little, and Anita Hill, demanded bodily integrity and exemplified the inextricable links between racial and gendered justice. Speaking up and out formed what historian Darlene Clark Hill called a "culture of dissemblance." Within this protective measure, the actions and attitudes of Black women "created the appearance of openness and disclosure but actually shielded the truth of their inner lives and selves from their oppressors."[39] While Black women were outspoken in their activism, Hill explains, they left their personal narratives and experiences quiet.

Yet, the #MeToo movement, developed for women and girls of color in 2006 by Tarana Burke, often uses disclosure and personal narratives to instigate organizing and social change. When the movement gained traction after film producer Harvey Weinstein's decades-long crimes of sexual abuse became public, social media and personal narratives connected women across race, gender, class, and sexuality.[40] As the movement grew, Burke insisted that Black women and women of color, disabled women, queer and trans women must continue to be at the center of #MeToo, lest they become only a footnote in histories of feminist activism.[41] In the #MeToo era, Black feminist comedians are using comedy to dissect the nuances of racialized sexual violence.

Unconcerned with respectability politics or shielding truths about their inner worlds, Seales and Jay examine the frustrations with and fears of sexual harassment and violence. Centering their own bodies and subjectivities within the public sphere, Seales and Jay detail how mundane acts, such as walking down the street or taking an Uber, require shielding oneself against harassment and potential violent acts. Each comic details the mental and emotional labor of Black womanhood and navigating threats of sexual assault, while seeking freedom in everyday mobility.

In *I Be Knowin'*, Seales performs a well-known bit sparked by Seales's 2014 appearance on CNN where she debated author Steve Santagati about the differences between street harassment and what constitutes a "compliment." On the program, Seales explained the difficulty of living in New York City and her frustration with catcalling. Santagati countered Seales saying that, "There is nothing more than a woman loves to hear is that how pretty she is."[42] Seales, outraged by his assertion than women enjoy catcalling, came after her debate partner without restraint, and the video clip of their confrontation became viral. In her stand-up special *I Be Knowin'*, Seales recalls this incident and further explains why catcalling is not, after all, complimentary. "Anyone who identifies as a woman understands, it's a journey. . . . We dealin' with things people don't know that we're dealin' with. . . . Women are still dealing with catcalling." In a high-pitched voice, she sighs, "Whyeee?"[43]

She explicates: "If I'm in Brooklyn at midnight. And a Jamaican man appears from the shadows . . . ." The audience, seemingly familiar with this bit and/or the experience of being catcalled, laughs and claps in response. Seales begins doing exaggerated body rolls, each hand in a gun shape, pointing her index and middle fingers toward the audience. "Sweetness," she begins with a thick Jamaican accent. She lets the "s" sound linger, snake-like. "Ya look like a vanilla ice cream." Seales dangles her microphone from her crotch and swings it back and forth for a moment. Then, tossing and catching the mic, she continues in her hyperbolic accent, "Me wanna lick ya." She switches into her own serious voice and declares, "That's not a compliment. That's a threat."[44] Seales asks the audience to fully see her from an objective standpoint. "If I'm in" places her body directly in the world of this comedic, yet uneasy scene. And although the man she characterizes is meant to be funny, his slithering voice and body rolls show that a man's "sensual" behavior toward a woman, on a dark street, is predatory.

To continue her point, Seales moves to another New York borough and Black male stereotype. "If I'm in Harlem and some brothers pause their dice game … And they like, 'Yooooo.'" Once more Seales elongates the greeting. This time her voice is low with a thick New York accent. Seales speaks in the man's voice, "Shorty rockin' rough and stuff with one afro puff and the jacket and the pants with the da da da da da da on it, I see you Ma! What's really good?" She raises her eyebrows and states with condescension, "Yeah, it's not a compliment. It's an observation." The catcall is a mere description of what Seales is wearing: a pant/jacket combo with an elaborate pattern and a high ponytail with natural curls on top of her head. Her bit builds in frustration: "Then, they want you to smile! 'Why you mad? Let me see them pearly whites. Yo, why you ain't smiling Ma?'" Holding the microphone in two hands, standing stiffly, Seales responds, "You know why I'm not smiling?" She performs holding back rage, speaking slowly with a steel look in her eyes and explains, "'Cause I just spent the last twenty minutes in a public bathroom fashioning a makeshift maxi pad out of a long-ass CVS receipt. Just so I don't gotta walk around here lookin' like a dire wolf bit me in the pussy!"[45]

Seales synthesizes the layers of frustration, fear, and humor in street harassment in these two scenarios. Seales plays the male intruders as exaggerated stereotypes, their masculinity so excessive to reveal the absurdity of gender performativity. Seales crosses gender performance much like Jackie "Moms" Mabley's old man impersonations. Through vocal impression and almost slap-stick physical comedy, Seales transforms her poised self to masculine caricatures. Their over-the-top "threats" masked as observations and compliments empower Seales and her audience to render the men ridiculous rather than threatening.

Seales laments that anonymity is lost for women in the urban public sphere, and that women must also conceal themselves and their rage simply to maintain safety. By the end of her build to the final punchline, her face is tense and ready to lash out. Her anger is directed at both the catcallers, but also the systems in place that normalize women's passivity and ask them to accept a subpar status quo. She expresses the inconvenience and injustice of lack of access to free menstrual products in public restrooms, joking that she fashions a maxi pad out of a "long-ass CVS receipt." Her punchlines express how women, particularly those who experience menstrual cycles, must go to great "lengths" just to maintain dignity in the public sphere.

Sam Jay also relays the stressors of mobility as a Black woman. In the 2018 Netflix comedy special *The Lineup*, Jay jokes that her masculine appearance hopefully, "keeps her rape numbers down." Yet, even in her satirical description of her gender performance and aesthetic, Jay communicates that women have scant freedom from having to be overly cautious. Jay directs her frustration at white men, who are "desperate" and "losin' it" and "getting reported every day for touching people too much." Like Seales, Jay laments the emotional labor of being on guard for a potentially violent encounter. Jay explains,

> As a woman, I hate that. I hate that I have to think about it, you know? Like every time I'm in an Uber, I'm like, "What the fuck are you doing in this Uber with your *whole vagina*? Are you stupid?" I know I'm not the only woman in here like, "What the fuck? This is stupid. Gonna get in this car with a strange man and a whole pussy. Am I dumb?" Like, I'm just dumb 'cause I wanna get to the club like ten minutes quicker. I'm an idiot. Shit is scary.[46]

Jay initially seems to be directing the joke inward ("I'm an idiot"). But she also knows she's "not the only woman" who experiences this. Jay articulates and satirizes how women and queer folks internalize threats of sexual assault. Systems of anti-Black and misogynist violence ask that the labor of safety falls on those who experience abuse, rather than those most likely to perpetuate it. Wanda Sykes suggested in her 2006 special *Sick and Tired* that life as a woman would be easy if you could have a "detachable pussy," thus avoiding rape.[47] Jay employs a similar joke, but goes further: a woman going anywhere with her body fully intact requires constant assessment of how much danger she may be willing to put herself in order to obtain mobility.

The "rape joke" has been a source of feminist comedic backlash, especially since 2012 when white male comedian Daniel Tosh targeted a "heckler" who challenged him in the middle of a "joke" about sexual assault. The audience member shouted to him onstage that his joke was not funny and Tosh retorted, "Wouldn't it be funny if that girl got raped by, like, five guys right now?"[48] Countless comics fired back with demonstrations of how "rape jokes" can be funny or thought-provoking if they reveal systems of violence rather than harm audiences.[49] Jay exemplifies that by lamenting the ways women are in a constant state of vigilance in attempt to protect themselves, maintain safety, and travel alone. Jay expounds, "Every woman has her rape contingency plan. You have to. You think about this shit." The audience laughs. I assume many in the crowd do so in recognition. Jay makes her hand in a fist and demonstrates, "Most women it's like, 'I'll take my keys, turn them into a talon, claw his neck out.' Which is very fucking ambitious, you know? Who the fuck do you think you are, Dwayne 'The Rock' Johnson? You're gonna take some blunt keys and claw a guy's neck out. It's a bad plan."[50] Jay counters with her own idea:

> My plan is to bite the dick off. Better plan. Bite the dick. It's solid, and it makes the most sense. 'Cause men are dumb. Can never forget that. They're fucking idiots. He'll be like, "Hey it's time." And I'm like, "Let me suck your dick." And even though he's a rapist he's gonna be like "Okay." Cause they're stupid. And I'm gonna bite that shit. Get free.[51]

Jay tells this joke like it is a sales pitch; her tone is optimistic and clear. If the labor of "thinking of this shit" is exhausting and confusing, Jay's joke creates a matter-of-fact solution in which "the dick" becomes the object of attack, rather than her "whole vagina." By distilling the complex systems that perpetuate sexual violence to genitalia, Jay presents an empowering "plan" that offers a solution to the fear of potential violence, while de-humanizing predators. This comedy as cultural commentary and activism from Seales and Jay crack up the notion that Black women must remain stoic amidst very real threats of intimidation and violence. In telling their stories onstage, they let loose the ways Black women are gaslighted to take responsibility for harassment and sexual assault. Both comics reposition themselves as rageful, and unyeilding in their willingness to accept misogyny and rape culture as the status quo.

Nobody Wanna See Your Dick

Many comedic "legends" in the United States, such as Bill Cosby, Richard Pryor, and Louis C.K., are/were abusers.[52] As the #MeToo movement gained momentum, Black feminist comics have extended their performances to critique the misogyny and sexual violence within the world of comedy. Like much of the entertainment industry, stand-up has a history of celebrating and supporting misogyny and racism. Women, queer people, and people of color often navigate precarious situations in comedy clubs, touring alone, and being subject to inhospitable and prejudiced colleagues and/or audiences. Some comedians have used the momentum of the #MeToo movement to address sexual violence in stand-up communities. Buteau's and Zamata's recent comedic performances speak directly to power structures and naming/addressing their colleagues as perpetrators.

In the 2018 Netflix comedy special *The Comedy Line Up*, Buteau hones in on her male comedian friends who come to her grappling with their privilege and anxieties about toxic masculinity. Buteau uses a comedic segue usually employed when a comedian begins a self-deprecating bit: "It's been a very interesting year for me because—" she pauses and quickly pivots the subject of analysis away from herself, "a lot of my guy friends have come out."[53] Her eyebrows are raised and her face serious. She takes a longer pause and then states with a blunt staccato, "As predators." The audience laughs at this punchline, yet Buteau is deadpan. She looks around the room, blinking slowly, resigned and unimpressed. The laughter fades. She purses her lips and nods. In a sarcastic, empathetic tone, she elaborates, "Yeah. Like I always knew, but it was really *their* journey to figure it out."[54] Again, the audience laughs, and she shakes her head, not in disbelief, but in vexation. Buteau takes on the role of a parent or wiser friend who, within the closet paradigm, "always knew" of their loved one's identity. Buteau's furrowed brows and somewhat disgusted face signal that, instead of the confession being one of marginalization, she will not let her male friends play the victim.

She quickens the pace and continues, "Good guy friends. Comedian guys. Call me up. Talkin' 'bout 'I don't know if I assaulted somebody. I don't know if I offended somebody.'" Buteau's eyes get wide, and she allows her response to crescendo, "I'm like, 'How do you not motherfuckin' *know*?'" The word "know" is elongated and guttural as she yells into the microphone and continues in exasperation, "Read the goddamn room, man! If she looks like she's breathing bad air, and has said 'no' three or four times, it's a *no*!"[55] She slightly crosses her eyes looking up at the ceiling, and rolls them back down at the audience. Reversing a masculinist punchline typically aimed at degrading a woman subject, the butt of Buteau's joke is men's ignorance. She di-

Michelle Buteau in The Comedy Lineup, *2018. Netflix.*

rects her frustration at her male friends and the structures that allow them to remain unaware to their own predatory behavior. "Know" and "no" become Buteau's central punchlines and public service announcements. She simplifies the cues of consent, while at the same time laments the emotional unintelligence of the comics who have "come out" to her ("read the goddamn room, man!"). From Buteau's perspective, male comics are not innocent, nor is consent a complicated matter. Her bit both makes fun of the men's ignorance, but also demands that they take responsibility for their actions and behaviors.

Broadening the roasting of her friends' lack of common sense, Buteau begins what has become one of her most widely known bits. "Also, guys, don't take your dick out! Who's takin' they dick out? Nobody wanna see your dick! *Nobody wanna see your dick.*"[56] She directs the men to what consent sounds like: "You know somebody wanna see your dick if they say, 'Lemme see your dick!'" Buteau explains, leaning forward with a smile on her face and desire and delight in her voice, "I wanna see that dick." She finishes her lesson by concluding, "That's how you know somebody wanna see your dick, guys."[57]

Here, Buteau is certainly referencing the many men in the entertainment industry who have feigned ignorance around consent and women's desire as a way to perpetuate sexual violence. This bit continues to build in tension and frustration as she lists the public figures who have been accused and/or prosecuted for sexual harassment and assault. She laments with precise rhythm and escalating anger. "Come on. Matt Lauer? Nobody wanna see your crusty, bitter dick! Yuck. Louis C.K.? Nobody wanna see that ginger dick, no thank you. Harvey Weinstein? Nobody wanna see that pastrami mess. Yuck. Charlie Rose? How did he get his adult diaper off to show his dick? I don't know! What?"[58]

In a contemporary version of Jackie "Moms" Mabley's "old men" jokes, Buteau renders each celebrity abject, accruing increasingly grotesque insults on their genitalia. In content and performance, she plays the dozens, worsening her insults for each object of her ridicule. "Nobody wanna see your dick," repeated after each insult, mirrors the structure of "yo mama" jokes, and builds in exaggeration with each punchline. Buteau crafts her insults to a crescendo of abjection, performing her disgust affectively and corporeally. Her mouth deeply frowns and her voice drops as she calls Lauer's penis "crusty, bitter." She renders him even more despicable with a declarative, "Yuck." She quickly writes off C.K. in pace, a simple "no thank you," as if she is passing up a menu item without thought. Buteau's reprimand of Weinstein includes a guttural retching sound after calling him a "pastrami mess." By her punchline on Rose's incontinence, she has adjudged the men to be completely repulsive. [59] Through joke-telling, Buteau turns confusion and blame away from the people who have been victims of sexual abuse, and instead directs anger, indignation, and abjection toward perpetrators.

The joke takes one more unexpected turn. For the last name on her list of white men accused of sexual harassment and assault, Buteau names: "James Franco? Put a pin in that! I wanna see his dick." Buteau reinforces her script for consent, leaning forward toward the center of the audience. "James Franco, I wanna see your dick!"[60] Buteau reverses the masculinist joke form again, this time centering male genitalia as the object of desire and the punchline. Both "nobody wanna see your dick" and "I wanna see your dick" employ a hard (pun intended?) "c" sound, punctuating the joke in such a way to elicit laughs directed at the male's private parts. Buteau puts the men on display—up for scrutiny and objectification. Additionally, she reverses power structures in diminishing Franco. She does not want to see him fully, she wants to see his dick. Mabley's disgust for old men almost always accompanied mention of her desire for younger ones ("I don't want nothin' old, but some old money. And I'm gonna use it to put an ad in the paper for some young man!").[61] Similarly, Buteau refuses to foreclose desire in her critique of patriarchal/misogynist structures. Rather than separating consent and sexual agency/desire, Buteau asserts herself as sexual subject not in opposition to, but alongside empowering language about consent and self-determination.

In a return to her thesis, she implores to the audience, "If you come to a party at my house. Please do not bring your dick. Bring rosé and hummus." The bit seems to have wrapped up with this quippy punchline, but she decides to direct her mantra to the audience. Buteau turns to a man sitting in the front row and repeats herself, "Nobody wanna see your dick." The audience laughs at her heckle and she relays to the crowd, "Oh my god. Now he talkin' to his friend." The man in the front row has just proved her point, that men do not understand her straightforward command. Buteau delights in being able to relay this to the rest of the crowd. In semi-serious exasperation, she turns back to him and yells, "Yeah, man I'm tellin' you! I got a special, microphone, lashes. *Nobody wanna see your dick*!"[62] Buteau positions herself as authority, disintegrating the anonymity of the audience and, throughout the bit, a range of men. From her good guy friends, to celebrities, to fans of Buteau, she cracks up the assumption that only particular types of men engage in predatory behavior, and the possibility that they remain inconspicuous or invisible in her own audience.

Sasheer Zamata has also taken up the stage to call out sexual violence in stand-up comedy. In a viral performance at Los Angeles's Dynasty Typewriter, Zamata directed her attack on comedy's most widely known predator in the #MeToo movement, Louis C.K. A highly visible and commercially famous US comic, writer, and producer, C.K. admitted to sexual harassment allegations just weeks after accusations against Harvey Weinstein became public and as the #MeToo movement gained national momentum. In November

2017, five women reported to the *New York Times* that C.K. had either masturbated in front of them without their consent or asked them to watch him masturbate.[63] These rumors had been circulating in the comedy world, but had never been confirmed until the *Times* article's publication. Although C.K. was professionally and somewhat publicly shunned (Netflix canceled an upcoming stand-up special; a film he wrote, directed, and starred in was never released; and HBO, FX, and his writing partner Pamela Aldon severed professional ties to him), he faced no legal ramifications.

Less than a year after the allegations became public, C.K. returned to performing stand-up comedy at a small, unannounced performance at the Comedy Cellar in New York City. Then, in 2018, he performed a new hour-long set in Long Island. The performance was secretly recorded and leaked to YouTube. C.K., whose previously nuanced comedy often broached issues of race and American identity, took an angry and bigoted turn. The performance ranged from lamenting his financial losses to racist diatribes aimed at Asian men. In a particularly scathing section of his performance, C.K. delivered "jokes" directed at young people in the United States who challenge gender binaries and students from Parkland, Florida, who responded to the mass shooting at their high school through activism around gun reform.

> They tell you what to call them: "You should address me as 'they/them' because I identify as gender-neutral." Okay. You should address me as "there" because I identify as a location, and the location is your mother's cunt.... They testify in front of Congress, these kids? What the fuck? What are you doing? You're young, you should be crazy, you should be unhinged! Not in a suit saying, "I'm here to tell you ..." Fuck you, you're not interesting 'cause you went to a high school where kids got shot.[64]

Many critics, fellow comedians, and former fans of C.K. publicly expressed their disapproval of his new work, while others used the performance as an example of how comedians should be able to engage in any material they want. One month later, Sasheer Zamata directly addressed and criticized C.K. during her own stand-up set at Dynasty Typewriter on January 9, 2019. Zamata's set exposes how joke-telling can dismantle myths of comedy "greats" and challenge "free speech" rhetoric that excuses how comedians have historically used jokes to reinforce oppressive structures.

As she begins, Zamata signposts to her audience exactly what she was about to perform and why. Her tone is straightforward and casual:

> Now, this next joke I wanna do is not necessarily a new joke for me. Instead, I rewrote one of Louis C.K.'s bits that he did recently. I'm sure most of you have heard, he was recorded doing a set in Long Island where he talked about the Parkland victims and Asian men and their genitalia. Yeah. And just [the] topics that I would expect from a comedian who is desperately trying to avoid talking about the masturbation in the room. Now, some people were trying to defend him, saying this is the same kind of material he's always been doing. That's what he does. He's *edgy*. He goes there.[65]

She then cites C.K.'s joke about wanting to be called, "there," revising, "But if there is a location, the location is the toilet because that was some lazy ass shit." She goes on to explain why she believes this new material is, indeed, different from previous performances by C.K.:

> And also, that's *not true*! This isn't the same kind of material he's always been doing. I used to think he was really thought provoking. But this wasn't it, and Louis fans should be able to tell the difference. It's like you go to your favorite restaurant, and instead of getting chicken that you ordered, they serve you pigeon. It may taste the same at first, but the more you chew on it, the more you realize the quality has decreased. And then if you try to complain about it to the manager, he takes his dick out and calls you the N—word.[66]

Introducing the bit by saying "this next joke," Zamata asks the audience to come along with in her line of thinking and artistry. To refer to her joke as such invokes what Limon calls the "metajoke." The metajoke invites audiences to reject their passivity and analyze both the joke being told and its contextual references. Limon explains, "If the best jokes are metajokes, this joke's superiority derives from its reflection not just on itself but on every joke."[67] That is, metajokes ask audiences to think about the content and structure of comedic performance at large. In Zamata's bit, her metajoke destabilizes C.K. as comedic authority by showing how his performance was *not* comedy, but she can rewrite the "lazy ass shit" to transform it into comedic material. "The next joke I wanna do" reveals Zamata's labor to her audience. To state one is about to "do" a joke implies that one created the joke, and invites the audience to pay attention to its framework. What initially sounds like a rant not structurally dissimilar to C.K.'s, ends with a punchline ("he takes his dick out and calls you the N— word") that gets to the heart of Zamata's critique. She turns her angry rant into a surprising distillation of what she calls C.K.'s "decreased quality" as a comic.

Zamata takes her time. She lets the joke's set-up build in energy, but not in volume. She remains calm, countering C.K.'s irrational anger. Continuing, Zamata also addresses arguments that stand-up comedy is a genre that is supposed to push limits on "political correctness."

> Some people heard that set and they thought, "He's a comedian! He can say whatever he wants on stage as long as it's funny." And I actually agree with that. I don't think any topic should be off limits. You should be able to say whatever you want to onstage. But *you have to have a take.* You can't just get up onstage and say blatantly racist transphobic victim blaming statements without a punchline. Like who are you? All of our uncles?[68]

The audience claps and laughs heartily. Zamata proves how C.K.'s white masculinist rage is not isolated and can be found among most families (presumably even her own). Zamata paints C.K. as a stand-in representative for toxic masculinity. Arguments a comic has the right to say whatever they want do not hold weight, especially, as she argues, if the jokes do not prove a point, but instead take up space. Continuing her metajoke and set-up, Zamata explains, "So, I reworked his Parkland bit. And in his, he says that the survivors of the shooting shouldn't be spending their time talking to Congress about gun control. Instead they should be finger fucking each other." She pauses, signaling this is her joke-write: "But who's to say they're *not*? They can do both. They're teenagers! Of course, they're finger fucking each other! They're probably fucking each other more on that bus ride to DC because they're so jacked up with adrenaline." With that, it seems like the joke is over. It is funny, and the audience is still laughing,

Sasheer Zamata at the 2018 Tribeca Film Festival.
Wikimedia Commons; photograph by Ryan McGrady, 2018.

but there is something dissatisfying about its ending. Thus, Zamata comes in for her final punchline that seals her roast of C.K., declaring slowly and with a dry tone, "They just know how to separate sex from work. Which I understand is a hard concept for Louis to grasp. Which is ironic because we all know how much Louis loves to grasp hard concepts."[69]

Altogether, Zamata's joke lasts five minutes, which is a relatively long bit. Her audience loves it. They clap and cheer loudly when she finishes her final punchline. It is not so much the actual joke, which is an easy pun ("hard to grasp"), but rather Zamata performs a slow and steady dissection of C.K.'s comedic "genius." Her long pauses and metajoke set-ups ("I reworked this bit") grant the audience access to new possibilities for stand-up comedy as a medium in which a white male's rage is not lauded as "edgy." Less a response to the joke itself, but what the joke represents, the audience laughs in the face of misogynistic and racist symbols of power. Their laughter, like Zamata's bit, is calculated and satisfactory, as the joke rests on a slow burn, not on quick misdirection. Given that several audience members who protested C.K.'s presence in comedy clubs when he returned to stand-up were censored or asked to leave the venue where he performed, Zamata makes space in a comedy club to protest C.K.'s appearances and critique what his defenders (both fans and managers of comedy clubs) call his right to free speech.

Buteau and Zamata employ strategies of abjection and the metajoke to dismiss men's power in broader cultural contexts and in the specific, theatrical space of the stand-up venue. Historically, women and people of color have been asked to sit passively as the comic uses their bodies for an objectifying and dehumanizing laugh. From minstrel performances to the racist and sexist work of comics such as Larry the Cable Guy—whose audience shouted his most famous punchline with him, "Get 'er done!"—white men have dominated the comedy world at the expense of racialized and gendered "others."[70] Reclaiming stand-up, Buteau and Zamata crack up the assumed credibility of men in the entertainment and comedy industry, celebrate their own skillful labor as artists and Black feminist critics, and empower audiences to delight in the dissolution of old power structures that use laughter as a tool to harm, rather than heal.

Esther, Hannah, and Becky: Cracking Up White Feminism

As feminism becomes taken up by a broader swath of women in the United States (especially in the midst of a Trump presidency), Black feminist comedians are engaging in call-outs that point to the nuanced ways white women continue to hold on to their racialized/gendered power in institutional spaces at the expense of Black women and people of color. For example, Michelle Buteau performed live in Washington, DC for a special episode of the *2 Dope Queens* podcast taped after the 2017 Women's March on Washington. Buteau tackled the racial politics of the march, pointing out its lack of diversity and the ways that white feminists isolated women of color in the event's organizing. "Today was so magical.... Took the Amtrak in from Brooklyn this morning .... I had my sign, 'Yes We Can.' Fuckin' went out; saw, like, a gang of Meryl Streeps. Just a gang of old white bitches. I was like, 'Were you my teacher?' Like it was so ... 'Is your name Esther?'"[71] Buteau depicts the white women who crowded the march as endearing, yet ignorant in their understanding of what sustained struggle and resistance looks like for women of color. She also exemplifies the need for Black feminist interventions within spaces that are built to sustain and privilege white heteronormativity.

White people and their behavioral mysteries, complicity in racism, subpar feminism, and fragility have long been subjects of scrutiny for Black comics in the United States.[72] Richard Pryor analyzed the strange mood swings of white men, who will be overly "nice to a group of Black men," but become unreasonably angry if someone cuts them in line.[73] One of Mo'Nique's most famous bits on *The Queens of Comedy* tour was a comparison between the way white women and Black women fight with their husbands, namely that white women will protect their husband's masculine pride and send them off to work, while Black women will fight all the way to her husband's place of employment. In Mo'Nique's impression of a white woman, she is meek and saccharine sweet, apologizing, "Hey, Peter. All that shit I said? I'm sorry!"[74] These examples identify the ways comedians have dissected and mocked the subtleties of passive aggressive behaviors associated with white culture. Contemporary Black feminist comics are critiquing the more implicit and explicit ways white people, and in particular white women, deny their place in and uphold white privilege.

Seales's and Jay's performances dissect white women's deployment of white fragility, cracking up white feminists' notions of universal sisterhood.

In *I Be Knowin'*, Seales reenacts and names white fragility for women of color seeking commune, and also to rid white women of their power over workplace culture. Seales astutely analyzes how white women, even those who understand and seek to dismantle their privilege, still benefit from and perpetuate racial hierarchies in the workplace. Seales describes her theory that there are two kinds of white people: Hannahs and Beckys. Hannahs are people who "happen to be white." She explains that Hannahs, "know and understand that there ain't no truth to whiteness ... It was only created for the sole purpose of oppression ... They know to use their privilege to give access to those who don't have access to that privilege." Beckys, on the other hand, "believe the lie! That whiteness makes them better!"[75] Seales implicates both well-intentioned and ill-intentioned white women throughout her set because, "the entire world has been taught to protect white women and women who happen to be white. At the threat of death!" Harkening to the cultural haunting of lynching and violence enacted against Black people in the name of white femininity, Seales acknowledges the stakes of her material. She is not just a twenty-first century commentator, but a Black feminist comic who understands and contextualizes the ways the past is imbued in the present. Seales continues to connect how this history presents itself in daily life: "And so, what has happened is similar to like when kids aren't exposed to germs and their immune systems don't develop. White women and women who happen to be white ain't been exposed to criticism, so now they all fragile and they be cryin' all the goddamn time. And now, all of us gotta deal with that shit." She pauses and drops her voice carefully enunciating, "Every day at work." The audience knowingly applauds as Seales continues, "Now because of this fragility, no one is tellin' white women and women who happen to be white about their problematic behaviors." Again, she pauses and allows a knowing grin to spread across her face, places her hand on her hip, and leans slightly, bringing the microphone closer to her lips, "Well tonight's the night!"[76] The audience applauds in approval, knowing a comedic roast is coming.

Seales likens white women's fragility to a disease, one in which exposure to their privilege and interracial missteps brings about the classic scripts of white fragility. Robin DiAngelo describes in her study, *White Fragility*, that the structures of white supremacy and white people's failure to recognize their responsibility in systems of racism shut down difficult discussions about their offenses. This often means people of color are left to deal with the aftermath of white people's inept behavior. "Though white fragility is triggered by discomfort and anxiety," DiAngelo describes, "it is born of superiority and entitlement."[77] White women crying because they had not before been exposed to criticism is a classic way white people "reinstate white equilibrium as they repel the challenge [and] maintain our dominance within the racial hierarchy."[78] The white woman "crying all the time," gets no sympathy in Seales's performance. Instead, she shows how white superiority (masked as hurt feelings), is simultaneously toxic and absurd.

Signaling the pervasiveness of white women's fragility and their efforts to reinstate white equilibrium, Seales claims that this happens constantly in professional settings: "Right now there is a woman benefiting from white privilege who is storming into a break room in a huff." Seales quickly walks across the stage with wide strides, fists at her sides, head down, and sighing dramatically. She stops at one end of the stage and looks around with exaggerated turns of her head, manically pivoting her body back and forth. She juts her chin out and cocks her head to one side, bringing the microphone to her mouth. "Did you see Ranita?" Seales asks in a voice completely unlike her own, higher pitched, a bit nasally, and staccato. "Last week, she had an adorbs pixie cut," Seales continues. She says this with a smile, then shifts to a troubled look. Brows furrowed, mouth agape, comedically searching for the right words. The audience delights in this skillful impression. "And today, she showed up with dreadlocks!" Seales pauses again, this time frowning, and holding back fake tears. The audience immediately recognizes this move, laughing and clapping. Head down and lips slightly quivering, Seales bursts out quickly, "And I didn't recognize her on the elevator! And now she thinks I'm a racist!"[79] She throws her hands in the air and leans on the microphone stand burying her head in exaggerated embarrassment.

Performing, through linguistic whiteface and a child-like frustration, Seales breaks down the Hannah or Becky's false neutrality in the workplace. Jennifer Lynn Stoever's analysis of the "inaudibility of whiteness" that, as she argues, perpetuates whiteness as neutral or impossible to criticize. Stoever explains, "The inaudibility of white-ness stems from its considerably wider palette of representation and the belief that white presentations stand in for 'people' in general, rather than 'white people' in particular."[80] Yet, Seales's impression of the workplace Becky/Hannah, through her own vocal virtuosity cracks up white supremacy in the workplace. Through this impression, Seales makes both audible and visible the ways white women hold professional power while feigning innocence or responsibility for their interpersonal behaviors and microaggressions. Seales enacts a linguistic whiteface that, when placed onto Seales's Black body, reveals the particularly self-centered nature of white fragility in professional settings.

Seales switches scenes in this workplace scenario to the Black woman who was on the elevator with her white colleague: "Ranita is in her office. She is aware," Seales pauses and then shouts, "but she don't care! She ain't got time to care, because she is composing an email that she has written four times. And had to delete, delete, delete, delete. 'Cause she was telling the *truth*! But it's gonna send her to HR." For her final implication of white women, Seales melds a punchline and a firm declaration: "Since y'all done turned passive aggression into a synonym for *professionalism*!"[81] Just as skilled as comics such as Mabley, Pryor, and Mo'Nique in employing linguistic whiteface and observational humor on white culture, Seales proves the pervasiveness of white women's fragility and white privilege as the dominant force around which Black professionals must constantly navigate.

Seales's pointed discussion about white fragility addresses the everyday ways Black women must navigate interpersonal racism and microaggressions. On a broader national level, however, the rise of white supremacist organizing and visibility since the 2016 presidential election has been a painful and violent reminder of how inept white people in the United States are at addressing their role in ending both structural and overtly violent forms of racism. In *Donna's Daughter*, Sam Jay's track, "Nazis" narrates a timely pedagogical manual for white anti-racist action. Jay performs a mix of exhaustion and ambivalence: "We gotta talk about Nazis, right? It's like what the fuck, but you have to right? I don't—." She pauses and lets out a sigh, signaling that she feels an obligation to address the issue, but is uninterested in leading the charge. Instead, she offers a generalized observation: "I feel like everyone is just being dumb. Everyone is blaming Trump. That's stupid. It's not Trump's fault there's Nazis. It's Trump's fault that Nazis are coming *outside*."[82]

White nationalist organizing and a rise of white supremacist terrorism has been a hallmark of the Trump presidency. In the months following his election, emboldened and empowered by the nation's new president, neo-Nazi groups, the Ku Klux Klan (KKK), and members of alt-right groups leapt out from the anonymity of online forums and secret meetings and increased their visibility through public rallies and "protests." The 2017 Unite the Right rally in Charlottesville, Virginia was a catalytic event that encouraged future white supremacist rallies across the United States, and went uncondemned by the Trump administration. Mostly absent from these public events, however, were the women who support the men behind the torches and Klan robes. Despite their perceived invisibility in these movements, Jay squarely places blame on this one group for white supremacists and far-right violence: "White women."[83]

"I really feel like it's y'all fault there's Nazis." Jay says this quietly, matter of fact. Much of her audience does not audibly respond during her pause, but there is one woman who resounds from the crowd in a moment of near complete silence. She laughs loud and long in auditory recognition that seemingly affirms Jay's theory. The length of the laugh cuts through the relatively quiet audience, imploring Jay to continue. More as a declaration than a question, Jay asks,

> Who else is to blame? Y'all be deflecting. White women are classic deflectors. Y'all have been doing this shit for years. Centuries, even. Just doin' it. "That black man looked at me!" After you sucked his dick. Y'all do this! This is what y'all do. If everybody gotta own they shit, y'all gotta own your classic victim maneuvering bullshit y'all do. And that's why I blame Nazis on y'all.[84]

Like Seales, Jay speaks about how protection of white femininity shaped white supremacy in the United States. "Y'all have been doing this shit for years. Centuries, even," places a direct spotlight on white women's complicity in and contributions to anti-Black violence and white nationalist movements. In the Reconstruction Era following the Civil War, Southern whites seeking to retain a racial hierarchy did so by enforcing anti-Black terrorism. Organizations like the

KKK were founded post-emancipation, and their ideologies thrived on white anxieties about Black men's growing political clout. Historian Martha Hodes explains that Klansmen justified their brutal attacks on Black men by conflating "the newly won political and economic power of black men with alleged sexual liaisons with white women."[85] Hodes also notes that white women who were accused of having sexual relationships with Black men were often physically and sexually attacked by the KKK if they were not deemed morally worthy or imbued with middle- and upper-class propriety. These are just a few of the ways accusations of rape laid the groundwork for justifications of widespread lynching and other forms of anti-Black violence.

Buried in the shadows of white nationalist, white supremacist, and neo-Nazi movements are the white women who uplift and support the men at the forefront. The KKK had an all-women's branch of its organization in 1920 that attracted nearly half a million women.[86] The branch itself was short-lived, but the KKK at-large adopted many of its subtle advertising strategies that focused on protection of the family and the nation.[87] "Blaming Nazis" on white women is a way for Jay to historicize how white women have been used as tools for anti-Black violence *and* white women's centrality in the formulation of white nationalist ideologies in the United States, especially under the guise of moral superiority and self-protection/preservation.

Moving to the present, Jay critiques the way well-intentioned white women (or, "Hannahs" as Seales calls them), also deflect their relationships to white supremacy, even as they participate in social justice movements. "Y'all do this weird thing where you act like you don't know." Jay fakes an incredulous tone, "Just like, Nazis? How? Where? Who?'" She switches back to her low, gruff voice and fires back, "Like, bitch your Dad! Who? Your *father*! You knew this n— was a Nazi! Help this n— brah! Y'all be so ready to help! Y'all be at the Black Lives Matter rally with your aloe vera water, granola. Bring it to them n—! They need it! They're sad. Hug them n—! Fuckin' do somethin'! They belong to *you*!"[88]

White feminists, after the election of Donald Trump and subsequent rise of white nationalist fervor, quickly aligned themselves with anti-racist causes such as Black Lives Matter. Jay's joke points out the ways white feminists have ignored their own relationships to white supremacy in historical, individual, and familial contexts. Jay calls out white supremacy as a system that must "shift the locus of change onto white people, where it belongs. It also points [white people] in the direction of the lifelong work that is uniquely [for white people], challenging our complicity with and investment in racism."[89] Jay implores white women to focus their attention on their close proximity to toxic masculinity and white supremacy, and take their anti-racist strategies to the place where it may do the most good: the home space.

Just as Seales likened white fragility to a lack of a healthy immune system, Jay calls Nazis "sad" white men who are crying for help, who are just "spiraling." Reflecting Toni Morrison's description of racism as a state of bereavement, Jay also aptly states the mental dis-ease of white supremacy. "People who practice racism are bereft," Morrison identified in a 1993 interview. "There is something distorted about their psyche. . . . It's a profound neurosis that no one examines."[90] The "no one" Morrison refers to is, of course, white people themselves. James Baldwin famously wrote that white Americans engage in forms of extreme denial, but that "for their own sakes" must "face their history" and recognize the ways their passivity "hideously menaces this country."[91] Jay places herself in a lineage of Black feminist and Black queer public intellectuals who recognize white supremacy as something to be cured within communities of white people. Like Morrison and Baldwin, Jay argues that white Americans, and white women in particular, must be the ones to fix what is psychically, spiritually, and nationally broken.

The audience strongly laughs as Jay finishes this bit. But when their collective noise fades, that singular voice once again bursts forth. Again, it is the woman with the hearty, cackling laugh. Her voice echoes on the album, a clap-back to Jay's truth-telling, an out-loud response to what has remained too quiet in stories of US racism. The resonating laugh signals a desire to release the burden of solving anti-Black violence, and place the duty back in the hands of those most responsible to fix it. Seales and Jay call out white women's fragility and their place in perpetuating oppressive systems, and call on them to know and do better.

Lift Every Voice and Sing

The artists in this last chapter of *Cracking Up* usher in new forms of comedic protest that place center stage the celebration of Black, feminist, and queer lives often depicted as marginal to US culture. Taken together, these comics represent a cohort of artists who dissect the complexities of past and present, anti-Black racism, the mundane and systemic ways that misogyny permeates US culture, and modes of living that refuse to comply with white heteropatriarchy.

These comics use their time onstage to crack up homonormativity, sexual violence, and white supremacy, and white feminism in the Trump era. In a current surge of opportunities for more diverse comedic performances to reach wide-ranging audiences, these comics are doing important labor as cultural critics and Black feminist trailblazers. As contemporary as their work is, however, I also read them as deeply aligned with the comedic styles of Jackie Mabley, whose work was rooted in the traditions of Black vernacular performance practices and aimed at using comedy to further a civil rights agenda. Linking these women to Mo'Nique, their comedy reaches broad audiences, but privileges Black women, women of color, and queer women of color, giving those witnessing their work a space to celebrate and name some of their common experiences in the United States. Like Wanda Sykes, these comics see citizenship as a precarious notion for Black and Black queer women. Amanda Seales, Michelle Buteau, Sam Jay, and Sasheer Zamata epitomize what is forthcoming in Black feminist comedic excellence.

A moment in Seales's *I Be Knowin'* illustrates the ways contemporary Black feminist comedy celebrates and relishes in movements toward freedom, borrowing from the past and remixing it for present and future modes of empowerment. As discussed in chapter 1, Mabley's comedic routines often included spiritual hymns and songs rewritten so that the lyrics expressed futures of Black liberation and racial harmony. So too, does Amanda Seales employ song as a central form of community-building alongside joke-telling. In the middle of *I Be Knowin'*, Seales expresses frustration and grief over not having learned about Black history as a young person, both at home and in school. She explains to her audience, "They really didn't teach us shit. Black history, we had to figure it out. Most of us, we didn't even learn about the Negro National Anthem. They kept that real hush hush."[92] The Negro National Anthem, formally titled "Lift Every Voice and Sing," has been a pillar of Black communion and a song of both celebration and resistance since the early 1900s. Imani Perry writes that the song is a prime example of formalism, a practice "primarily internal to the black community, rather than those based upon a white

Amanda Seales and I Be Knowin' *audience sing*
Lift Every Voice and Sing, *2019. HBO.*

gaze or an aspiration for white acceptance."[93] A "ritual engagement
in performative, musical, literary, institutional, and social culture,"
formalism, according to Perry, is often "practiced seriousness" that
moves away from vernacular expression like comedy.[94]

Seales makes fun of this seriousness when she states that no matter
what, Black people always begin the song "Like you're at your man's
mama house, for the first time." The audience laughs as Seales poses
regally, one knee bent, palm flat on her thigh, polite smile on her face
and asks her audience, "Shall we?" She hums a note with a pantomimed harmonica to keep the audience in tune. Not mocking, but in
an enjoyable performance of formality, Seales and many of her audience members join together singing the first stanza: *Lift every voice
and sing / 'Til earth and heaven ring / Ring with the harmonies of
liberty.* Seales jokes, "Then someone starts a double clap." The audience, without skipping a beat does so and they all continue loudly:
*Let our rejoicing rise / high as the list'ning skies / let it resound loud
as the rolling sea.* "Stop!" Seales commands. "There are white people

in here right now who are like—" Seales looks suspiciously from left to right, then brings one finger to her ear as if wearing a security guard's earpiece, "'They're having meetings.'" Making fun of the ways white people both surveil and are ignorant to Black enjoyment and celebration of culture, Seales continues, "There are people watching this right now that *just found out* there's a Negro National Anthem! And that it is not a song from *Hamilton*!"[95] Blending the communal and formal seriousness of the anthem with comedic boldness, Seales and much of her audience continue singing loudly, joyfully: *Sing a song full of the hope that the present has brought us.* The anthem concludes with loud applause and cheers. Seales grandly punctuates the song as well. In a gesture that harkens to histories of Black power and pride and continuing commitment to liberty and justice for all, she stands with her feet wide, microphone in one hand and lifting her other hand in a fist high in the air. Seales and the audience belt grandly: *Facing the rising sun of our new day begun / Let us march on 'til victory is won.*

Conclusion

n December 2019, a touching display of Black feminist comedic genealogy donned the small screen when Wanda Sykes guest starred in the Amazon series *The Marvelous Mrs. Maisel* as Moms Mabley at the Apollo Theatre.[1] Sykes as Moms appears in a blue dress with pineapple print, resembling an overcoat Mabley often wore in the later years of her career. In Moms's other signature costume items, floppy hat and house shoes, Sykes's posture is slightly hunched, her hands either on her hips or dangling at her sides. The fictionalized audience cheers uproariously as they do in Mabley's *Live at the Apollo* album. Sykes performs a truncated version of the "good old days" bit in which Moms laments the old man she married as a teenager. "My daddy picked out this old man." She then repeats "old man," elongating "old" just as Mabley did in the 1961 *Apollo* album. "My daddy liked him. *My daddy shoulda married him!*"[2]

Sykes brought a sweetness to her performance that made her admiration of Mabley obvious. The impression was both spot on and slightly off. Sykes's timing and tone mimicked Mabley, but the gruffness in Mabley's voice was replaced with a softer reverence. As Sykes hit Moms's famous punchlines, she relishes the moment and kindly smiles instead of pursing her lips like Mabley often did. Sykes described this performance as a dream role and Mabley as her idol, without whom she "probably wouldn't even be doing stand-up."[3] Sykes cracks up time in this guest appearance, collapsing the boundaries between self and performance, and pays homage to her comedic hero. With Mabley as the temporal pinpoint, a comedic and civil rights trail-

Wanda Sykes as Moms Mabley at the Apollo Theater in
The Marvelous Mrs. Maisel. *Screen grab, Amazon, 2019.*

blazer, whose Black queer aesthetic practices reach beyond a containing archive, twenty-first century Black feminist comics like Sykes
and the rest of the artists in this book have followed in her footsteps
and melded joke-telling and political/cultural protest.

Cracking Up positions the Black feminist comic as storyteller,
truth-teller, protest leader, and critical historiographer. Each of the
artists in this book plays important roles in both reflecting and shaping Black feminist thought, Black performance traditions, and civil
rights movements. Linking comedy and protest, their work extends
beyond the ephemeral theatre, the recorded album, or the digital
platform. They inspect our national past and present, and they crack
up the veneers of power that attempt to normalize racism, sexism,
homophobia, and white supremacy. They demonstrate that the stakes
of Black feminist performance are, indeed, high in terms of shaping
and reshaping national ideologies around citizenship and belonging.

In line with Black feminist aesthetic practices, the artists in *Cracking Up* exercise "the instrumentality of the black female body as an

artistic and public flashpoint," revealing the embodied possibilities of protest via the stage.[4] Mabley's civil rights comedy alongside her Black feminist and queer performance persona forged paths for future Black women comics to subvert racialized and gendered stereotypes and assert the clout of a laugh. While overlooked in theatre and performance histories, Mabley used Black feminist and Black queer performance strategies to innovate stand-up comedy as a form of Black/queer resistance. Mo'Nique's performance in *I Coulda Been Your Cellmate!* exemplified the coalitional potential of Black feminist comedy, and showed how audiences are vital spect-actors and shapers of theatrical experience. Superseding the panoptical power of the state, Mo'Nique and her audience created resonant movements toward freedom and collective bonding. Wanda Sykes's comedy in the era of an Obama presidency grappled with citizenship, and comedically and poignantly performed the complex vertigo of "progress" as experienced from her intersecting standpoints as a Black lesbian. The assemblage of comics in chapter 4 script what performative protest can be, and is both inspired by and furthers a Black feminist comedic genealogy.

In this genealogy, "cracking up" is the descriptor of joyful, resistant, Black feminist/queer comedic performance practices. It is also the resulting embodied and critical work of their stand-up. The artists analyzed and celebrated in this text crack us up: they make us burst out in laughter, but also ask us to look closer, through the interstices their performances create. What gets cracked up, be it whiteness, US history, or linear time, becomes something new. Both the laughs and the fresh perspectives their performances expose give audiences more space, more critical thinking, more joy, more life. Cracking up in these performances means that the performing and laughing body functions as epistemology divergent from dominant logics and confined modes of knowledge production and community formation.

Shining a spotlight on popular entertainment as a form of cultural protest, I also offer "cracking up" as an intervention in theatre and performance studies. The artists in the preceding pages contribute to, what Johnson names as the vital "material, intellectual, and aesthetic matrix that is black theatre and performance."[5] They work outside the realm of avant garde, performance art, or commercial theatre, but are nonetheless integral to the study of live performance and theatre histories. Cracking up as a methodology proposes a way of thinking, archiving, and theorizing that centers the explosive, the breaks in the mundane, and the distilled punchline as rich historiographical and ideological sources. Cracking up deconstructs boundaries in exchange for interdisciplinarity, Black/queer temporality, and richer histories told from the margins.

I must say that, of course, the irony of this book's tone is not lost on me—that nearly two hundred pages devoted to comedy takes itself so seriously. Yet, I have attempted to reconcile a scholarly seriousness with the pleasures meant to be evoked by popular entertainment. At the nexus between these two points is where I attempt to both theorize and reveal particular desires, practices, and patterns of cultural formations, and where the labor of these artists can be given much due props. Anyhow, my attempts at humor would not come close to the mastery of the comics in *Cracking Up*. If anything, it is my hope that I was able to do the nuances of their style, tone, and timing some justice. If this has not been the case, I cannot recommend highly enough that the reader seek out the brilliant comedic performances documented here for themselves.

My contention that Black feminist comedy is a kind of performance that unites communities reflects Dolan's idea of the theatre as a Utopia—that performance and politics intertwine to give hope for our lives to be as "emotionally voluminous, generous, aesthetically striking, and intersubjectively intense" as theatrical experience can and should be.[6] Because Black feminist comedy so often negates the separations between performer and audience members, because laughter is inherently communal, and because Black feminist comedy affirms racialized, gendered, and queer experiences as valid, it holds the potential to bring Black women and their allies together in such a way where many other performances might fail or remain fleeting, even alienating.

At the heart of *Cracking Up* is a deep commitment to archiving Black feminist artists who believe in the political and cultural power of a laugh, and for a joke to resonate in our individual and collective imaginaries. Laughter carries and connects. It is deeply individual, but also communal. It is both explosively improvisational and carries deep historical weight. In short, laughter is a distinct kind of action, a corporeal and affective response that can solidify collectivity just as much as it can express individual desires, fears, histories and delights. The performances I explore in *Cracking Up* evoke what

Ashon T. Crawley calls an "otherwise possibility."[7] This "otherwise" mode of Black feminist and Black queer performance conjures communal, embodied, strategies that resist the state, and generate alternative and liberative ways of being.[8] Performances of a Black feminist/Black queer "otherwise" are particularly vital at this juncture in the United States. As I complete this manuscript, a global pandemic rages, shamefully and disproportionately so in Black, Brown, and Indigenous communities. A national rebellion spawned by yet more unjust murders of Black people by police officers has ignited the largest surge of the Black Lives Matter movement to date. If the brilliant performances in *Cracking Up* are any proof, there is little doubt that Black feminist comics will help lead the charge in this urgent national reckoning, articulating and staging what social and political equity require, and asserting Black feminist power and presence in the world.

I return now to Jackie "Moms" Mabley's memorialized words at the National Museum of African American History and Culture: "I just tell the truth. If you don't want the truth, don't come to Moms." The assemblage of comics in this book illuminates Black/feminist/queer subjectivities, particularly as they relate to US citizenship, past and present. Cracking up protocols of respectability and refusing fixed narratives of US history, they compose movements toward freedom that produce embodied moments of commune for their audiences, both live and mediated. In short, they tell the truth—be those difficult to confront or those that aptly affirm the lived experiences of minoritarian groups. They facilitate laughter that functions as release and out-loud protest. To crack up is to express a desire for something different and something more. To crack up is to both break down injustice and suture its coinciding pain. To crack up is to insist on telling stories of a more complex past and to demand a more just and joyous future.

Notes

Introduction

1. See "Museum Maps," National Museum of African American History and Culture, accessed July 1, 2018, https://nmaahc.si.edu/visit/maps.

2. This quote is part of the permanent exhibit *Taking the Stage* at National Museum of African American History and Culture, Washington, DC.

3. Phoebe Robinson and Jessica Williams, *2 Dope Queens*, "New York," directed by Tig Notaro, HBO, 2018 (emphasis mine).

4. Robinson and Williams, *2 Dope Queens* (emphasis mine). Robinson is speaking of Sally Hemings, an enslaved woman inherited by Thomas Jefferson upon his marriage to Martha Jefferson. Here, Robinson is also referring to language that framed Jefferson and Hemings in a romantic partnership rather than one based on violence and power. Hemings was not, however, without agency. For example, she negotiated freedom for any children she bore by Jefferson. For a thorough account of the Hemings family, see Annette Gordon-Reed, *The Hemingses of Monticello: An American Family* (New York: W.W. Norton & Co, 2008).

5. Stephanie Leigh Batiste, *Darkening Mirrors: Imperial Representation in Depression-Era African American Performance* (Durham, NC: Duke University Press, 2011), 19.

6. Clarence Major, *Juba to Jive: A Dictionary of African-American Slang* (New York: Viking, 1994), 120.

7. Emily J. Lordi. *Black Resonance: Iconic Women Singers and African American Literature* (New Brunswick, NJ: Rutgers University Press, 2013), 8–9.

8. Daphne Brooks, *Bodies in Dissent: Spectacular Performances of Race and Freedom, 1850–1910* (Durham, NC: Duke University Press, 2006), 10.

9. Matt Richardson, *The Queer Limit of Black Memory: Black Lesbian Literature and Irresolution* (Columbus: Ohio State University Press, 2013), 10.

10. Patricia Hill Collins, "The Social Construction of Black Feminist Thought," *Signs* 14, no. 4 (1989): 750.

11. Kara Keeling, *Queer Times, Black Futures* (New York: New York University Press, 2019), xiii.

12. Omi Osun Joni L. Jones, *Theatrical Jazz: Performance, Àṣẹ, and the Power of the Present Moment* (Columbus: Ohio State University Press, 2015).

13. Thomas F. DeFrantz and Anita Gonzalez, "Introduction: From 'Negro Expression' to 'Black Performance,'" in *Black Performance Theory*, ed. Thomas F. DeFrantz and Anita Gonzalez (Durham, NC: Duke University Press, 2014), xii.

14. E. Patrick Johnson, "Black Performance Studies: Genealogies, Politics, Futures," in *The Sage Handbook of Performance Studies*, ed. D. Soyini Madison and Judith Hamera (Thousand Oaks: Sage, 2006), 452.

15. Jones, *Theatrical Jazz.*

16. Patricia Hill Collins, *Fighting Words: Black Women and the Search for Justice* (Minneapolis: University of Minnesota Press, 1998), 279.

17. Pearl Cleage, "A Hollering Place," *The Dramatists Guild Quarterly* Summer (1994): 12.

18. bell hooks, *Black Looks: Race and Representation* (Cambridge, MA: South End Press, 1992), 51.

19. Audre Lorde, "Scratching the Surface: Some Notes on Barriers to Women and Loving," in *Sister Outsider: Essays & Speeches by Audre Lorde* (Freedom: The Crossing Press, 1984), 46.

20. M. Jacqui Alexander, *Pedagogies of Crossing: Meditations on Feminism, Sexual Politics, Memory and the Sacred* (Durham, NC: Duke University Press, 2005), 300.

21. For more on Black feminist transformation of institutional spaces to sites of resistance and bonding, see Evelyn Brooks Higginbotham, *Righteous Discontent: The Women's Movement in the Black Baptist Church, 1880–1920* (Cambridge, MA: Harvard University Press, 1994); Koritha Mitchell, *Living with Lynching: African American Lynching Plays, Performance, and Citizenship, 1890–1930* (Champaign: University of Illinois Press, 2011); and Aimee Meredith Cox, *Shapeshifters: Black Girls and the Choreography of Citizenship* (Durham, NC: Duke University Press, 2015).

22. Diana Taylor, *The Archive and the Repertoire: Performing Cultural Memory in the Americas* (Durham, NC: Duke University Press, 2003), 15.

23. For more on Black performance traditions that engage transformation, see Fred Moten, *In the Break: The Aesthetics of the Black Radical Tradition* (Minneapolis: University of Minnesota Press, 2003).

24. Brooks, *Bodies in Dissent*, 8.

25. DeFrantz and Gonzalez, "From 'Negro Expression' to 'Black Performance,'" vii.

26. Eric Lott, *Love and Theft: Blackface Minstrelsy and the American Working Class* (New York: Oxford University Press, 1993).

27. Harry L. Newton, *A Bundle of Burnt Cork Comedy: Original Cross-Fire Conversations, Gags, Retorts, Minstrel Monologues and Stump Speeches* (Minneapolis: T.S. Denison & Co, 1905), 101.

28. Yuval Taylor and Jake Austen, *Darkest America: Black Minstrelsy from Slavery to Hip-Hop* (New York: W.W. Norton and Company, 2012), 34.

29. W. E. B. Du Bois, *The Souls of Black Folk*, Oxford World Classics (New York: Oxford University Press, 2007), 9.

30. David Krasner, *Resistance, Parody, and Double Consciousness in African American Theatre, 1895–1910* (New York: St. Martin's Press, 1997), 1.

31. Annemarie Bean, "Black Minstrelsy and Double Inversion, Circa 1890," in *African American Performance and Theatre History: A Critical Reader*, ed. Harry J. Elam, Jr. and David Krasner (New York: Oxford University Press, 2001), 187.

32. Megan Pugh, *America Dancing: From the Cakewalk to the Moonwalk* (New Haven: Yale University Press, 2015), 17.

33. Bean, "Black Minstrelsy and Double Inversion," 184.

34. Mel Watkins, *African American Humor: The Best Black Comedy from Slavery to Today* (Chicago: Lawrence Hill Books, 2002), xi.

35. Bambi Haggins, *Laughing Mad: The Black Comic Persona in Post-Soul America* (New Brunswick, NJ: Rutgers University Press, 2007).

36. See John Limon, *Stand-Up Comedy in Theory, Or, Abjection in America* (Durham, NC: Duke University Press, 2000), and Watkins, *African American Humor.*

37. Haggins, *Laughing Mad*, 7.

38. Glenda Carpio, *Laughing Fit to Kill: Black Humor in the Fictions of Slavery* (New York: Oxford University Press, 2008), 15.

39. Carpio, *Laughing Fit to Kill*, 230–31.

40. Athelia Knight, "In Retrospect: Sherman H. Dudley—He Paved the Way for T.O.B.A.," *The Black Perspective in Music* 15, no. 2 (1987): 171–72.

41. Michelle R. Scott, "These Ladies Do Business with a Capital B: The Griffin Sisters as Black Businesswomen in Early Vaudeville," *Journal of African American History* 101, no. 4 (2016): 469–503.

42. Angela Y. Davis, *Blues Legacies and Black Feminism: Gertrude "Ma" Rainey, Bessie Smith, and Billie Holiday* (New York: Pantheon Books, 1998).

43. L. H. Stallings, *Mutha' Is Half a Word: Intersections of Folklore, Vernacular, Myth, and Queerness in Black Female Culture* (Columbus: Ohio State University Press, 2007), 115–16.

44. See Wayne Federman and Andrew Steven, "The Apollo and the Chitlin' Circuit," audio podcast, *The History of Standup*, June, 18, 2019, https://player.fm/series/the-history-of-standup-2424926/s2-ep-03-the-apollo-and-the-chitlin-circuit.

45. For more on LaWanda Page, see Jessyka Finley, "Raunch and Redress: Interrogating Pleasure in Black Women's Stand-Up Comedy," *Journal of Popular Culture* 49, no. 4 (2016): 780–98. Page played an imperative role in Black comedy in the 1970s and influenced artists who flourished in the 1980s and 1990s, such as Adele Givens and Mo'Nique.

46. Kara Hunt, "Off the Record: A Critical Perspective on Def Comedy Jam," *Journal of Popular Culture* 48, no. 5 (2015): 837.

47. See Finley, "Raunch and Redress."

48. bell hooks, *Talking Back: Thinking Feminist, Thinking Black* (Boston: South End Press, 1989), 9.

49. See Regina Barreca's *They Used to Call Me Snow White . . . But I Drifted: Women's Strategic Use of Humor* (New York: Penguin Books, 1991), 53; Sigmund Freud, *Jokes and Their Relation to the Unconscious* (New York: Norton, 1963), 176.

50. Samuel A. Floyd, Jr., *The Power of Black Music: Interpreting Its History from Africa to the United States* (New York: Oxford University Press, 1996), 43–45.

51. Augusto Boal, *Theatre of the Oppressed* (New York: Theatre Communications Group, 1985), 143–44.

52. Henri Bergson, *Laughter: An Essay On the Meaning of the Comic*, trans. Fred Rothwell and Cloudesley Brereton (New York: The Macmillan Company, 1921), 5.

53. Rebecca Krefting, *All Joking Aside: American Humor and Its Discontents* (Baltimore: Johns Hopkins University Press, 2014).

54. See Anne Cheng's *The Melancholy of Race: Psychoanalysis, Assimilation,*

and *Hidden Grief* (New York: Oxford University Press, 2001); Ann Cvetkovich, *Depression: A Public Feeling* (Durham, NC: Duke University Press, 2012); Frank B. Wilderson, "The Vengeance of Vertigo: Aphasia and Abjection in the Political Trials of Black Insurgents," *InTensions* 5 (2011): 1–41.

55. Haggins, *Laughing Mad*, 1.

56. Diane Davis, *Breaking Up (at) Totality: A Rhetoric of Laughter* (Carbondale: Southern Illinois University Press, 2000), 208.

57. Limon, *Stand-Up Comedy in Theory*, 12.

58. Michael Warner, *Publics and Counterpublics* (New York: Zone Books, 2002), 24.

59. Diana Taylor describes performance's primary function as an act of transfer, "transmitting social knowledge, memory, and a sense of identity." See Taylor, *The Archive and the Repertoire*, 2.

60. I see the artists in this book demonstrating an understanding of and balance between what D. Soyini Madison calls in *Acts of Activism* the "process/product dyad." While comedic performance may always be reaching for the end goal of a laugh, the comedy I document does not take an easy punchline, but rather weaves together the political content with comedic effects. See D. Soyini Madison, *Acts of Activism: Human Rights as Radical Performance* (Cambridge, UK: Cambridge University Press, 2010), 111.

61. Stuart Hall, "Whose Heritage? Un-Settling 'The Heritage,' Re-Imagining the Post-Nation," in *The Politics of Heritage: The Legacies of "Race,"* ed. Jo Littler and Koshi Naidoo (New York: Routledge, 2005), 26.

62. Hall, "Whose Heritage?"

63. Patricia Hill Collins, "Like One of the Family: Race, Ethnicity, and the Paradox of US National Identity," *Ethnic and Racial Studies* 24, no. 1 (2001): 9.

64. Fred Moten, *Black and Blur* (Durham, NC: Duke University Press, 2017), 164.

65. Moten, *Black and Blur*, xxiii.

66. Saidiya V. Hartman, *Scenes of Subjection: Terror, Slavery, and Self-Making in Nineteenth-Century America* (New York: Oxford University Press, 1997), 77.

67. Darieck Scott, *Extravagant Abjection: Blackness, Power, and Sexuality in the African American Literary Imagination* (New York: New York University Press, 2010), 9.

68. Carpio, *Laughing Fit to Kill*, 8.

69. Limon, *Stand-Up Comedy in Theory*, 4.

70. Christina Elizabeth Sharpe, *In the Wake: On Blackness and Being* (Durham, NC: Duke University Press, 2016), 22.

71. Megan Alrutz and Lynn Hoare, *Devising Critically Engaged Theatre for Youth: The Performing Justice Project* (New York: Routledge, 2020), xx.

72. Ta-Nehisi Coates, "In Defense of a Loaded Word," *The New York Times*, November 23, 2013, https://www.nytimes.com/2013/11/24/opinion/sunday/coates-in-defense-of-a-loaded-word.html.

73. Dwight Conquergood, "Performing as a Moral Act: Ethical Dimensions of the Ethnography of Performance," *Literature in Performance* 5, no. 2 (1985): 1–14.

Chapter 1: Laughter in the Archives

1. Gordon "Doc" Anderson served as the unofficial house photographer for the Apollo Theatre from the 1940s–80s. The New York Public Library's biography on Anderson in the Gordon Anderson Collection described his work as notably candid, and that he "would sometimes include himself in some of his images. His style is often recognized by the distinctive photomontages he created of Apollo Theatre performers." See, https://digitalcollections.nypl.org/collections/gordon-anderson-collection. Currently, Anderson's estate has not been, according to the New York Public Library, "resolved." Thus, his photographs are not available for reproduction. However, a small digital version of this photograph can be viewed here at https://digitalcollections.nypl.org/collections/gordon-anderson-collection#/?tab=about.

2. M. Cordell Thompson, "Moms Mabley Raps About Old Women, Young Love," *Jet*, January 3, 1974, 61.

3. Thompson, "Moms Mabley Raps," 62.

4. These resources include her twenty-eight LPs (almost all out of print), four films starring Mabley (she plays herself in two), the one biography written about Mabley, various periodicals, a play by Alice Childress titled, *Moms*, and her few television appearances in the late 1960s and early 1970s. Primary documents from the New York Public Library and the Schomburg Center for Research in Black Culture also shed light on Mabley's work, yet there is still no official residency for Mabley's full archive.

5. José Esteban Muñoz, *Cruising Utopia: The Then and There of Queer Futurity* (New York: New York University Press, 2009), 49.

6. Michel-Rolph Trouillot, *Silencing the Past: Power and the Production of History* (Boston: Beacon Press, 1995), 73.

7. Trouillot, *Silencing the Past*, 97.

8. Whoopi Goldberg, *Whoopi Goldberg Presents: Moms Mabley*, directed by Whoopi Goldberg (Los Angeles: HBO, 2013).

9. Goldberg, *Whoopi Goldberg Presents*.

10. Goldberg.

11. Goldberg.

12. Goldberg.

13. Anne Meara was part of the original Second City comedy group that formed in 1959 in Chicago. Meara also performed as a comedy duo with husband, Jerry Stiller. See Lawrence J. Epstein, *The Haunted Smile: The Story of Jewish Comedians in America* (New York: Public Affairs, 2001).

14. Anne Meara quoted in *Whoopi Goldberg Presents: Moms Mabley*.

15. Roderick A. Ferguson, *Aberrations in Black: Toward a Queer of Color Critique* (Minneapolis: University of Minnesota Press, 2004).

16. Matt Richardson, "Our Stories Have Never Been Told: Preliminary Thoughts on Black Lesbian Cultural Production as Historiography in the Watermelon Woman," *Black Camera: An International Film Journal (the New Series)* 2, no. 2 (2011): 110.

17. Haggins, *Laughing Mad*, 5.

18. "Moms Mabley: She Finally Makes the Movies," *Ebony*, April 1974, 88.

19. Elsie A. Williams, *The Humor of Jackie Moms Mabley: An African American Comedic Tradition* (New York: Garland, 1995), 45.

20. GHB Archives, "Moms Mabley," October 18, 2011, YouTube Video, 5:20, https://www.youtube.com/watch?v=PWW-96BouIU.

21. Mark Jacobson, "Amazing Moms," *New York Magazine*, April 13, 1974, 46.

22. Christine Acham, *Revolution Televised: Prime Time and the Struggle for Black Power* (Minneapolis: University of Minnesota Press, 2004), 12.

23. Acham, *Revolution Televised*, 12.

24. Harry J. Elam, Jr. and David Krasner, eds. *African American Performance and Theatre History: A Critical Reader* (Oxford: Oxford University Press, 2001), 139.

25. Preston Lauterbach, *The Chitlin' Circuit and the Road to Rock 'N' Roll* (New York: W.W. Norton, 2011).

26. Jackie "Moms" Mabley, *Boarding House Blues*, directed by Josh Binney, All-American News, 1948.

27. Jackie Mabley, "Jackie 'Moms' Mabley Talks About Her Life and Career as a Comedian," Best of Studs Turkel, WFMT, Chicago, IL, June 13, 1961.

28. Jackie "Moms" Mabley, *The Funny Sides of Moms Mabley* (Jewel Records, LP, 1964).

29. Mabley, *Funny Sides*.

30. E. Patrick Johnson, "'Quare' Studies, or (Almost) Everything I Know about Queer Studies I Learned from My Grandmother," in *Black Queer Studies: A Critical Anthology*, ed. E. Patrick Johnson and Mae G. Henderson (Durham, NC: Duke University Press, 2005), 127.

31. For a more detailed description and historicization of the mammy caricature, see Patricia A. Turner, *Ceramic Uncles & Celluloid Mammies: Black Images and Their Influence on Culture* (Charlottesville: University of Virginia Press, 2002).

32. Jackie "Moms" Mabley, *Moms Mabley at Geneva Conference* (Chess Records, LP, 1963).

33. Roberta Mock, "Stand-Up Comedy and the Legacy of the Mature Vagina," *Women & Performance: A Journal of Feminist Theory* 22, no. 1 (2012): 9–28.

34. L. H. Stallings, *Mutha' Is Half a Word*, 113.

35. Jackie "Moms" Mabley, *Live at Sing Sing* (Mercury Records, LP, 1970) (emphasis mine).

36. Mabley, *Live at Sing Sing*.

37. Mabley.

38. Mabley.

39. Mabley.

40. Frankie Valli, "Can't Take My Eyes Off of You," *Frankie Valli Solo* (Phillips Records, LP, 1967).

41. Mabley, *Live at Sing Sing*.

42. Meta DuEwa Jones, *The Muse Is Music: Jazz Poetry from the Harlem Renaissance to Spoken Word* (Urbana: University of Illinois Press, 2011), 54.

43. Jackie "Moms" Mabley, *Out on a Limb* (Mercury Records, LP, 1964).

44. Deborah, Paredez, *Selenidad: Selena, Latinos, and the Performance of Memory* (Durham, NC: Duke University Press, 2009), 8.

45. Jackie "Moms" Mabley, *Moms Mabley Live at the Apollo* (Jewel Records, CD, 1998).

46. Haggins, *Laughing Mad*, 149.

47. Mabley, *Moms Mabley Live at the Apollo.*

48. Williams, *The Humor of Jackie Moms Mabley.*

49. Elin Diamond, *Unmaking Mimesis: Essays on Feminism and Theatre* (London: Routledge, 1997), 13.

50. Henry Louis Gates, Jr., *The Signifying Monkey: A Theory of African-American Literary Criticism* (New York: Oxford University Press, 1988), 71.

51. Gates, *The Signifying Monkey*, 87.

52. Shane Vogel, "Lena Horne's Impersona," *Camera Obscura* 23, no. 67 (2008): 13.

53. The 1948 film *Boarding House Blues* shows an early version of Mabley's stand-up.

54. Jackie "Moms" Mabley, *Moms Wows* (Chess Records, LP-1486, 1964) (emphasis mine).

55. Mabley, *Moms Wows.*

56. Raymond Arsenault, *Freedom Riders: 1961 and the Struggle for Racial Justice* (New York: Oxford University Press, 2006).

57. Dewy "Pigmeat" Markham was also an important star of the Black vaudeville and comedy circuits. For more on Markham, see Brenda Dixon Gottschild's *Waltzing in the Dark: African American Vaudeville and Race Politics in the Swing Era* (New York: St. Martin's Press, 2000), 67–70.

58. Mabley, *Best of Moms Mabley and Pigmeat Markham*, Vol. 1 (Chess Records, LP, 1961).

59. Mabley, *Best of Moms.*

60. Koritha Mitchell, "LOVE In ACTION Noting Similarities Between Lynching Then and Anti-LGBT Violence Now," *Callaloo* 36, no. 3 (2013): 694.

61. For more on feminine drag and Black queer performance, see Kortney Ziegler, "Black Sissy Masculinity and the Politics of Dis-Respectability," in *No Tea, No Shade: New Writings in Black Queer Studies*, ed. E. Patrick Johnson (Durham, NC: Duke University Press, 2016), 196–215.

62. Mary Russo, *The Female Grotesque: Risk, Excess, and Modernity* (New York: Routledge, 1995), 23.

63. Russo, *Female Grotesque*, 26.

64. Also, see, Jackie "Moms" Mabley on *The Merv Griffin Show*, directed by Dick Carson, Season 7, Episode 1, aired August 18, 1969, on CBS. Mabley also performed a version of this bit where she sang her Civil Rights anthem, "Abraham, Martin and John."

65. Faedra Carpenter, *Coloring Whiteness: Acts of Critique in Black Performance* (Ann Arbor: University of Michigan Press, 2014), 195.

66. Carpio, *Laughing Fit to Kill*, 86.

67. Carpio, 86.

68. Mabley, *Moms Mabley at The Playboy Club* (Chess Records, LP, 1961).

69. Jackie "Moms" Mabley, *Moms Mabley Live at the U.N.* (Chess Records, LP, 1961).

70. Mabley, *Live at the U.N.*

71. Mabley.

72. Jackie "Moms" Mabley, *Moms Mabley Breaks it Up* (Chess Records, LP, 1968).

73. Deborah Paredez, "Lena Horne and Judy Garland: Divas, Desire, and Discipline in the Civil Rights Era," *TDR: The Drama Review* 58, no. 4 (2014): 107.

74. Mabley, *Moms Mabley Breaks it Up.*

75. Jonathan P. Rossing. "Critical Race Humor in a Postracial Moment: Richard Pryor's Contemporary Parrhesia," *Howard Journal of Communications* 25, no. 1 (2014): 16–33.

76. Mabley, *Moms Mabley Breaks it Up.*

77. Jason King, "Don't Stop 'Til You Get Enough: Presence, Spectacle, and Good Feeling in Michael Jackson's *This Is It*," in *Black Performance Theory*, ed. Thomas F. DeFrantz and Anita Gonzalez (Durham, NC: Duke University Press, 2014), 184.

78. Daphne A. Brooks, "Afro-sonic Feminist Praxis: Nina Simone and Adrienne Kennedy in High Fidelity," in *Black Performance Theory*, ed. Thomas F. DeFrantz and Anita Gonzalez (Durham, NC: Duke University Press, 2014), 204–22.

79. Ana-Maurine Lara, "Of Unexplained Presences, Flying Ife Heads, Vampires, Sweat, Zombies, and Legbas," *GLQ: A Journal of Lesbian & Gay Studies* 18, no. 2/3 (2012): 349.

Chapter 2: I Love You Bitches Back

1. Mo'Nique, *I Coulda Been Your Cellmate!*, directed by Gary Binkow (Enliven Entertainment, 2007), DVD.

2. Mo'Nique, *Cellmate.*

3. Mo'Nique.

4. Jonathan Chambers-Letson, *After the Party: A Manifesto for Queer of Color Life* (New York: New York University Press, 2018), 42.

5. Angela Y. Davis, *Are Prisons Obsolete?* (New York: Seven Stories Press, 2003), 67.

6. Les Back, "How Blue Can You Get? BB King, Planetary Humanism and the Blues Behind Bars," *Theory Culture & Society* 32, no. 7–8 (2015): 284.

7. Anna Deavere Smith's *Notes from the Field*, for example, is a documentary theatre piece in which Deavere employs her well-known style of solo performance. The piece splices interviews from a wide range of people whose lives are impacted by incarceration. Preceding this, *The Exonerated* is a widely performed, documentary-style theatre piece that explores the aftermath of people who had been wrongly convicted of crimes and then exonerated from the criminal justice system in the United States. See Anna Deavere Smith, *Notes from the Field* (New York: Anchor Publishing, 2019), and Jessica Blank and Eric Jensen, *The Exonerated* (New York: FSG Adult, 2005).

8. See Rena Fraden, *Imagining Medea: Rhodessa Jones and Theatre for Incarcerated Women* (Chapel Hill: University of North Carolina Press, 2001).

9. See "Ohio Reformatory for Women," Ohio Department of Rehabilitation and Correction, accessed September 26, 2019, https://drc.ohio.gov/orw.

10. "Ohio Reformatory for Women."

11. Jonathon Shailor, *Performing New Lives: Prison Theatre* (Philadelphia: Jessica Kingsley Publishers, 2011), 19.

12. Finley, "Raunch and Redress."

13. Katelyn Hale Wood, "Standing Up: Black Feminist Comedy in the Twentieth and Twenty-First Centuries," in *The Routledge Companion to African American Theatre and Performance*, ed. Kathy A. Perkins, Sandra L. Richards, Renée Alexander Craft, and Thomas F. DeFrantz (New York: Routledge, 2018), 326–27.

14. See, Mo'Nique, *One Night Stand*, directed by Leslie Smalls (Filmrise, 2004), DVD.

15. *The Parkers* was a sitcom that ran from 1999–2004 on the UPN network. The show centered around mother/daughter team Nikki (Mo'Nique) and Kim Parker (Countess Vaughn). Nikki decides to attend junior college at the same time her daughter is enrolled.

16. *Flavor of Love* was a VH1 reality dating show in which women contestants vied for a romantic relationship with the rapper Flavor Flav.

17. Shirley Henderson, "Mo'Nique Charms the World," *Ebony* 62, no. 10 (August 2007): 69.

18. Henderson, "Mo'Nique Charms," 70.

19. Michael Balfour, *Theatre In Prison: Theory and Practice* (Bristol, UK: Intellect, 2004), 3.

20. Mo'Nique, *Cellmate* (emphasis mine).

21. Blondie Cant U C, "Bow Down (Big Girl World)," written by Blondie Cantuc and Terry Lewis, 2007.

22. Mo'Nique, *Cellmate*.

23. José Esteban Muñoz, *Disidentifications: Queers of Color and the Performance of Politics* (Minneapolis: University of Minnesota Press, 1999), 161.

24. Muñoz, *Disidentifications*, 11.

25. Muñoz, 56.

26. Mo'Nique, *Cellmate* (emphasis mine).

27. Mo'Nique, *Cellmate*.

28. Joseph R. Roach, *Cities of the Dead: Circum-Atlantic Performance* (New York: Columbia University Press, 1996), 2.

29. Robin Bernstein, *Racial Innocence: Performing American Childhood from Slavery to Civil Rights* (New York: New York University Press, 2011), 23.

30. Mo'Nique, *Cellmate*.

31. Muñoz, *Disidentifications*, 121.

32. Muñoz, 128.

33. Paredez, *Selenidad*, 160.

34. Mo'Nique, *Cellmate* (emphasis mine).

35. Mo'Nique.

36. Mo'Nique.

37. Nancy Fraser, "Rethinking the Public Sphere: A Contribution to the Critique of Actually Existing Democracy," *Social Text* 25/26 (1990): 67.

38. Muñoz, *Disidentifications*, 179.

39. Jacques Derrida, *Writing and Difference*, trans. Alan Bass (Chicago: University of Chicago Press, 1978).

40. Uri McMillan, *Embodied Avatars: Genealogies of Black Feminist Art and Performance* (New York: New York University Press, 2015), 81.

41. Mo'Nique, *Cellmate*.

42. Audre Lorde, *Sister Outsider*, 56.

43. Lorde, 57.

44. Lyndon Kamaal Gill, *Erotic Islands: Art and Activism in the Queer Caribbean* (Durham, NC: Duke University Press, 2018), 9–11.

45. Nancy Walker, *A Very Serious Thing: Women's Humor and American Culture* (Minneapolis: University of Minnesota Press, 1988), 9.

46. Alexander, *Pedagogies of Crossing*, 22.

47. Shoniqua Roach, "Black Pussy Power: Performing Acts of Black Eroticism in Pam Grier's Blaxploitation Films," *Feminist Theory* 19, no. 1 (2018): 14.

48. Evelynn M. Hammonds, "Black (W)holes and the Geometry of Black Female Sexuality," *Differences: A Journal of Feminist Cultural Studies* 6, nos. 2–3 (1995): 132.

49. Collins, *Fighting Words*, 47.

50. Mo'Nique, *Cellmate*.

51. Kara Keeling, "'Ghetto Heaven': Set It Off and the Valorization of Black Lesbian Butch-Femme Sociality," *Black Scholar* 33, no. 1 (2003): 42.

52. Mo'Nique, *Cellmate* (emphasis mine).

53. Mo'Nique (emphasis mine).

54. Omise'eke Natasha Tinsley, "Black Atlantic, Queer Atlantic: Queer Imaginings of the Middle Passage," *GLQ: A Journal of Lesbian and Gay Studies* 14, no.2 (2008): 199.

55. Boal, *Theatre of the Oppressed*.

56. Muñoz, *Disidentifications*, 161.

57. Muñoz,162–63.

58. Mo'Nique, *Cellmate* (emphasis mine).

59. Mo'Nique.

60. Mo'Nique.

61. Alice Rayner, "Creating the Audience: It's All in the Timing," in *The Laughing Stalk: Live Comedy and Its Audiences*, ed. Judy Batalion (Anderson: Parlor Press, 2012), 33.

62. See Richard Butsch, *The Making of American Audiences: From Stage to Television, 1750–1990* (New York: Cambridge University Press, 2000), 115–16.

63. Neil Martin Blackadder, *Performing Opposition: Modern Theatre and the Scandalized Audience* (Westport: Praeger, 2003), xii.

64. Blackadder, *Performing Opposition*, x.

65. Michel Foucault, *Discipline and Punish: The Birth of the Prison*, 2nd Vintage Books ed. (New York: Vintage Books, 1995), 196–200.

66. Mo'Nique, *Cellmate* (emphasis mine).

67. D. Scott, *Extravagant Abjection*, 15.

68. Mo'Nique, *Cellmate*.

69. Mo'Nique.

70. Saladdin Ahmed, "Panopticism and Totalitarian Space," *Theory In Action* 11, no. 1 (2018): 13.

71. Mo'Nique.

72. This song, although never explicitly cited in the film credits is a gospel song written by Ira Forest Stanpill in 1950. It is called "I Know Who Holds Tomorrow."

73. Mo'Nique, *Cellmate*.

74. Mo'Nique.

75. bell hooks, "Performance as a Site of Opposition," in *Let's Get It On: Politics of Black Performance*, ed. Catherine Ugwu (Seattle: Bay Press, 1995), 211.

76. Gayle Wald, "Sound Vibrations: Black Music and Black Freedom in Sound and Space," *American Quarterly* 63, no. 3 (2011): 675.

77. Mo'Nique, *Cellmate*.

78. Chambers-Letson, *After the Party*, 25.

79. Chambers-Letson, 25.

Chapter 3: The Black Queer Citizenship of Wanda Sykes

1. Wanda Sykes, "Wanda Sykes Comes Out at Las Vegas Equality Rally," The CenterLV, November 15, 2008, YouTube video, 4:41, https://www.youtube.com/watch?v=S6UdoCIYvIw.

2. Eve Kosofsky Sedgwick, *Epistemology of the Closet*, 2nd ed. (Berkeley: University of California Press, 2008), 70.

3. Here, I am referencing Lady Gaga's 2011 anthem, "Born This Way," which very much reflects the ways "coming out" narratives and LGBTQ pride has been commodified and simplified to promise that a singular declaration will lead to affective freedom.

4. See Jessie McKinley and Laurie Goodstein, "Bans in 3 States on Gay Marriage," *The New York Times*, November 5, 2008, https://www.nytimes.com/2008/11/06/us/politics/06marriage.html.

5. Sykes discusses coming out at the event on the radio program *Fresh Air*. See, Wanda Sykes "Comic Wanda Sykes," radio interview, *Fresh Air*, August 1, 2019, https://www.npr.org/programs/fresh-air/2019/08/01/747288552/fresh-air-for-august-1-2019-comic-wanda-sykes.

6. Sykes, "Wanda Sykes Comes Out."

7. Jack Halberstam, *In a Queer Time and Place: Transgender Bodies, Subcultural Lives* (New York: New York University Press, 2005).

8. Halberstam, *In a Queer Time*, 2.

9. Sykes, "Comic Wanda Sykes."

10. For a summary of the LGBT youth suicide prevention campaign, "It Gets Better" as well as how critiques of the campaign pointed out its homonormative/linear progress structure, see Dustin Goltz, "It Gets Better: Queer Futures, Critical Frustrations, and Radical Potentials," *Critical Studies in Media Communication* 30, no. 2 (2013): 135–51.

11. Sykes does not refer to herself as queer, to my knowledge. Publicly, she seems to most often use the term gay or lesbian. I use the term queer to describe some of her work as I see Sykes making distinct intersectional connections among Blackness, gender, sexuality, and how those intersections dramatize or actualize alternatives to linear temporality, binds of homonormativity, and the complications of being a racialized, queer subject in the United States.

12. Sykes also created, produced, and served as a writer for the show.

13. Haggins, *Laughing Mad*, 175.

14. Haggins, 175.

15. *Sick and Tired*, directed by Michael Drumm, performed by Wanda Sykes (Image Entertainment, 2006), DVD.

16. Lisa Duggan, *The Twilight of Equality?: Neoliberalism, Cultural Politics, and the Attack on Democracy* (Boston: Beacon Press, 2003), 50.

17. Mary Bernstein, "Same-Sex Marriage and the Assimilationist Dilemma: A Research Agenda on Marriage Equality and the Future of LGBTQ Activism, Politics, Communities, and Identities," *Journal of Homosexuality* 65, no. 14 (2018): 1941–56.

18. Michelle M. Wright, *The Physics of Blackness: Beyond the Middle Passage Epistemology* (Minneapolis: University of Minnesota Press: 2015), 46.

19. Carolyn Dinshaw et al., "Theorizing Queer Temporalities: A Roundtable Discussion," *GLQ: A Journal of Lesbian and Gay Studies* 13, no. 2 (2007): 180.

20. Siobhan B. Somerville, "Queer *Loving*," *GLQ: A Journal of Lesbian & Gay Studies* 11, no. 3 (2005): 335.

21. Elizabeth Freeman, *Time Binds: Queer Temporalities, Queer History* (Durham, NC: Duke University Press, 2010), x.

22. Freeman, *Time Binds*.

23. "US Capitol Visitor Center," Architect of the Capitol, https://www.aoc.gov /capitol-buildings/us-capitol-visitor-center.

24. Michelle Obama, "Remarks by the First Lady at the Sojourner Truth Bust Unveiling," The White House, April 28, 2009, https://obamawhitehouse.archives .gov/the-press-office/remarks-first-lady-sojourner-truth-bust-unveiling.

25. Alexander, *Pedagogies of Crossing*, 7.

26. In 1992, Paula Poundstone was the first woman comic to perform at the WHCA Dinner.

27. Calvin Coolidge in 1924 was the first president to attend the dinner. The early years of the dinner included a variety of entertainment, such as song and dance between courses, short skits, and an after-dinner show with a number of celebrity performers. See George Condon, "The WHCA at 100," *White House Correspondents' Association*. Accessed May 8, 2011. https://whca.press/about/history/.

28. President Trump, who has not attended the Dinner during his presidency, canceled the tradition of a comedic keynote address after Michelle Wolf's pointed and critical performance in 2018. See Laura Bradley, "The White House Correspondents' Dinner Has Given Up on Comedy," *Vanity Fair*, November 19, 2018, https:// www.vanityfair.com/hollywood/2018/11/white-house-correspondents-dinner-ron -chernow-no-comedian-michelle-wolf.

29. Obama, himself, used comedic performance to "crack up" notions of white su-

premacy and national heritage in his 2011 WHCA Dinner performance. In it, he made fun of "birther" conspiracies that claimed he was not a US citizen by showing his "birth video," a scene from the Disney animated film *The Lion King*. See Barack Obama, "President Obama at White House Correspondents' Dinner (2011)." Washington, DC: White House, 2011. Video. https://www.youtube.com/watch?v=lX16OrIVfeQ.

30. Wanda Sykes, Public Address, White House Correspondents' Dinner, Washington, DC, April 8, 2009, https://www.youtube.com/watch?v=zmyRog2w4DI.

31. Hall, "Whose Heritage?," 26.

32. Hall, 23.

33. Elizabeth Freeman, "The Queer Temporalities of Queer Temporalities," *GLQ: A Journal of Lesbian & Gay Studies* 25, no. 1 (2019): 93.

34. James Edward Young, *The Texture of Memory: Holocaust Memorials and Meaning* (New Haven: Yale University Press, 1993), 183.

35. Young, *Texture of Memory*, 183.

36. Tavia Nyong'o, *The Amalgamation Waltz: Race, Performance, and the Ruses of Memory* (Minneapolis: University of Minnesota Press, 2009), 3.

37. Sykes, White House Correspondents' Dinner (emphasis mine).

38. Richardson, *Queer Limit of Black Memory*, 10.

39. Wanda Sykes, *I'ma Be Me*, directed by Beth McCarthy-Miller (Sykes Entertainment, 2009), DVD.

40. Sykes, *I'ma Be Me*.

41. Sykes.

42. Sykes (emphasis mine).

43. Sykes.

44. Wilderson, "Vengeance of Vertigo," 3 (emphasis mine).

45. Wilderson, 3.

46. Sykes, *I'ma Be Me*.

47. Sykes.

48. Sykes.

49. Sykes.

50. Sykes.

51. Marlon Ross, "Beyond the Closet as Raceless Paradigm," in *Black Queer Studies: A Critical Anthology*, edited by E. Patrick Johnson and Mae Henderson (Durham, NC: Duke University Press, 2005), 163.

52. See Eve Kosofsky Sedgwick's "Queer and Now," in *Tendencies* (Durham, NC: Duke University Press, 1993).

53. Cindy L. Griffin and Karma R. Chávez, "Introduction: Standing at the Intersections of Feminisms, Intersectionality, and Communication Studies," in *Standing at the Intersection: Feminist Voices, Feminist Practices in Communication Studies*, ed. Karma R. Chávez and Cindy L. Griffin (Albany: State University of New York Press, 2012), 10.

54. See Jill Dolan's historicization of this trope in *Theatre and Sexuality* (New York: Palgrave Macmillan, 2010), 7–8.

55. Richardson, *Queer Limit of Black Memory*, 160.

56. Sykes, *I'ma Be Me*.

57. Patricia Hill Collins, *Black Feminist Thought: Knowledge, Consciousness, and the Politics of Empowerment* (New York: Routledge Classics, 2009), 247–51.

58. Lindsey Bever, "Six Predominately Black Southern Churches Burn Within a Week, Arson Suspected in at Least Three," *The Washington Post*, June 29, 2015, https://www.washingtonpost.com/news/morning-mix/wp/2015/06/29/six-predominately-black-southern-churches-burn-within-a-week-with-arson-suspected-in-at-least-three/?noredirect=on&utm_term=.c9facfaa1ae8.

59. Alex Schmider, "2016 Was the Deadliest Year on Record for Transgender People," *GLAAD BLOG*, November 9, 2016, https://www.glaad.org/blog/2016-was-deadliest-year-record-transgender-people.

60. Wanda Sykes, *What Happened, Ms. Sykes?*, directed by Liz Patrick, performed by Wanda Sykes (Push It Productions, 2017); emphasis mine.

61. Sykes, *What Happened* (emphasis mine).

62. Sykes (emphasis mine).

63. Wanda Sykes, "Wanda Sykes's Free Ancestors," PBS Video, *Finding Your Roots*, May 13, 2012, https://www.pbs.org/video/finding-your-roots-wanda-sykess-free-ancestors-1600s-and-1700s/.

64. Sykes, *What Happened* (emphasis mine). Sykes is referring here to the film *12 Years a Slave*, an Oscar winning film that fictionalized the life of Solomon Northup, a free black man who was sold into slavery.

65. Sykes, *What Happened*.

66. Stefanie K. Dunning, *Queer in Black and White: Interraciality, Same Sex Desire, and Contemporary African American Culture* (Bloomington: Indiana University Press, 2009), 16.

67. Sykes, *What Happened*.

68. Dunning, *Queer in Black and White*, 11.

69. Sykes, *What Happened*.

70. Evelynn M. Hammonds, "Toward a Genealogy of Black Female Sexuality: The Problematic of Silence," in *Feminist Genealogies, Colonial Legacies, Democratic Futures*, ed. M. Jacqui Alexander and Chandra Talpade Mohanty (New York: Routledge, 1997): 170–82.

71. Sykes, *What Happened*.

72. Sykes.

73. Micki McElya, *Clinging to Mammy: The Faithful Slave in Twentieth-Century America* (Cambridge, MA: Harvard University Press, 2007), 83.

74. Sykes, *What Happened*.

75. Sykes.

76. Ianna Hawkins Owen, "Still, Nothing: Mammy and Black Asexual Possibility," *Feminist Review* 120, no. 1 (2018): 70–84.

77. Owen, "Still, Nothing," 76.

78. See Arthur Jones, *Wade in the Water: The Wisdom of the Spirituals* (Maryknoll: Orbis Books, 1993).

79. Sykes, *What Happened*.

80. Sara Ahmed, *Queer Phenomenology: Orientations, Objects, Others* (Durham, NC: Duke University Press, 2006), 2–3.

81. Sykes, *What Happened* (emphasis mine).

82. Sykes.

83. Freeman, *Time Binds*, 72.

Chapter 4: Contemporary Truth-Tellers

1. See Negin Farsad, *How to Make White People Laugh* (New York: Grand Central Publishing, 2016), and Krefting, *All Joking Aside*.

2. Amanda Seales, *I Be Knowin'*, directed by Stan Lathan, HBO, 2019, film.

3. Seales, *I Be Knowin'*.

4. Seales.

5. Seales.

6. Seales.

7. Amanda Seales, "Amanda Seales's Catcalling," audio podcast, *Good One: A Podcast About Jokes*, July 8, 2019, Head Gum, https://headgum.com/good-one-a-pod cast-about-jokes/amanda-sealess-catcalling.

8. While vinyl album (comedy included) is having a resurgence in sales, what I mean to say is that distribution of comedy has become more individualized and speedier due to YouTube and subscription service platforms like Netflix and Spotify. See, Elias Leight, "Vinyl Is Poised to Outsell CDs for the First Time Since 1986," *Rolling Stone*, September 6, 2019, https://www.rollingstone.com/music/music -news/vinyl-cds-revenue-growth-riaa-880959/.

9. Cameron Tung, "How Podcasts Conquered Comedy," *The New Yorker*, August 26, 2013, https://www.newyorker.com/tech/elements/how-podcasts-conquered -comedy.

10. See Yvyonne Villarreal, "For Tiffany Haddish and Six Unsung Comedians, Netflix's New Special Is Worth Crying Over," *The Los Angeles Times*, August 12, 2019, https://www.latimes.com/entertainment-arts/tv/story/2019-08-12/netflix-tif fany-haddish-stand-up-comedy-they-ready.

11. "Mo'Nique is back and she's not sorry about the Netflix boycott," *The Washington Post*, February 7, 2019, YouTube video, 4:25, https://www.youtube.com/watch ?v=_eiAvl1B_JY.

12. See Courtney Garcia, "SNL's Jay Pharoah on a mission to bring a black woman on cast: 'They need to pay attention,'" *The Grio*, September 27, 2013, http:// thegrio.com/2013/09/27/snls-jay-pharoah-on-a-mission-to-bring-a-black-woman -on-cast-they-need-to-pay-attention.

13. See Joanna Robinson, "Why Did a Third *SNL* Cast Member Silently Leave the Show Last Night?," *Vanity Fair*, May 21, 2017, https://www.vanityfair.com/holly wood/2017/05/sasheer-zamata-snl-leaving-bobby-moynihan-vanessa-bayer.

14. See Sasheer Zamata, "Racist Radio," posted by Official Comedy Standup, May 21, 2013, YouTube Video, 4:02, https://www.youtube.com/watch?list=PLZQfnFyel TBOQ15kmHSgEbdjzLMWzZpL7&v=jI_SFm-txRI.

15. See Kelly Maxwell, "Funny Lady Gets Flashed and Then Makes a Video About It, Obviously," *BUST*, https://bust.com/general/10223-funny-lady-gets-flashed-and -then-make-a-video-about-it-obviously.html; Anna Breslaw, "Comedian Gets Awesomely Meta About Her Encounter With a Flasher," *Jezebel*, July 25, 2012, https://

jezebel.com/comedian-gets-awesomely-meta-about-her-encounter-with-a-5928 839.

16. See Nicole Byer and Sasheer Zamata, "Best Friends with Nicole Byer and Sasheer Zamata," audio podcast, Earwolf, 2019, https://podcasts.apple.com/us/podcast/best-friends-with-nicole-byer-and-sasheer-zamata/id1464766741.

17. Alexis Soloski, "Sasheer Zamata Finds Humor at the A.C.L.U.," *The New York Times*, October 4, 2019, https://www.nytimes.com/2019/10/04/style/sasheer-zamata-snl-aclu.html.

18. Sam Jay, *The Comedy Lineup*, directed by Christopher Storer, Netflix, July 3, 2018.

19. Michelle Buteau, "Phoebe and Michelle Get Cozy," audio podcast, *So Many White Guys*, May 21, 2019, WNYC Studios, https://www.wnycstudios.org/podcasts/whiteguys/episodes/phoebe-and-michelle-buteau.

20. Michelle Buteau, *The Comedy Lineup*, directed by Christopher Storer, Netflix, July 3, 2018 (emphasis mine).

21. Seales, "Amanda Seales's Catcalling."

22. Sam Jay, *Donna's Daughter*, Comedy Central Records, 2018.

23. Jay, *Donna's Daughter* (emphasis mine).

24. Jay.

25. Judith Butler, *Frames of War: When Is Life Grievable?* (New York: Verso, 2009), 1.

26. Keeling, *Queer Times, Black Futures*, 19.

27. Jay, *Donna's Daughter*.

28. Jay often uses the N—word in her sets. I mentioned in this book's introduction that as a white woman, I choose not to type the word in its entirety. I do not believe the ways Jay employs the word are for me to analyze or quote. Thus, in place of the actual word, I will use, "n— ." I am following Ta-Nehisi Coates's opinion that the N—word is a "signpost that reminds us that old crimes do not disappear," and that for white people, the word is a place "they can never go." See Ta-Nehisi Coates, "In Defense of a Loaded Word," *The New York Times*, November 23, 2013, https://www.nytimes.com/2013/11/24/opinion/sunday/coates-in-defense-of-a-loaded-word.html.

29. Jay, *Donna's Daughter*.

30. Savannah Shange, "Play Aunties and Dyke Bitches: Gender, Generation, and the Ethics of Black Queer Kinship," *Black Scholar* 49, no. 1 (2019): 41.

31. Jay, *Donna's Daughter*.

32. Tina M. Campt, *Listening to Images* (Durham, NC: Duke University Press, 2017), 32.

33. Campt, *Listening to Images*, 10.

34. Halberstam, *In a Queer Time*, 36–37.

35. Muñoz, *Cruising Utopia*, 4.

36. Jafari S. Allen, "Black Queer Diaspora at the Current Conjecture," *GLQ: A Journal of Lesbian and Gay Studies* 18, no. 2–3 (2012): 217.

37. Keeling, *Queer Times, Black Futures*, 19.

38. Danielle L. McGuire, *At the Dark End of the Street: Black Women, Rape, and*

Resistance—a New History of the Civil Rights Movement from Rosa Parks to the Rise of Black Power (New York: Vintage Books, 2011), 63.

39. Darlene Clark Hine, "Rape and the Inner Lives of Black Women in the Middle West," *Signs* 14, no. 4 (1989): 912.

40. See Ronan Farrow, "From Aggressive Overtures to Sexual Assault: Harvey Weinstein's Accusers Tell Their Stories," *The New Yorker*, October 10, 2017, https://www.newyorker.com/news/news-desk/from-aggressive-overtures-to-sexual-assault-harvey-weinsteins-accusers-tell-their-stories.

41. See Tarana Burke, "#MeToo was started for black and brown women and girls. They're still being ignored," *The Washington Post*, November 9, 2017, https://www.washingtonpost.com/news/post-nation/wp/2017/11/09/the-waitress-who-works-in-the-diner-needs-to-know-that-the-issue-of-sexual-harassment-is-about-her-too/?utm_term=.2b7fc74f8ca3.

42. Steve Santagati, "Catcalling Video Goes Viral," CNN, November 2, 2014, YouTube video, 2:18, https://www.youtube.com/watch?time_continue=1&v=-HI4DC18wCg.

43. Seales, *I Be Knowin'*.

44. Seales.

45. Seales, *I Be Knowin'*.

46. Jay, *The Comedy Lineup* (emphasis mine).

47. Sykes, *Sick and Tired*.

48. See Jason Zinoman, "Toe-to-Toe at the Edge of the Comedy Club Stage," *The New York Times*, July 17, 2012, https://www.nytimes.com/2012/07/18/arts/television/when-the-comic-and-the-heckler-both-take-offense.html.

49. See Jessica Valenti, "Anatomy of a Successful Rape Joke," *The Nation*, July 12, 2012, https://www.thenation.com/article/anatomy-successful-rape-joke/; Ainara Tiefenthäler, "Female Comics Take on the Rape Joke," *The New York Times* video, 5:13, from *The #MeToo* Moment video series, December 20, 2017, https://www.nytimes.com/video/arts/100000005534134/female-comics-sexual-harassment.html; Cameron Esposito, *Rape Jokes*, directed by Paul Bonanno (Young and Sharp Productions, 2018), video, 1:01:09, https://www.cameronesposito.com/.

50. Jay, *The Comedy Lineup*.

51. Jay.

52. Bill Cosby was convicted of rape in 2018 and sixty women have come forward with allegations against Cosby. Richard Pryor admitted in a 1986 interview with Barbara Walters to being physically abusive toward women. In 2017 Louis C.K. admitted to sexually harassing fellow comics after the *New York Times* published allegations against him.

53. Buteau, *The Comedy Lineup*.

54. Buteau (emphasis mine).

55. Buteau.

56. Buteau (emphasis mine).

57. Buteau.

58. Buteau.

59. Leticia Alvarado discusses in *Abject Performances: Aesthetic Strategies in*

Latino Cultural Production (Durham, NC: Duke University Press, 2018), "abjection's affective impulse to disrupt identity" (40). Alvarado's work analyzes aesthetic strategies of Latinx performance. While differing from Mabley and Buteau's work, Alvarado analyzes a rich archive of abjection as a performance strategy for resistance and minoritarian worldmaking.

60. Buteau, *The Comedy Lineup*.

61. Mabley, *Live at Sing Sing*.

62. Buteau, *The Comedy Lineup* (emphasis mine).

63. Melena Ryzik, Cara Buckley, and Jodi Kantor, "Louis C.K. Is Accused by 5 Women of Sexual Misconduct," *The New York Times*, November 9, 2017, https://www.nytimes.com/2017/11/09/arts/television/louis-ck-sexual-misconduct.html.

64. Louis C.K., "Louis C.K. New Set 2019 / Louis C.K. leaked set 2019," filmed August 2018 at Louis C.K.'s stand-up set at Governor's Comedy Club, Levittown, Long Island, New York. YouTube video, 45:09, posted by Agustin Alva, March 13, 2019, https://www.youtube.com/watch?v=BOdFIvPp4ko.

65. Sasheer Zamata, "Sasheer Zamata on Louis C.K.'s Parkland Bit," from a Sasheer Zamata stand-up set, posted by user *Vulture. SoundCloud*, audio clip, 4:47, https://soundcloud.com/user-517669847/sasheer-zamata-on-louis-cks-parkland-bit (emphasis mine).

66. Zamata, "Zamata on Louis C.K." (emphasis mine).

67. Limon, *Stand-Up Comedy in Theory*, 18.

68. Zamata, "Zamata on Louis C.K." (emphasis mine).

69. Zamata (emphasis mine).

70. Larry the Cable Guy, *Get-R-Done*, directed by Michael Drumm (Los Angeles: Image Entertainment, 2004), film.

71. Michelle Buteau, "The 2 Dope Queens Go Marching," audio podcast, *2 Dope Queens*, January 31, 2017, WNYC Studios.

72. Carpio, *Laughing Fit to Kill*, 86.

73. Richard Pryor, *Richard Pryor Live in Concert*, directed by Jeff Margolis (Elkins Entertainment and SEE Theater Network, 1979), film.

74. Mo'Nique, *The Queens of Comedy*, directed by Steve Purcelle (Lantham Entertainment and Paramount Pictures, 2001), film.

75. Seales, *I Be Knowin'*.

76. Seales.

77. Robin DiAngelo, *White Fragility: Why It's So Hard for White People to Talk about Racism* (Boston: Beacon Press, 2018), 3.

78. DiAngelo, *White Fragility*.

79. Seales, *I Be Knowin'*.

80. Jennifer Lynn Stoever, *The Sonic Color Line: Race and the Cultural Politics of Listening* (New York: New York University Press, 2016), 12.

81. Seales, *I Be Knowin'*.

82. Jay, *Donna's Daughter*.

83. Jay.

84. Jay.

85. Martha Hodes, "The Sexualization of Reconstruction Politics: White Women and Black Men in the South after the Civil War," *Journal of the History of Sexuality* 3, no. 3 (1993): 407.

86. Linda Gordon, *The Second Coming of the KKK: The Klu Klux Klan of the 1920s and the American Political Tradition* (New York: Liveright Publishing, 2017), 109.

87. Gordon, *Second Coming*, 59.

88. Jay, *Donna's Daughter* (emphasis mine).

89. DiAngelo, *White Fragility*, 33.

90. Toni Morrison, "Toni Morrison," *Charlie Rose*, PBS video, 55:04, May 7, 1993, https://charlierose.com/videos/18778.

91. James Baldwin, "The White Man's Guilt," *Ebony*, August 1965, 47–48. Online at https://books.google.com/books?id=N94DAAAAMBAJ&lpg=PA47&dq=%22white%20man's%20guilt%22&pg=PA47#v=onepage&q&f=false.

92. Seales, *I Be Knowin'*.

93. Imani Perry, *May We Forever Stand: A History of the Black National Anthem* (Chapel Hill: University of North Carolina Press, 2018), 8.

94. Perry, *May We Forever Stand*, 12.

95. Seales, *I Be Knowin'* (emphasis mine).

Conclusion

1. This episode also reifies some of the arguments I make in chapter 1 about Mabley as a sidelined figure in performance history. In the episode, Mrs. Maisel (a white woman) bumps Moms to the slot of opening act. She's discussed in the episode as a comedic legend who received about four minutes of screen time. In a particularly hard-to-believe scene, Mrs. Maisel easily wins over the famously harsh Apollo audience simply by complimenting the food that was left for performers backstage.

2. *The Marvelous Mrs. Maisel*, episode "A Jewish Girl Walks into the Apollo . . . ," featuring Wanda Sykes, December 6, 2019, Amazon Studios (emphasis mine).

3. Stevie Wong, "On My Screen: Wanda Sykes' Childhood Hero in 'The Marvelous Mrs. Maisel,' Marvel Dreams & The Kids' Movie That Makes Her Cry," *Deadline*, August 23, 2020, https://deadline.com/2020/08/the-marvelous-mrs-maisel-star-wanda-sykes-on-my-screen-interview-news-1203018705/.

4. McMillan, *Embodied Avatars*, 198.

5. E. Patrick Johnson, "Poor 'Black' Theatre: Mid-America Theatre Conference Keynote Address, March 7, 2009." *Theatre History Studies* (2010): 1–13.

6. Jill Dolan, *Utopia in Performance: Finding Hope at the Theater* (Ann Arbor: University of Michigan Press, 2005), 5.

7. Ashon T. Crawley, *Blackpentecostal Breath: The Aesthetics of Possibility* (New York: Fordham University Press, 2016), 7.

8. Crawley, *Blackpentecostal Breath*, 24.

Bibliography

Acham, Christine. *Revolution Televised: Prime Time and the Struggle for Black Power.* Minneapolis: University of Minnesota Press, 2004.

Ahmed, Saladdin. "Panopticism and Totalitarian Space." *Theory In Action* 11, no. 1 (2018): 1–16.

Ahmed, Sara. *Queer Phenomenology: Orientations, Objects, Others.* Durham, NC: Duke University Press, 2006.

Alexander, M. Jacqui. *Pedagogies of Crossing: Meditations on Feminism, Sexual Politics, Memory and the Sacred.* Durham, NC: Duke University Press, 2005.

Allen, Jafari S. "Black Queer Diaspora at the Current Conjecture." *GLQ: A Journal of Lesbian and Gay Studies* 18, no. 2–3 (2012): 212–48.

Alrutz, Megan, and Lynn Hoare. *Devising Critically Engaged Theatre for Youth: The Performing Justice Project.* New York: Routledge, 2020.

Alvarado, Leticia. *Abject Performances: Aesthetic Strategies in Latino Cultural Production.* Durham, NC: Duke University Press, 2018.

Arsenault, Raymond. *Freedom Riders: 1961 and the Struggle for Racial Justice.* New York: Oxford University Press, 2006.

Back, Les. "How Blue Can You Get? B.B. King, Planetary Humanism and the Blues Behind Bars." *Theory Culture & Society* 32, no. 7–8 (2015): 274–85.

Baldwin, James. "The White Man's Guilt." *Ebony*, August 1965.

Balfour, Michael. *Theatre in Prison: Theory and Practice.* Bristol, UK: Intellect, 2004.

Barreca, Regina. *They Used to Call Me Snow White … But I Drifted: Women's Strategic Use of Humor.* New York: Penguin Books, 1991.

Batiste, Stephanie Leigh. *Darkening Mirrors: Imperial Representation in Depression-Era African American Performance.* Durham, NC: Duke University Press, 2011.

Bean, Annemarie. "Black Minstrelsy and Double Inversion, Circa 1890." In *African American Performance and Theatre History: A Critical Reader*, edited by Harry J. Elam, Jr. and David Krasner, 171–91. New York: Oxford University Press, 2001.

Bergson, Henri. *Laughter: An Essay on the Meaning of the Comic.* Translated by Fred Rothwell and Cloudesley Brereton. New York: The Macmillan Company, 1921.

Bernstein, Mary. "Same-Sex Marriage and the Assimilationist Dilemma: A Research Agenda on Marriage Equality and the Future of LGBTQ Activism, Politics, Communities, and Identities." *Journal of Homosexuality* 65, no. 14 (2018): 1941–56.

Bernstein, Robin. *Racial Innocence: Performing American Childhood from Slavery to Civil Rights*. New York: New York University Press, 2011.

Bever, Lindsey. "Six Predominately Black Southern Churches Burn Within a Week, Arson Suspected in at Least Three." *The Washington Post*, June 29, 2015. https://www.washingtonpost.com/news/morning-mix/wp/2015/06/29/six-predominately-black-southern-churches-burn-within-a-week-with-arson-suspected-in-at-least-three/?noredirect=on&utm_term=.c9facfaa1ae8.

Blackadder, Neil Martin. *Performing Opposition: Modern Theatre and the Scandalized Audience*. Westport: Praeger, 2003.

Blank, Jessica, and Eric Jensen. *The Exonerated*. New York: FSG Adult, 2005.

Boal, Augusto. *Theatre of the Oppressed*. New York: Theatre Communications Group, 1985.

Bradley, Laura. "The White House Correspondents' Dinner Has Given Up on Comedy." *Vanity Fair*, November 19, 2018. https://www.vanityfair.com/hollywood/2018/11/white-house-correspondents-dinner-ron-chernow-no-comedian-michelle-wolf.

Breslaw, Anna. "Comedian Gets Awesomely Meta About Her Encounter With a Flasher." *Jezebel*, July 25, 2012. https://jezebel.com/comedian-gets-awesomely-meta-about-her-encounter-with-a-592883.

Brooks, Daphne A. "Afro-sonic Feminist Praxis: Nina Simone and Adrienne Kennedy in High Fidelity." In *Black Performance Theory*, edited by Thomas F. DeFrantz and Anita Gonzalez, 204–22. Durham, NC: Duke University Press, 2014.

———. *Bodies in Dissent: Spectacular Performances of Race and Freedom, 1850–1910*. Durham, NC: Duke University Press, 2006.

Burke, Tarana. "#MeToo was started for black and brown women and girls. They're still being ignored." *The Washington Post*, November 9, 2017. https://www.washingtonpost.com/news/post-nation/wp/2017/11/09/the-waitress-who-works-in-the-diner-needs-to-know-that-the-issue-of-sexual-harassment-is-about-her-too/?utm_term=.2b7fc74f8ca3.

Buteau, Michelle. "The 2 Dope Queens Go Marching." Audio podcast. *2 Dope Queens*, January 31, 2017. WNYC Studios. https://www.wnycstudios.org/podcasts/dopequeens/episodes/2-dope-queens-podcast-bonus-episode-2-dope-queens-go-marching.

———. *The Comedy Lineup*. Directed by Christopher Storer. Netflix, July 3, 2018.

———. "Phoebe and Michelle Get Cozy." Audio podcast. *So Many White Guys*, May 21, 2019. WNYC Studios. https://www.wnycstudios.org/podcasts/whiteguys/episodes/phoebe-and-michelle-buteau.

Butler, Judith. *Frames of War: When Is Life Grievable?* New York: Verso, 2009.

Butsch, Richard. *The Making of American Audiences: From Stage to Television, 1750–1990*. New York: Cambridge University Press, 2000.

Byer, Nicole, and Sasheer Zamata. *Best Friends with Nicole Byer and Sasheer Zamata*. Audio podcast. Earwolf, 2019. https://podcasts.apple.com/us/podcast/best-friends-with-nicole-byer-and-sasheer-zamata/id1464766741.

Campt, Tina M. *Listening to Images*. Durham, NC: Duke University Press, 2017.

Cant U C, Blondie. "Bow Down (Big Girl World)." Written by Blondie Cantuc and Terry Lewis, 2007.

Carpenter, Faedra. *Coloring Whiteness: Acts of Critique in Black Performance.* Ann Arbor: University of Michigan Press, 2014.

Carpio, Glenda. *Laughing Fit to Kill: Black Humor in the Fictions of Slavery.* New York: Oxford University Press, 2008.

Carson, Dick, dir. *The Merv Griffin Show.* Season 7, episode 1. Aired August 18, 1969, on CBS.

Chambers-Letson, Jonathan. *After the Party: A Manifesto for Queer of Color Life.* New York: New York University Press, 2018.

Cheng, Anne. *The Melancholy of Race: Psychoanalysis, Assimilation, and Hidden Grief.* New York: Oxford University Press, 2001.

C.K., Louis. "Louis C.K. New Set 2019 / Louis C.K. leaked set 2019." Louis C.K.'s stand-up set filmed August 2018 at Governor's Comedy Club, Levittown, Long Island, New York. YouTube video, 45:09. Posted by Agustin Alva, March 13, 2019, https://www.youtube.com/watch?v=BOdFIvPp4ko.

Cleage, Pearl. "A Hollering Place." *The Dramatists Guild Quarterly* Summer (1994): 12–15.

Coates, Ta-Nehisi. "In Defense of a Loaded Word." *The New York Times,* November 23, 2013. https://www.nytimes.com/2013/11/24/opinion/sunday/coates-in -defense-of-a-loaded-word.html.

Collins, Patricia Hill. *Black Feminist Thought: Knowledge, Consciousness, and the Politics of Empowerment.* New York: Routledge Classics, 2009.

———. *Fighting Words: Black Women and the Search for Justice.* Minneapolis: University of Minnesota Press, 1998.

———. "Like One of the Family: Race, Ethnicity, and the Paradox of US National Identity." *Ethnic and Racial Studies* 24, no. 1 (2001): 3–28.

———. "The Social Construction of Black Feminist Thought." *Signs* 14, no 4 (1989) 745–73.

Condon, George. "The WHCA at 100." *White House Correspondents' Association.* Accessed May 8, 2011. https://whca.press/about/history/.

Conquergood, Dwight. "Performing as a Moral Act: Ethical Dimensions of the Ethnography of Performance." *Literature in Performance* 5, no. 2 (1985): 1–14.

Cox, Aimee Meredith. *Shapeshifters: Black Girls and the Choreography of Citizenship.* Durham, NC: Duke University Press, 2015.

Crawley, Ashon T. *Blackpentecostal Breath: The Aesthetics of Possibility.* New York: Fordham, University Press, 2017.

Cvetkovich, Ann. *Depression: A Public Feeling.* Durham, NC: Duke University Press, 2012.

Davis, Angela Y. *Are Prisons Obsolete?* New York: Seven Stories Press, 2003.

———. *Blues Legacies and Black Feminism: Gertrude "Ma" Rainey, Bessie Smith, and Billie Holiday.* New York: Pantheon Books, 1998.

Davis, Diane. *Breaking Up (at) Totality: A Rhetoric of Laughter.* Carbondale: Southern Illinois University Press, 2000.

DeFrantz, Thomas F., and Anita Gonzalez. "Introduction: From 'Negro Expression' to 'Black Performance.'" In *Black Performance Theory*, edited by Thomas F. DeFrantz and Anita Gonzalez, 1–18. Durham, NC: Duke University Press, 2014.

Derrida, Jacques. *Writing and Difference*. Translated by Alan Bass. Chicago: University of Chicago Press, 1978.

Diamond, Elin. *Unmaking Mimesis: Essays on Feminism and Theater*. London: Routledge, 1997.

DiAngelo, Robin. *White Fragility: Why It's So Hard for White People to Talk about Racism*. Boston: Beacon Press, 2018.

Dinshaw, Carolyn, Lee Edelman, Roderick A. Ferguson, Carla Freccero, Elizabeth Freeman, Jack Halberstam, Annamarie Jagose, Christopher Nealon, and Tan Hoang Nguyen. "Theorizing Queer Temporalities: A Roundtable Discussion." *GLQ: A Journal of Lesbian and Gay Studies* 13, no. 2 (2007): 177–95.

Dolan, Jill. *Theatre and Sexuality*. New York: Palgrave Macmillan, 2010.

———. *Utopia in Performance: Finding Hope at the Theater*. Ann Arbor: University of Michigan Press, 2005.

Du Bois, W. E. B. *The Souls of Black Folk*. Oxford World Classics. New York: Oxford University Press, 2007.

Duggan, Lisa. *The Twilight of Equality?: Neoliberalism, Cultural Politics, and the Attack on Democracy*. Boston: Beacon Press, 2003.

Dunning, Stefanie K. *Queer in Black and White: Interraciality, Same Sex Desire, and Contemporary African American Culture*. Bloomington: Indiana University Press, 2009.

Elam, Harry J., Jr., and David Krasner, eds. *African American Performance and Theater History: A Critical Reader*. Oxford: Oxford University Press, 2001.

Epstein, Lawrence J. *The Haunted Smile: The Story of Jewish Comedians in America*. New York: Public Affairs, 2001.

Esposito, Cameron. *Rape Jokes*. Directed by Paul Bonanno. Young and Sharp Productions, 2018. Video, 1:01:09. https://www.cameronesposito.com/.

Farrow, Ronan. "From Aggressive Overtures to Sexual Assault: Harvey Weinstein's Accusers Tell Their Stories." *The New Yorker*, October 10, 2017. https://www .newyorker.com/news/news-desk/from-aggressive-overtures-to-sexual-assault -harvey-weinsteins-accusers-tell-their-stories.

Farsad, Negin. *How to Make White People Laugh*. New York: Grand Central Publishing, 2016.

Federman, Wayne, and Andrew Steven. "The Apollo and the Chitlin' Circuit." Audio podcast. *The History of Standup*, June 18, 2019. https://player.fm /series/the-history-of-standup-2424926/s2-ep-03-the-apollo-and-the -chitlin-circuit.

Ferguson, Roderick A. *Aberrations in Black: Toward a Queer of Color Critique*. Minneapolis: University of Minnesota Press, 2004.

Finley, Jessyka. "Raunch and Redress: Interrogating Pleasure in Black Women's Stand-Up Comedy." *Journal of Popular Culture* 49, no. 4 (2016): 780–98.

Floyd, Samuel A., Jr. *The Power of Black Music: Interpreting Its History from Africa to the United States*. New York: Oxford University Press, 1996.

Foucault, Michel. *Discipline and Punish: The Birth of the Prison.* 2nd Vintage Books ed. New York: Vintage Books, 1995.

Fraden, Rena. *Imagining Medea: Rhodessa Jones and Theatre for Incarcerated Women.* Chapel Hill: University of North Carolina Press, 2001.

Fraser, Nancy. "Rethinking the Public Sphere: A Contribution to the Critique of Actually Existing Democracy." *Social Text* no. 25/26 (1990): 56–80.

Freeman, Elizabeth. "The Queer Temporalities of Queer Temporalities." *GLQ: A Journal of Lesbian & Gay Studies* 25, no. 1 (2019): 91–95.

———. *Time Binds: Queer Temporalities, Queer History.* Durham, NC: Duke University Press, 2010.

Freud, Sigmund. *Jokes and Their Relation to the Unconscious.* New York: Norton, 1963.

Garcia, Courtney. "SNL's Jay Pharoah on a mission to bring a black woman on cast: 'They need to pay attention.'" *The Grio,* September 27, 2013. http://thegrio.com/2013/09/27/snls-jay-pharoah-on-a-mission-to-bring-a-black-woman-on-cast-they-need-to-pay-attention.

Gates, Henry Louis, Jr. *The Signifying Monkey: A Theory of African-American Literary Criticism.* New York: Oxford University Press, 1988.

GHB Archives. "Moms Mabley." October 18, 2011. YouTube Video, 5:20. https://www.youtube.com/watch?v=PWW-96BouIU.

Gill, Lyndon Kamaal. *Erotic Islands: Art and Activism in the Queer Caribbean.* Durham, NC: Duke University Press, 2018.

Goldberg, Whoopi. *Whoopi Goldberg Presents: Moms Mabley.* Directed by Whoopi Goldberg. Los Angeles: HBO, 2013.

Goltz, Dustin Bradley. "It Gets Better: Queer Futures, Critical Frustrations, and Radical Potentials." *Critical Studies in Media Communication* 30, no. 2 (2013): 135–51.

Gordon, Linda. *The Second Coming of the KKK: The Ku Klux Klan of the 1920s and the American Political Tradition.* New York: Liveright Publishing, 2017.

Gordon-Reed, Annette. *The Hemingses of Monticello: An American Family.* New York: W.W. Norton & Co, 2008.

Gottschild, Brenda Dixon. *Waltzing in the Dark: African American Vaudeville and Race Politics in the Swing Era.* New York: St. Martin's Press, 2000.

Griffin, Cindy L., and Karma R. Chávez. "Introduction: Standing at the Intersections of Feminisms, Intersectionality, and Communication Studies." In *Standing at the Intersection: Feminist Voices, Feminist Practices in Communication Studies,* edited by Karma R. Chávez and Cindy L. Griffin, 1–34. Albany: State University of New York Press, 2012.

Haggins, Bambi. *Laughing Mad: The Black Comic Persona in Post-Soul America.* New Brunswick, NJ: Rutgers University Press, 2007.

Halberstam, Jack. *In a Queer Time and Place: Transgender Bodies, Subcultural Lives.* New York: New York University Press, 2005.

Hall, Stuart. "Whose Heritage? Un-Settling 'The Heritage,' Re-Imagining the Post-Nation." In *The Politics of Heritage: The Legacies of "Race,"* edited by Jo Littler and Koshi Naidoo, 21–31. New York: Routledge, 2005.

Hammonds, Evelynn M. "Black (W)holes and the Geometry of Black Female Sexuality." *Differences: A Journal of Feminist Cultural Studies* 6, nos. 2–3 (1995): 126–45.

———. "Toward a Genealogy of Black Female Sexuality: The Problematic of Silence." In *Feminist Genealogies, Colonial Legacies, Democratic Futures*, edited by M. Jacqui Alexander and Chandra Talpade Mohanty, 170–82. New York: Routledge, 1997.

Hartman, Saidiya V. *Scenes of Subjection: Terror, Slavery, and Self-Making in Nineteenth-Century America*. New York: Oxford University Press, 1997.

Henderson, Shirley. "Mo'Nique Charms the World." *Ebony* 62, no. 10 (August 2007): 64–70.

Higginbotham, Evelyn Brooks. *Righteous Discontent: The Women's Movement in the Black Baptist Church, 1880–1920*. Cambridge, MA: Harvard University Press, 1994.

Hine, Darlene Clark. "Rape and the Inner Lives of Black Women in the Middle West." *Signs* 14, no. 4 (1989): 912–20.

Hodes, Martha. "The Sexualization of Reconstruction Politics: White Women and Black Men in the South after the Civil War." *Journal of the History of Sexuality* 3, no. 3 (1993): 402–17.

hooks, bell. *Black Looks: Race and Representation*. Cambridge, MA: South End Press, 1992.

———. "Performance as a Site of Opposition." In *Let's Get It On: Politics of Black Performance*, edited by Catherine Ugwu, 210–19. Seattle: Bay Press, 1995.

———. *Talking Back: Thinking Feminist, Thinking Black*. Boston: South End Press, 1989.

Hunt, Kara. "Off the Record: A Critical Perspective on Def Comedy Jam." *Journal of Popular Culture* 48, no. 5 (2015): 836–58.

Jacobson, Mark. "Amazing Moms." *New York Magazine*, April 13, 1974.

Jay, Sam. *The Comedy Lineup*. Directed by Christopher Storer. Netflix, July 3, 2018.

———. *Donna's Daughter*. Comedy Central Records. 2018.

Johnson, E. Patrick. "Black Performance Studies: Genealogies, Politics, Futures." In *The Sage Handbook of Performance Studies*, edited by D. Soyini Madison and Judith Hamera, 446–63. Thousand Oaks: Sage, 2006.

———. "Poor 'Black' Theatre: Mid-America Theatre Conference Keynote Address, March 7, 2009." *Theatre History Studies* 30 (2010): 1–13.

———. "'Quare' Studies, or (Almost) Everything I Know about Queer Studies I Learned from My Grandmother." In *Black Queer Studies: A Critical Anthology*, edited by E. Patrick Johnson and Mae G. Henderson, 124–57. Durham, NC: Duke University Press, 2005.

Jones, Arthur. *Wade in the Water: The Wisdom of the Spirituals*. Maryknoll: Orbis Books, 1993.

Jones, Meta DuEwa. *The Muse Is Music: Jazz Poetry from the Harlem Renaissance to Spoken Word*. Urbana: University of Illinois Press, 2011.

Jones, Omi Osun Joni L. *Theatrical Jazz: Performance, Àṣẹ, and the Power of the Present Moment*. Columbus: Ohio State University Press, 2015.

Keeling, Kara. "'Ghetto Heaven': Set It Off and the Valorization of Black Lesbian Butch-Femme Sociality." *Black Scholar* 33, no. 1 (2003): 33–46.

———. *Queer Times, Black Futures*. New York: New York University Press, 2019.

King, Jason. "Don't Stop 'Til You Get Enough: Presence, Spectacle, and Good Feeling in Michael Jackson's *This Is It*." In *Black Performance Theory*, edited by Thomas F. DeFrantz and Anita Gonzalez, 184–203. Durham, NC: Duke University Press, 2014.

Knight, Athelia. "In Retrospect: Sherman H. Dudley—He Paved the Way for T.O.B.A." *The Black Perspective in Music* 15, no. 2 (1987): 153–81.

Krasner, David. *Resistance, Parody, and Double Consciousness in African American Theatre, 1895–1910*. New York: St. Martin's Press, 1997.

Krefting, Rebecca. *All Joking Aside: American Humor and Its Discontents*. Baltimore: Johns Hopkins University Press, 2014.

Lara, Ana-Maurine. "Of Unexplained Presences, Flying Ife Heads, Vampires, Sweat, Zombies, and Legbas." *GLQ: A Journal of Lesbian & Gay Studies* 18, no. 2/3 (2012): 347–60.

Larry the Cable Guy. *Get-R-Done*. Directed by Michael Drumm. Los Angeles: Image Entertainment, 2004.

Lauterbach, Preston. *The Chitlin' Circuit and the Road to Rock 'N' Roll*. New York: W.W. Norton, 2011.

Leight, Elias. "Vinyl Is Poised to Outsell CDs for the First Time Since 1986." *Rolling Stone*, September 6, 2019. https://www.rollingstone.com/music/music -news/vinyl-cds-revenue-growth-riaa-880959/.

Limon, John. *Stand-Up Comedy in Theory, Or, Abjection in America*. Durham, NC: Duke University Press, 2000.

Lorde, Audre. *Sister Outsider: Essays & Speeches by Audre Lorde*. Freedom: The Crossing Press, 1984.

Lordi, Emily J. *Black Resonance: Iconic Women Singers and African American Literature*. New Brunswick, NJ: Rutgers University Press, 2013.

Lott, Eric. *Love and Theft: Blackface Minstrelsy and the American Working Class*. New York: Oxford University Press, 1993.

Mabley, Jackie "Moms." *Best of Moms Mabley and Pigmeat Markham*, Vol. 1. Chess Records. LP, 1961.

———. *Boarding House Blues*. Directed by Josh Binney. All-American News, 1948.

———. *The Funny Sides of Moms Mabley*. Jewel Records. LP, 1964.

———. "Jackie 'Moms' Mabley Talks About Her Life and Career as a Comedian." Best of Studs Turkel, WFMT. Chicago, IL: June 13, 1961.

———. *Live at Sing Sing*. Mercury Records. LP, 1970.

———. *Moms Mabley at Geneva Conference*. Chess Records. LP, 1963.

———. *Moms Mabley at The Playboy Club*. Chess Records. LP, 1961.

———. *Moms Mabley Breaks it Up*. Chess Records. LP, 1968.

———. *Moms Mabley Live at the Apollo*. Jewel Records. CD, 1998.

———. *Moms Mabley Live at the U.N.* Chess Records. LP, 1961.

———. *Moms Wows*. Chess Records. LP-1486, 1964.

———. *Out on a Limb*. Mercury Records. LP, 1964.

Madison, D. Soyini. *Acts of Activism: Human Rights as Radical Performance.* Cambridge, UK: Cambridge University Press, 2010.

Major, Clarence. *Juba to Jive: A Dictionary of African-American Slang.* New York: Viking, 1994.

The Marvelous Mrs. Maisel. Episode "A Jewish Girl Walks into the Apollo …," featuring Wanda Sykes. December 6, 2019, Amazon Studios.

Maxwell, Kelly. "Funny Lady Gets Flashed and Then Makes a Video About It, Obviously." *BUST.* https://bust.com/general/10223-funny-lady-gets-flashed-and-then-make-a-video-about-it-obviously.html.

McElya, Micki. *Clinging to Mammy: The Faithful Slave in Twentieth-Century America.* Cambridge, MA: Harvard University Press, 2007.

McGuire, Danielle L. *At the Dark End of the Street: Black Women, Rape, and Resistance—a New History of the Civil Rights Movement from Rosa Parks to the Rise of Black Power.* New York: Vintage Books, 2011.

McKinley, Jessie, and Laurie Goodstein. "Bans in 3 States on Gay Marriage." *The New York Times*, November 5, 2008. https://www.nytimes.com/2008/11/06/us/politics/06marriage.html.

McMillan, Uri. *Embodied Avatars: Genealogies of Black Feminist Art and Performance.* New York: New York University Press, 2015.

Mitchell, Koritha. *Living with Lynching: African American Lynching Plays, Performance, and Citizenship, 1890–1930.* Champaign: University of Illinois Press, 2011.

———. "LOVE In ACTION Noting Similarities Between Lynching Then and Anti-LGBT Violence Now." *Callaloo* 36, no. 3 (2013): 687–717.

Mock, Roberta. "Stand-Up Comedy and the Legacy of the Mature Vagina." *Women & Performance: A Journal of Feminist Theory* 22, no. 1 (2012): 9–28.

"Moms Mabley: She Finally Makes the Movies." *Ebony*, April 1974.

Mo'Nique. *I Coulda Been Your Cellmate!* Directed by Gary Binkow. Enliven Entertainment, 2007. DVD.

———. *One Night Stand.* Directed by Leslie Smalls. Filmrise, 2004.

———. *The Queens of Comedy.* Directed by Steve Purcelle. Lantham Entertainment and Paramount Pictures, 2001.

"Mo'Nique is back and she's not sorry about the Netflix boycott." *The Washington Post*, February 7, 2019. YouTube video, 4:25. https://www.youtube.com/watch?v=_eiAvl1B_JY.

Morrison, Toni. "Toni Morrison," *Charlie Rose.* PBS video, 55:04. May 7, 1993. https://charlierose.com/videos/18778.

Moten, Fred. *Black and Blur.* Durham, NC: Duke University Press, 2017.

———. *In the Break: The Aesthetics of the Black Radical Tradition.* Minneapolis: University of Minnesota Press, 2003.

Muñoz, José Esteban. *Cruising Utopia: The Then and There of Queer Futurity.* New York: New York University Press, 2009.

———. *Disidentifications: Queers of Color and the Performance of Politics.* Minneapolis: University of Minnesota Press, 1999.

New York Public Library. "Encore—Gordon Anderson Collection [Graphic]."
NYPL Catalog. Accessed September 26, 2019. https://digitalcollections.nypl
.org/collections/gordon-anderson-collection.

Newton, Harry L. *A Bundle of Burnt Cork Comedy: Original Cross-Fire
Conversations, Gags, Retorts, Minstrel Monologues and Stump Speeches.*
Minneapolis: T.S. Denison, 1905.

Nyong'o, Tavia. *The Amalgamation Waltz: Race, Performance, and the Ruses of
Memory.* Minneapolis: University of Minnesota Press, 2009.

Obama, Barack. "President Obama at White House Correspondents' Dinner
(2011)." Washington, DC: White House, 2011. Video. https://www.youtube
.com/watch?v=lX16OrIVfeQ.

Obama, Michelle. "Remarks by the First Lady at the Sojourner Truth Bust
Unveiling." The White House. April 28, 2009. https://obamawhitehouse
.archives.gov/the-press-office/remarks-first-lady-sojourner-truth-bust
-unveiling.

Ohio Department of Rehabilitation and Correction. "Ohio Reformatory for
Women." Accessed September 26, 2019. https://drc.ohio.gov/orw.

Owen, Ianna Hawkins. "Still, Nothing: Mammy and Black Asexual Possibility."
Feminist Review 120, no. 1 (2018): 70–84.

Paredez, Deborah. "Lena Horne and Judy Garland: Divas, Desire, and Discipline
in the Civil Rights Era." *TDR: The Drama Review* 58, no. 4 (2014): 105–19.

———. *Selenidad: Selena, Latinos, and the Performance of Memory.* Durham, NC:
Duke University Press, 2009.

Perry, Imani. *May We Forever Stand: A History of the Black National Anthem.*
Chapel Hill: University of North Carolina Press, 2018.

Pryor, Richard. *Richard Pryor Live in Concert.* Directed by Jeff Margolis. Elkins
Entertainment and SEE Theater Network, 1979.

Pugh, Megan. *America Dancing: From the Cakewalk to the Moonwalk.* New
Haven: Yale University Press, 2015.

Rayner, Alice. "Creating the Audience: It's All in the Timing." In *The Laughing
Stalk: Live Comedy and Its Audiences,* edited by Judy Batalion, 28–39.
Anderson: Parlor Press, 2012.

Richardson, Matt. "Our Stories Have Never Been Told: Preliminary Thoughts
on Black Lesbian Cultural Production as Historiography in the Watermelon
Woman." *Black Camera: An International Film Journal (the New Series)* 2,
no. 2 (2011): 100–13.

———. *The Queer Limit of Black Memory: Black Lesbian Literature and
Irresolution.* Columbus: Ohio State University Press, 2013.

Roach, Joseph R. *Cities of the Dead: Circum-Atlantic Performance.* New York:
Columbia University Press, 1996.

Roach, Shoniqua. "Black Pussy Power: Performing Acts of Black Eroticism in Pam
Grier's Blaxploitation Films." *Feminist Theory* 19, no. 1 (2018): 7–22.

Robinson, Joanna. "Why Did a Third *SNL* Cast Member Silently Leave the Show
Last Night?" *Vanity Fair,* May 21, 2017. https://www.vanityfair.com/holly
wood/2017/05/sasheer-zamata-snl-leaving-bobby-moynihan-vanessa-bayer.

Robinson, Phoebe, and Jessica Williams. *2 Dope Queens*. "New York." Directed by Tig Notaro. HBO, 2018.

Ross, Marlon. "Beyond the Closet as Raceless Paradigm." In *Black Queer Studies: A Critical Anthology*, edited by E. Patrick Johnson and Mae Henderson, 161–89. Durham, NC: Duke University Press, 2005.

Rossing, Jonathan P. "Critical Race Humor in a Postracial Moment: Richard Pryor's Contemporary Parrhesia." *Howard Journal of Communications* 25, no. 1 (2014): 16–33.

Russo, Mary. *The Female Grotesque: Risk, Excess, and Modernity*. New York: Routledge, 1995.

Ryzik, Melena, Cara Buckley, and Jodi Kantor. "Louis C.K. Is Accused by 5 Women of Sexual Misconduct." *The New York Times*, November 9, 2017. https://www.nytimes.com/2017/11/09/arts/television/louis-ck-sexual-misconduct.html.

Santagati, Steve. "Catcalling Video Goes Viral." CNN, November 2, 2014. YouTube video, 2:18. https://www.youtube.com/watch?time_continue=1&v=-HI4DC18wCg.

Schmider, Alex. "2016 Was the Deadliest Year on Record for Transgender People." *GLAAD BLOG*, November 9, 2016. https://www.glaad.org/blog/2016-was-deadliest-year-record-transgender-people.

Scott, Darieck. *Extravagant Abjection: Blackness, Power, and Sexuality in the African American Literary Imagination*. New York: New York University Press, 2010.

Scott, Michelle R. "These Ladies Do Business with a Capital B: The Griffin Sisters as Black Businesswomen in Early Vaudeville." *Journal of African American History* 101, no. 4 (2016): 469–503.

Seales, Amanda. "Amanda Seales's Catcalling." Audio podcast. *Good One: A Podcast About Jokes*, July 8, 2019. Head Gum. https://headgum.com/good-one-a-podcast-about-jokes/amanda-sealess-catcalling.

———. *I Be Knowin'*. Directed by Stan Lathan. HBO, 2019.

Sedgwick, Eve Kosofsky. *Epistemology of the Closet*, 2nd ed. Berkeley: University of California Press, 2008.

———. *Tendencies*. Durham, NC: Duke University Press, 1993.

Shailor, Jonathon. *Performing New Lives: Prison Theatre*. Philadelphia: Jessica Kingsley Publishers, 2011.

Shange, Savannah. "Play Aunties and Dyke Bitches: Gender, Generation, and the Ethics of Black Queer Kinship." *Black Scholar* 49, no. 1 (2019): 40–54.

Sharpe, Christina Elizabeth. *In the Wake: On Blackness and Being*. Durham, NC: Duke University Press, 2016.

Smith, Anna Deavere. *Notes from the Field*. New York: Anchor Publishing, 2019.

Soloski, Alexis. "Sasheer Zamata Finds Humor at the A.C.L.U." *The New York Times*, October 4, 2019. https://www.nytimes.com/2019/10/04/style/sasheer-zamata-snl-aclu.html.

Somerville, Siobhan B. "Queer *Loving*." *GLQ: A Journal of Lesbian & Gay Studies* 11, no. 3 (2005): 335–70.

Stallings, L. H. *Mutha' Is Half a Word: Intersections of Folklore, Vernacular, Myth, and Queerness in Black Female Culture*. Columbus: Ohio State University Press, 2007.

Stoever, Jennifer Lynn. *The Sonic Color Line: Race and the Cultural Politics of Listening*. New York: New York University Press, 2016.

Sykes, Wanda. "Comic Wanda Sykes." Radio interview. *Fresh Air*, August 1, 2019. https://www.npr.org/programs/fresh-air/2019/08/01/747288552/fresh-air-for -august-1-2019-comic-wanda-sykes.

———. *I'ma Be Me*. Directed by Beth McCarthy-Miller. Sykes Entertainment, 2009.

———. Public Address. White House Correspondents' Dinner, Washington, DC. April 8, 2009. https://www.youtube.com/watch?v=zmyR0g2w4DI.

———. *Sick and Tired*. Directed by Michael Drumm. Image Entertainment, 2006.

———. "Wanda Sykes Comes Out at Las Vegas Equality Rally." The CenterLV, November 15, 2008. YouTube video, 4:41. https://www.youtube.com/watch ?v=S6UdoCIYvIw.

———. "Wanda Sykes's Free Ancestors." PBS Video. *Finding Your Roots*, May 13, 2012. https://www.pbs.org/video/finding-your-roots-wanda-sykess-free -ancestors-1600s-and-1700s/.

———. *What Happened, Ms. Sykes?* Directed by Liz Patrick. Push It Productions, 2017.

Taylor, Diana. *The Archive and the Repertoire: Performing Cultural Memory in the Americas*. Durham, NC: Duke University Press, 2003.

Taylor, Yuval, and Jake Austen. *Darkest America: Black Minstrelsy from Slavery to Hip-Hop*. New York: W.W. Norton and Company, 2012.

Thompson, M. Cordell. "Moms Mabley Raps About Old Women, Young Love." *Jet*, January 3, 1974.

Tiefenthäler, Ainara. "Female Comics Take on the Rape Joke." *The New York Times* video, 5:13, from *The #MeToo* Moment video series, December 20, 2017. https://www.nytimes.com/video/arts/100000005534134/female-comics -sexual-harassment.html.

Tinsley, Omise'eke Natasha. "Black Atlantic, Queer Atlantic: Queer Imaginings of the Middle Passage." *GLQ: A Journal of Lesbian and Gay Studies* 14, no. 2 (2008): 191–215.

Trouillot, Michel-Rolph. *Silencing the Past: Power and the Production of History*. Boston: Beacon Press, 1995.

Tung, Cameron. "How Podcasts Conquered Comedy." *The New Yorker*, August 26, 2013. https://www.newyorker.com/tech/elements/how-podcasts-conquered -comedy.

Turner, Patricia A. *Ceramic Uncles & Celluloid Mammies: Black Images and Their Influence on Culture*. Charlottesville: University of Virginia Press, 2002.

"US Capitol Visitor Center." Architect of the Capitol. https://www.aoc.gov/capitol buildings/us-capitol-visitor-center.

Valenti, Jessica. "Anatomy of a Successful Rape Joke." *The Nation*, July 12, 2012. https://www.thenation.com/article/anatomy-successful-rape-joke/.

Valli, Frankie. "Can't Take My Eyes Off of You." *Frankie Valli Solo*. Phillips Records. LP, 1967.

Villarreal, Yvyonne. "For Tiffany Haddish and Six Unsung Comedians, Netflix's New Special Is Worth Crying Over." *The Los Angeles Times*, August 12, 2019. https://www.latimes.com/entertainment-arts/tv/story/2019-08-12/netflix-tiffany-haddish-stand-up-comedy-they-ready.

Vogel, Shane. "Lena Horne's Impersona." *Camera Obscura* 23, no. 67 (2008) 10–45.

Wald, Gayle. "Sound Vibrations: Black Music and Black Freedom in Sound and Space." *American Quarterly* 63, no. 3 (2011): 673–96.

Walker, Nancy. *A Very Serious Thing: Women's Humor and American Culture*. Minneapolis: University of Minnesota Press, 1988.

Warner, Michael. *Publics and Counterpublics*. New York: Zone Books, 2002.

Watkins, Mel. *African American Humor: The Best Black Comedy from Slavery to Today*. Chicago: Lawrence Hill Books, 2002.

Wilderson, Frank B. "The Vengeance of Vertigo: Aphasia and Abjection in the Political Trials of Black Insurgents." *InTensions* 5 (2011): 1–41.

Williams, Elsie A. *The Humor of Jackie Moms Mabley: An African American Comedic Tradition*. New York: Garland, 1995.

Wong, Stevie. "On My Screen: Wanda Sykes' Childhood Hero in 'The Marvelous Mrs. Maisel,' Marvel Dreams & The Kids' Movie That Makes Her Cry." *Deadline*, August 23, 2020. https://deadline.com/2020/08/the-marvelous-mrs-maisel-star-wanda-sykes-on-my-screen-interview-news-1203018705/.

Wood, Katelyn Hale. "Standing Up: Black Feminist Comedy in the Twentieth and Twenty-First Centuries." In *The Routledge Companion to African American Theatre and Performance*, edited by Kathy A. Perkins, Sandra L. Richards, Renée Alexander Craft, and Thomas F. DeFrantz, 323–29. New York: Routledge, 2018.

Wright, Michelle M. *The Physics of Blackness: Beyond the Middle Passage Epistemology*. Minneapolis: University of Minnesota Press, 2015.

Young, James Edward. *The Texture of Memory: Holocaust Memorials and Meaning*. New Haven: Yale University Press, 1993.

Zamata, Sasheer. "Racist Radio." Posted by Official Comedy Standup, May 21, 2013. YouTube Video, 4:02. https://www.youtube.com/watch?list=PLZQfnFyelTBOQ15kmHSgEbdjzLMWzZpL7&v=jI_SFm-txRI.

———. "Sasheer Zamata on Louis C.K.'s Parkland Bit." From a Sasheer Zamata stand-up set, posted by user *Vulture. SoundCloud*, audio clip, 4:47. https://soundcloud.com/user-517669847/sasheer-zamata-on-louis-cks-parkland-bit.

Ziegler, Kortney. "Black Sissy Masculinity and the Politics of Dis-Respectability." In *No Tea, No Shade: New Writings in Black Queer Studies*, edited by E. Patrick Johnson, 196–215. Durham, NC: Duke University Press, 2016.

Zinoman Jason. "Toe-to-Toe at the Edge of the Comedy Club Stage." *The New York Times*, July 17, 2012. https://www.nytimes.com/2012/07/18/arts/television/when-the-comic-and-the-heckler-both-take-offense.html.

Index

2 Dope Queens, 3–4, 137

abjection, 76–77; and Blackness, 8, 19–20, 43, 136; and queerness, 19–20, 76–77
Ace Theatre (Los Angeles), 102
Acham, Christine, 33
albums, comedy, 13, 27–28, 167n8
Alexander, M. Jacqui, 9, 68, 90
Allen, Jafari S., 122
Anderson, Gordon, 25, 157n1
Apollo Theatre (Harlem): Black comedic performances at, 12; famously harsh audiences of, 171n1; Mabley's connection to, 25, 41–43; *Moms Mabley Live at the Apollo*, 41–43; *Showtime at the Apollo*, 56
archives: Black lesbian, 100; and Black queer absence, 4, 27–28, 157n4
assimilation: and the American Dream, 87, 116; Black queer resistance to, 116. *See also* homonormativity critiques of
audience, 14–17, 71–76, 111–13; agency of, 14–17, 71–77, 111–13, 171n1; and Black feminist community, 14–15, 16–17, 53–82, 111–13; live versus mediated, 114; and power, 15, 71–77; as spect-actors, 14–17, 71–77, 171n1
authority: challenges to, 53–82

Baker, Josephine, 11
barbeque, 121–22. *See also* marriage
Baulfor, Michael, 57
Bean, Anne-Marie, 11
Becky. *See* white women
Belly, Lead, 48

Bergson, Henri, 16
Best of Moms Mabley and Pigmeat Vol. 1, 46–48, 159n57
Black comedy: and double consciousness, 10–11; and double inversion, 11; history of, 4–17, 19–20, 22–23, 27–31, 148–51, 157n4; and parody, 10–11, 44, 49, 51; and women, 11, 12–13, 24, 32–33, 127, 169n52
Black community, 8, 9, 23, 122, 143–46
Black feminism, 6–9. *See also* feminism
Black feminist comedy: archival record of, 22–23, 27–31, 157n4; as critical history, 3–4, 9, 40–44; defined, 150; as epistemology, 8–9, 87–88, 98, 149; genealogies of, 5–6, 8, 13, 50–51, 55, 86, 87, 111, 143, 147–50; history and analysis of, 4–17, 19–20, 148–51; influence of #MeToo on, 24; as protest, 4–5, 8–9, 19–20, 54–55, 81–82, 99, 113, 144, 149–50; as truth-telling, 1, 3–4, 9, 40–44, 86, 89–90, 151. *See also* #MeToo
Black feminist theory: and embodiment, 7; and performance, 6–9; and queer theory, 7, 22, 87–89
Black humor, 10–14. *See also* humor
Black Lives Matter, 110, 142–43
Black metronormativity, 121–22
Black performance: as epistemology, 8, 10, 14; marginalization of, 5; theory, 8, 10, 148. *See also* Black feminist comedy
Black queer time, 87–89, 95–101, 120–23
Black women: activism of, 24, 44–51, 81, 83–85, 110, 111, 115–17, 123–36,

169n41; in comedy, 4–17, 19–20, 22–23, 27–31, 148–51, 157n4; in/visibility of, 8–9, 21, 23, 35–36, 45–48, 68, 75–76, 100
Blackadder, Neil Martin, 74
Blank, Jessica, 55
BLM. *See* Black Lives Matter
Blondie Cant U C, 58
Boal, Augusto, 15, 71
Boarding House Blues, 33
bodies: of comedians, 35–36, 42–43, 56–57, 58–61, 67, 125–27; male, 35, 37–40, 42–43, 125, 129–31; as sites of resistance and change, 11, 17, 35–36, 42–43, 77–78, 93, 100. *See also* clothing; genitals; laughter; movement
Brooks, Daphne, 9, 51
Burke, Tarana, 123
Bush, George W., 86
BUST, 115
butch-femme identities, 70–71
Buteau, Michelle, 4, 24, 129; comedy specials of, 128–31; comic persona of, 116–17; podcasts of, 116–17, 137; professional career of, 116–17
Butler, Judith, 118
Butterbeans and Suzie, 32–33
Byer, Nicole, 116

camp, 62. *See also* clothing
Campt, Tina, 121
Carlos, Jordan, 117
Carpenter, Faedra, 47
Carpio, Glenda, 12, 47–48
Cash, Johnny, 55
catcalling, 124–25
Chambers-Letson, Jonathan, 54
Charles, Ray, 48
Charm School, 57
Chávez, Karma, 99
Chitlin' Circuit, 12
chrononormativity, 88–89, 95–101
citizenship: cracking up, 18–20, 87; as

gender inflected, 18–20, 85, 87; as racially inflected, 18–20, 87; and same-sex marriage, 85
civil rights, 44–51, 81, 83–84, 117
Civil Rights Bill, 48
C.K., Louis, 127, 130, 131–36, 169n52
Cleage, Pearl, 8
clothing: as aspect of performance, 1, 2, 36–37, 59–63, 65, 67, 91, 102, 147; muumuus, 36–37; prison uniforms, 59–63, 65, 70, 78, 80. *See also* disidentification
Coates, Ta-Nehisi, 21, 168n28
Collins, Patricia Hill, 18, 69
Comedy Cellar (New York City), 132
Comedy Central, 13
Comedy Factory Outlet (Baltimore), 56
comedy industry: misogyny and sexual violence in, 127–36
coming out: narrative scripts of, 83, 94–101, 128–29, 163n3. *See also* homonormativity critiques of
consent, 128–32
Cosby, Bill, 127, 169n52
counterpublic, 64
cracking up: and abjection, 19–20, 76–77, 169n59; citizenship, 18–20, 87; coming out narratives, 94–101; definition of, 5; as disruptive, 17; history, 3–4, 9, 23–24, 28, 40–44, 92–94; national heritage, 18, 23–24, 92–94; nostalgia, 40–44; performance history, 4, 10, 13–14, 23, 29, 171n1; time, 93–94, 95–101, 120–23; white supremacy, 18–20, 40–41, 44–51, 92–94, 137–43
Crawley, Ashon T., 151

Davis, Angela, 54
Davis, Diane, 17
Deavere Smith, Anna, 55, 160n7
Def Comedy Jam, 13
DeFrantz, Thomas, 10
Diamond, Elin, 43

DiAngelo, Robin, 139
dicks. *See* genitals
disidentification: and comedy, 23, 58–65, 72, 85; and costume, 59–63, 65; and set and stage design, 63–64
diva: Mabley as, 49–50; Mo'Nique as, 59, 70; Seales as, 112
Dolan, Jill, 150
domesticity, 91–92, 101–6, 107–8, 117–23. *See also* heteropatriarchy; homonormativity critiques of
Du Bois, W. E. B., 10
Duggan, Lisa, 87
Dunning, Stefanie K., 103
Dynasty Typewriter (Los Angeles), 131–36

Ebony, 32, 57
epistemology: and Black queer time, 87–88, 98; performance as, 8–9, 149; self-determination and, 8–9
eroticism, 65–71, 122, 134. *See also* sexuality

Facebook. *See* social media
Fanon, Frantz, 19
feminism: Black, 6–9; and queer theory, 7; white, 137–43
Ferguson, Roderick A., 31, 88
Ferguson protests, 103–4
Finding Your Roots, 102
Flavor of Love, 161n16
Forsyne, Ida, 11
Foucault, Michel, 75–76
Franco, James, 130–31
Fraser, Nancy, 64
Freedom Riders, 45–46, 50
Freeman, Elizabeth, 88–89, 93
Freud, Sigmund, 15–16
The Funny Sides of Moms Mabley, 35

gender: butch-femme identities, 70–71, 116; male impersonation, 11; non-conformity, 116; toxic masculinity,

127–36; white femininity, 137–39, 141–42
genitals: penises, 69–70, 127, 129–31; vulvas, 36–37, 125–27
Gill, Lyndon, 67–68
Givens, Adele, 13, 22
Goldberg, Whoopi, 22, 29–31
Gonzalez, Anita, 10
Gregory, Dick, 1, 13
Griffin, Cindy, 99
griot traditions, 11

Haddish, Tiffany, 114–15
Haggins, Bambi, 11–12, 32, 42, 86
Halberstam, Jack, 84, 121
Hall, Stuart, 18, 92–93
Hamer, Fanny Lou, 123
Hammonds, Evelynn, 68–69
Hannah. *See* white women
Hartman, Saidiya V., 19
HBO, 3–4, 111, 116, 117, 132
Hemings, Sally, 4, 153n4
heteropatriarchy: challenges to, 18–20, 36–40, 41–44; as embedded in national myths, 92–93. *See also* domesticity; marriage
Hill, Anita, 123
Hill, Darlene Clark, 123
history, 3–4, 9, 40–44. *See also* nostalgia; time
"hollering place," 8
homonormativity critiques of, 87, 101–6, 117–23; same-sex marriage and, 87, 117–23; white supremacy of, 98–99, 101–6, 107–8. *See also* domesticity; marriage
hooks, bell, 7, 8, 13–14, 79
Horne, Lena, 49
Hughes, Langston, 40
humor: as aggression and release, 15–16; Black, 10–14, 42–43, 130; the metajoke, 133–34; punching up versus punching down, 126–27, 134; types of, 42–43, 44, 46, 47–48, 130

I Coulda Been Your Cellmate! See
Mo'Nique
Instagram. *See* social media
interracial love, 101–6
intersectionality, 101–6
iTunes. *See* online platforms

Jay, Sam, 4, 24, 119; comedy albums of,
117–23, 140–42; gender nonconfor-
mity of, 116, 118; professional career
of, 116; on same-sex marriage, 117–
23; use of n-word by, 21
Jefferson, Thomas, 3–4, 9, 153n4
Jensen, Erik, 55
Jet Magazine, 25–26, 27
Jezebel, 115
Johnson, E. Patrick, 35, 149
Jones, Meta DuEwa, 40
Jones, Omi Osun Joni L., 7, 8
Jones, Rhodessa, 55
joy, 17, 19–20, 56, 100–101, 145–46. *See
also* laughter
"jumping the broom," 119–21. *See also*
marriage

Keeling, Kara, 7, 118
Kennedy, Bobby, 40–41, 44
King, B. B., 55
King, Jason, 51
King, Martin Luther Jr., 44
Krasner, David, 10–11
Ku Klux Klan, 41, 45, 141–42. *See also*
white supremacy

Lane, Artis, 89
Lauer, Matt, 130
laughter: as Black queer expression,
5–6, 15–16, 19–20, 66–69, 81, 91–92;
as radical act of belonging and resistance, 19–20, 66–69, 81, 111; as release, 15–16, 111. *See also* joy
lesbians. *See* Jay, Sam; Mabley, Jackie
"Moms"; Sykes, Wanda
"Lift Every Voice and Sing," 143–46

Limon, John, 20, 133
linearity. *See* progress; time
Little, Joan, 123
Lorde, Audre, 7, 8–9, 67
Lordi, Emily, 5
Lott, Eric, 10
lynching, 138

Mabley, Jackie "Moms," 4–5, 25–52;
comedic persona of, 1, 2, 25–26, 27,
28, 30–31, 34, 35–37, 40–41, 61, 147;
comedy albums of, 13, 35, 36–43,
46–51; documentation of, 27–28,
157n4; early life of, 32, 34, 42–43;
early performances of, 32–33; as
innovator and trail-blazer, 4–5,
21–23, 27, 51–52, 144, 149, 151; "Old
Man" jokes of, 35, 37–40, 42–43,
125, 130, 147; photographs of, 1, 2,
25–26, 27, 34; political comedy of,
13, 44–51, 85; portrayed by Wanda
Sykes, 147, 148, 171n1; queerness
of, 25–26, 28, 29–31, 40–41; racism
referenced by, 44–51; sexuality of,
28, 29–31, 35–37; as solo performer,
12–13, 32–33; songs and song parodies sung by, 39–40, 48–51, 81,
159n64; television appearances of,
44; as truth-teller, 1, 9, 40–44, 151
mammy, 36, 105
Markham, Dewy "Pigmeat," 159n57
marriage: alternatives to, 119–23; critiques of, 43, 87, 117–23; same-
sex, 83–85, 87, 95, 101, 117–22. *See
also* domesticity; heteropatriarchy;
homonormativity critiques of
Marvelous, Simply, 13
masturbation, 66, 67, 132, 133. *See also*
orgasm; sexuality
Meara, Anne, 31, 157n13
menstruation, 125–26
Merv Griffin Show, 44
#MeToo, 24, 110, 111, 123–36, 169n41
metronormativity, 121–22

Miller, Norma, 29–30
minstrels: Black, 10–11
minstrelsy, 10–11
Mitchell, Koritha, 46
Mock, Roberta, 37
Moms Mabley Breaks It Up, 49–51
Moms Mabley at Geneva Conference, 36–37
Moms Mabley Live at the Apollo, 41–43
Moms Mabley Live at Sing Sing, 37–40
Moms Mabley Live at the U.N., 48–49
Moms Mabley at the Playboy Club, 48
Mo'Nique, 4, 60, 65, 67, 80, 144, 149; activism of, 115; career of, 56–58; *Ebony* interview of, 57; film performances of, 56–57; *I Coulda Been Your Cellmate!*, 15, 20, 23, 53–82; physicality of, 56–61, 64; *The Queens of Comedy*, 137; queerness of, 69–71; sexual eroticism of, 65–71; television performances of, 56–58
Morrison, Toni, 143
Moten, Fred, 19
movement, 45–51, 54, 100, 123–25
Muñoz, José Esteban, 28, 59–60, 62, 72

national heritage, 18, 23–24, 92–94
National Museum of African American History and Culture, 1, 2
national myths, 92–94
neo-Nazis, 140–43. *See also* white supremacy
Netflix, 57–58, 114–15, 116, 128, 132. *See also* online platforms
normativity. *See* chrononormativity; homonormativity critiques of
nostalgia, 40–44. *See also* history; time
n-word, 21, 46–48, 133, 168n28

Obama, Barrack, 83–85, 94, 101–2, 164n29
Obama, Michelle, 89–90, 91–93

Ohio Reformatory for Women, 53–54, 55–56. *See also* Mo'Nique
online platforms, 114–15, 167n8
orgasm, 66–69. *See also* masturbation
"otherwise" possibility, 151
Out on a Limb, 40–41
Overton Walker, Aida, 11
Owen, Ianna Hawkins, 105

Page, LaWanda, 13, 22, 155n45
panopticon. *See* surveillance
Paredez, Deborah, 50
The Parkers, 57, 70, 161n15. *See also* Mo'Nique
Parks, Rosa, 123
parody, 10–11, 39–40, 48–51
party albums. *See* albums, comedy
patriarchy. *See* heteropatriarchy
performance, 8, 10–14, 156n59, 156n60
Perry, Imani, 144–45
Pharoah, Jay, 115
Playboy Club (Chicago), 45
playing the dozens, 42–43, 130
podcasts, 3, 116, 137. *See also* social media
Poundstone, Paula, 164n26
pouring tea, 11
prisons: comedic disruption of, 53–82; as expressions of state power, 54, 61–62, 65–66, 67–68, 75–78; performances in, 55–56. *See also* Mo'Nique
progress: narratives of, 87–101, 106–9, 120–23
Proposition 8, 83–85, 95
Pryor, Richard, 1, 13, 47–48, 127, 137, 169n52
pussy: detachable. *See* genitals

queer theory, 7; and Black feminist theory, 7, 22, 87–89
queerness: as antithetical to Blackness, 99–100; domestication of, 117–23; intersections with Blackness, 7,

101–6; as resistance and alternative, 70–71, 87–89. *See also* homonormativity critiques of; intersectionality

racism, 18–19, 44–51, 86, 111. *See also* white supremacy
rape and sexual violence, 123–27. *See also* violence
Regal Theater (Chicago), 12
Richardson, Matt, 6, 100
Roach, Joseph, 61
Robinson, Phoebe, 3–4. See also *2 Dope Queens*
Rock, Chris, 115
Rose, Charlie, 130
Ross, Marlon, 98
Rudolph, Maya, 115
Russo, Mary, 47

Saturday Night Live, 115
Schumer, Amy, 115
Scott, Darieck, 19, 76–77
Seales, Amanda, 24, 113; *I Be Knowin'*, 111–14, 117, 124–25, 138–40, 144–46; professional career of, 117
Sedgwick, Eve, 83
set and stage design, 63–64. *See also* disidentification
sexuality: of comedic personas, 28, 29–31, 36–37, 56–71; eroticism, 65–71, 122, 134. *See also* masturbation
Shailor, Jonathon, 56
Shange, Savannah, 120
Sharpe, Christina, 20
signifyin', 43
silence, 105. *See also* vocality
Snapchat. *See* social media
SNL. See *Saturday Night Live*
social media, 3, 111, 114
Somerville, Siobhan, 88
song: comedic use of, 39–40, 48–51; as resistance and freedom, 78–81, 105, 107, 143–46, 163n72

South, the, 44–51
spect-actors, 15, 71–75. *See also* audience
Spotify. *See* online platforms
stand-up comedy: history of, 4–17, 148–51; and minstrelsy, 10–11; scholarly studies of, 5–6; as social critique, 6, 21
state power: marriage as site of, 117–23; prisons as site of, 54, 61–62, 65–66, 67–68, 75–78
Stoever, Jennifer Lynn, 139–40
stump speech, 10. *See also* minstrelsy
surveillance: of Black people, 45, 46–47, 54, 61–62, 65–66, 75–78
Sutton, Norris, 26, 27
Sykes, Wanda, 4, 23–24, 92, 97, 108, 144, 149; activism of, 83–84, 117; background of, 102–3; career of, 86, 164n12; comedy specials of, 85–86, 94–106, 108–9, 126; coming out, 83–85, 94–101, 102–6, 164n11; domestic life of, 101–6; portrayal of Moms Mabley by, 147, 148; White House Correspondents' Dinner performances, 85, 90–94

Taylor, Diana, 9
television, 13–14, 56–58, 86, 111
Theatre Owners Booking Association (TOBA), 12, 32–33. *See also* vaudeville
Thompson, M. Cordell, 26
TikTok. *See* social media
Till, Emmett, 48
time: Black queer time, 87–89, 95–101, 120–23; cracking up, 93–94, 95–101, 120–23
Tinsley, Omise'eke, 70
TOBA. *See* Theatre Owners Booking Association (TOBA)
Tosh, Daniel, 126–27
toxic masculinity, 127–36
Tropicana, Carmelita, 62

Trump, Donald, 106, 108–9, 110,
    164n28
Truth, Sojourner, 89–92
truth-telling, 1, 3–4, 9, 86
Tung, Cameron, 114
Twitter. *See* social media

Underwood, Sheryl, 13
Unite the Right rally (2017), 141
Upright Citizens Brigade, 115
Uptown Theatre (Philadelphia), 12,
    48–49
Utopia, 150

Valli, Frankie, 39–40
vaudeville, 12, 74. *See also* Theatre
    Owners Booking Association
    (TOBA); Mabley's performances
violence: against Black people, 138,
    141–43. *See also* rape and sexual
    violence
vocality, 66, 68–69, 72–75, 124–25.
    See also laughter; song
Vogel, Shane, 43–44

Wanda at Large, 86
Warfield, Marsha, 22
Warner, Michael, 17
Warner Theatre (Washington, DC), 94
Weinstein, Harvey, 123, 130, 131
white feminism, 137–43
white fragility, 138–40
White House Correspondents' Dinner,
    85, 90–94, 164n26, 164n27, 164n28,
    164n29

white privilege, 137–43. *See also* white
    supremacy
white supremacy: in academic writ-
    ing, 21; challenges to, 18–20, 40–41,
    44–51, 92–94, 137–43; in citizen-
    ship, 18–19; in coming out narra-
    tives, 98–99; female supporters of,
    141–42; and Jim Crow, 44–51; as
    mental disorder, 143; in national
    myths, 92–94. *See also* racism;
    violence
white women, 21, 40–41, 137–43
whiteface: linguistic, 47–48, 105, 107,
    137, 139, 142
whiteness: as neutral, 138–40
*Whoopi Goldberg Presents: Moms
    Mabley*, 29–31
Wilderson, Frank, 95
Williams, Elise, 32
Williams, Jessica, 3–4. See also *2 Dope
    Queens*
Women's March on Washington (2017),
    137
Wright, Michelle M., 87–88

yo mama jokes. *See* playing the dozens
Young, James E., 93
YouTube, 57–58, 114, 167n8. *See also*
    social media

Zamata, Sasheer, 4, 24, 135; activism
    of, 115, 116; challenge to Louis C.K.,
    131–36; professional career of, 115–
    16; work on *Saturday Night Live*,
    115–16

Studies in Theatre History and Culture

*Actors and American Culture,
1880–1920*
by Benjamin McArthur

*The Age and Stage of George L. Fox,
1825–1877: An Expanded Edition*
by Laurence Senelick

*America in the Round: Capital, Race,
and Nation at Washington, DC's
Arena Stage*
by Donatella Galella

*The American Negro Theatre and the
Long Civil Rights Era*
by Jonathan Shandell

*American Theater in the Culture
of the Cold War: Producing and
Contesting Containment, 1947–1962*
by Bruce McConachie

*Athenian Tragedy in Performance:
A Guide to Contemporary Studies
and Historical Debates*
by Melinda Powers

*August Wilson: Completing the
Twentieth-Century Cycle*
edited by Alan Nadel

*Bloody Tyrants and Little Pickles:
Stage Roles of Anglo-American
Girls in the Nineteenth Century*
by Marlis Schweitzer

*Classical Greek Theatre:
New Views of an Old Subject*
by Clifford Ashby

*Cracking Up: Black Feminist Comedy
in the Twentieth and Twenty-First
Century United States*
by Katelyn Hale Wood

*Czech Theatre Design in the Twentieth
Century: Metaphor and Irony
Revisited*
edited by Joseph Brandesky

*Embodied Memory: The Theatre of
George Tabori*
by Anat Feinberg

*Fangs of Malice: Hypocrisy, Sincerity,
and Acting*
by Matthew H. Wikander

*Fantasies of Empire: The Empire
Theatre of Varieties and the
Licensing Controversy of 1894*
by Joseph Donohue

*French Theatre Today: The View from
New York, Paris, and Avignon*
by Edward Baron Turk

*From Androboros to the First
Amendment: A History of
America's First Play*
by Peter A. Davis

*Irish on the Move: Performing Mobility
in American Variety Theatre*
by Michelle Granshaw

*The Jewish Kulturbund Theatre
Company in Nazi Berlin*
by Rebecca Rovit

*Jews and the Making of Modern
German Theatre*
edited by Jeanette R. Malkin and
Freddie Rokem

*Kitchen Sink Realisms: Domestic
Labor, Dining, and Drama in
American Theatre*
by Dorothy Chansky

London in a Box: Englishness and Theatre in Revolutionary America
by Odai Johnson

London's West End Actresses and the Origins of Celebrity Charity, 1880–1920
by Catherine Hindson

The Making of Theatrical Reputations: Studies from the Modern London Theatre
by Yael Zarhy-Levo

Marginal Sights: Staging the Chinese in America
by James S. Moy

Melodramatic Formations: American Theatre and Society, 1820–1870
by Bruce A. McConachie

Meyerhold: A Revolution in Theatre
by Edward Braun

Modern Czech Theatre: Reflector and Conscience of a Nation
by Jarka M. Burian

Modern Hamlets and Their Soliloquies: An Expanded Edition
by Mary Z. Maher and Thomas Postlewait

Molière, the French Revolution, and the Theatrical Afterlife
by Mechele Leon

The Most American Thing in America: Circuit Chautauqua as Performance
by Charlotte M. Canning

Music for the Melodramatic Theatre in Nineteenth-Century London and New York
by Michael V. Pisani

Othello *and Interpretive Traditions*
by Edward Pechter

Our Moonlight Revels: A Midsummer Night's Dream *in the Theatre*
by Gary Jay Williams

The Performance of Power: Theatrical Discourse and Politics
edited by Sue-Ellen Case and Janelle Reinelt

Performing History: Theatrical Representations of the Past in Contemporary Theatre
by Freddie Rokem

Performing the Progressive Era: Immigration, Urban Life, and Nationalism on Stage
edited by Max Shulman and J. Chris Westgate

Performing Whitely in the Postcolony: Afrikaners in South African Theatrical and Public Life
by Megan Lewis

Poverty and Charity in Early Modern Theatre and Performance
by Robert Henke

The Recurrence of Fate: Theatre and Memory in Twentieth-Century Russia
by Spencer Golub

Reflecting the Audience: London Theatregoing, 1840–1880
by Jim Davis and Victor Emeljanow

Rehearsing Revolutions: The Labor Drama Experiment and Radical Activism in the Early Twentieth Century
by Mary McAvoy

Representing the Past: Essays in Performance Historiography
edited by Charlotte M. Canning and Thomas Postlewait

The Roots of Theatre: Rethinking Ritual and Other Theories of Origin
by Eli Rozik

Sex for Sale: Six Progressive-Era Brothel Dramas
by Katie N. Johnson

Shakespeare and Chekhov in Production: Theatrical Events and Their Audiences
by John Tulloch

Shakespeare on the American Yiddish Stage
by Joel Berkowitz

The Show and the Gaze of Theatre: A European Perspective
by Erika Fischer-Lichte

The Song Is You: Musical Theatre and the Politics of Bursting into Song and Dance
by Bradley Rogers

Stagestruck Filmmaker: D. W. Griffith and the American Theatre
by David Mayer

Staging Postcommunism: Alternative Theatre in Eastern and Central Europe after 1989
edited by Vessela S. Warner and Diana Manole

Strange Duets: Impresarios and Actresses in the American Theatre, 1865–1914
by Kim Marra

Susan Glaspell's Poetics and Politics of Rebellion
by Emeline Jouve

Textual and Theatrical Shakespeare: Questions of Evidence
edited by Edward Pechter

Theatre and Identity in Imperial Russia
by Catherine A. Schuler

Theatre, Community, and Civic Engagement in Jacobean London
by Mark Bayer

Theatre Is More Beautiful Than War: German Stage Directing in the Late Twentieth Century
by Marvin Carlson

Theatres of Independence: Drama, Theory, and Urban Performance in India since 1947
by Aparna Bhargava Dharwadker

The Theatrical Event: Dynamics of Performance and Perception
by Willmar Sauter

Traveler, There Is No Road: Theatre, the Spanish Civil War, and the Decolonial Imagination in the Americas
by Lisa Jackson-Schebetta

The Trick of Singularity: Twelfth Night *and the Performance Editions*
by Laurie E. Osborne

The Victorian Marionette Theatre
by John McCormick

Wandering Stars: Russian Emigré Theatre, 1905–1940
edited by Laurence Senelick

Women Adapting: Bringing Three Serials of the Roaring Twenties to Stage and Screen
by Bethany Wood

Writing and Rewriting National Theatre Histories
edited by S. E. Wilmer